CONSTRUCTION LAW

CONSTRUCTION LAW: AN INTRODUCTION FOR ENGINEERS, ARCHITECTS, AND CONTRACTORS

Gail S. Kelley

RSMeans

WILEY

John Wiley & Sons, Inc.

Library of Congress Cataloging-in-Publication Data:

Kelley, Gail S.
  Construction law : an introduction for engineers, architects, and contractors / Gail S. Kelley.
    p. cm.
  Includes index.
  ISBN 978-1-118-22903-3 (cloth); ISBN 978-1-118-35915-0 (ebk); ISBN 978-1-118-35916-7 (ebk); ISBN 978-1-118-35917-4 (ebk); ISBN 978-1-118-36073-6 (ebk); ISBN 978-1-118-36074-3 (ebk); ISBN 978-1-118-36075-0 (ebk)
  1. Construction contracts—United States. 2. Construction industry—Law and legislation—United States. I. Title.
  KF902.K45 2012
  343.7307'8624—dc23
                                                                      2012023643

This book is dedicated to my parents, with thanks for their support and encouragement.

CONTENTS

PREFACE

The material in this book is designed to provide construction professionals with practical information on legal issues commonly encountered in design and construction. It is primarily intended for nonlawyers working in the design and construction industry in the United States. This includes design professionals (architects, engineers, and surveyors), contractors, subcontractors, suppliers, construction managers, and owners' representatives. Although it is not intended for attorneys, those who are unfamiliar with the design and construction industries should find it of value.

Readers are cautioned to use this book only as a source of basic information. It is not intended to provide legal advice, rather its goal is to provide readers with an understanding of construction law so that they will be able to recognize the legal implications of the situations they find themselves in. Decisions concerning particular legal matters should not be made based on the information contained herein. Readers should consult an attorney or other professional advisor for help with such decisions.

The coverage of legal issues is intentionally limited and focused. The book is not written as a general legal treatise but as a discussion of issues that tend to be unique to the design and construction industries. Construction law is principally contract law; most of the book addresses issues related to the contracts between the various participants on a construction project. Coverage of topics such as bankruptcy, intellectual property law, and real property law is restricted to those issues directly related to the contracts between the project participants. Issues such as business structures and labor law, although important to the individuals working in design and construction, are generally no different than in other industries and are not covered at all.

Construction law is mostly common law, which means that it has developed from judicial decisions rather than statutes or regulations. Even when statutes such as mechanic's lien laws directly impact the construction and design industries, judicial decisions have interpreted the language of the statute. Further, construction law is mostly state law, which means that one state's decision on a particular dispute could be completely different from another state's. Likewise, relevant laws may vary considerably from state to state.

While this book discusses some of these differences, the discussion is necessarily very brief. Looking at how each of the fifty states addresses all of the issues that might arise on a construction project is well beyond the scope of this book, or for that matter, any book. A reader looking for more information is urged to consult a book that addresses either construction law specific to a particular state, or a so-called "fifty-state survey" of a particular issue. Such surveys are conducted by both the American Bar Association (ABA) and various industry trade associations.

This book is designed to be used as a reference; while the chapters are somewhat in the order that issues might arise on a construction project, there is generally no need to read the chapters in any particular order. Throughout the text, there are short case studies discussing the facts and rulings of selected cases. These case studies are not meant to summarize a point of law. Rather, they are meant to illustrate how a court looks at specific facts when ruling on a dispute. There is a glossary of legal terms in a construction context. In addition, Appendix C provides an overview of the notation used to identify published legal cases (case citations).

CONSTRUCTION LAW

1

LAW AND GOVERNMENT

1.1 INTRODUCTION

In simple terms, law is the rules that a government uses to protect the health and welfare of its citizens and those within its borders. The government of the United States is a federalist system, which means that lawmaking power is shared between the national (U.S.) government and the individual state governments.

Under the division of powers set out in the U.S. Constitution, the national government (also referred to as the *federal government*) is divided into three branches: legislative, executive, and judicial. The *legislative* branch (the U.S. Congress) is responsible for creating the laws, the *executive* branch (the president and federal agencies such as the Environmental Protection Agency) is responsible for implementing the laws, and the *judicial* branch (the federal court system) is responsible for interpreting the laws.

The powers of the state governments are divided similarly. The legislative branch is the state legislature; the executive branch includes the governor and state agencies such as the state department of motor vehicles; the judicial branch is the state court system.

1.1.1 The Powers of Governments

The powers of the federal government are limited to those expressly listed in the U. S. Constitution. Per the 10th Amendment to the Constitution, any power that is not specifically delegated to the federal government, or specifically prohibited to the states, is reserved to the states or to the people. The most significant power reserved to the states is the general police power to protect the health, safety, and welfare of their communities. The state's police power is used as the basis for enacting laws in areas such as land use, gambling, crime, licensing, liquor sales, and motor vehicles. With respect to construction, police power gives state governments the right to adopt and enforce building codes and to require that architects and engineers working within the state be licensed by the state. Although police power does not specifically refer to the right to create a police force, it does include that right.

Any exercise of the police power is subject to constitutional and statutory restrictions, however. One such restriction comes from the U.S. Constitution's prohibition that a government cannot "deprive any person of life, liberty, or property, without due process of law." Another is the Constitution's "Takings" Clause, which prohibits governments from taking private property for public use without the payment of just compensation. A third constitutional standard is equal protection, which prohibits governments from discriminatory actions. An exercise of the police power must also pass a test of reasonableness. Part of the test for reasonableness is whether there is some logical means-ends relationship, that is, whether the regulation bears some rational relationship to its stated objective.

1.1.2   City and County Governments

Cities and counties are political subdivisions of the state and must be delegated power by the state. Most states delegate considerable power, including police power, to the cities and counties. In many states, this is done through *home rule*. Home rule is a broad grant of power whereby cities and counties govern themselves by enacting and administering laws concerning local matters, within the bounds of the state and federal constitutions. Home rule can be granted either by the state's constitution or by an act of the state legislature. In states without home rule, local governments only have the authority expressly granted to them by state legislatures.

1.1.3   The Powers of the Federal Government

Although the federal government does not have police power, it does have quite extensive powers, primarily because of the authority to regulate interstate commerce given to it by Article 1, Section 8, Clause 3 of the U.S. Constitution (the Commerce Clause). In addition, in areas that are not reserved to the states, conflicts between state and federal law are governed by the Supremacy Clause (Article 6 of the Constitution). Under the Supremacy Clause, the federal Constitution, federal laws, and international treaties supersede state and local law. State and local laws that contradict federal laws or treaties are preempted.

A federal statute may explicitly waive preemption of state law, however. In such cases the federal law is applicable in states that have not enacted their own laws. In addition, some federal laws, particularly those related to environmental regulation, only create minimum standards; the states are free to enact stricter regulations. In some cases, primary implementation of a federal regulation may be delegated to the states, provided the states meet certain standards. When a state is delegated federal authority for environmental regulation, for example, the Environmental Protection Agency (EPA) and the state sign a Memorandum of Agreement establishing their respective responsibilities and necessary procedures. Many federal statutes provide grants, technical assistance, and other support to help the states in furthering national policies or programs.

1.2 THE SOURCES AND HIERARCHY OF LAW

In the United States, law comes from five sources: constitutions, statutes and ordinances, regulations promulgated by administrative agencies, international treaties, and appellate court opinions.

1.2.1 The Constitution

As the supreme law of the land, the Constitution of the United States provides the basis for the U.S. government and guarantees the freedom and rights of all U.S. citizens. No laws may contradict any of the Constitution's principles and no governmental authority in the United States is exempt from complying with the Constitution. The federal courts have the sole authority to interpret the Constitution and to evaluate the federal constitutionality of both federal and state laws. To the extent any statute or agency action is found to be unconstitutional, it is invalid. State constitutions are the supreme law within the state, subject to the U.S. Constitution. The statutes of a state must conform to that state's constitution.

1.2.2 Statutes and Ordinances

Laws passed by Congress and state legislatures are typically referred to as *statutes*; laws passed by cities and counties are typically referred to as *ordinances*. City ordinances apply to people, property, and activities within the city's corporate limits (the incorporated area). County ordinances (called *resolutions* in some states) are generally only applicable outside the corporate limits of cities. City and county ordinances are typically preempted by both state and federal law.

The U.S. Congress has exclusive authority to enact federal laws. A proposed law is referred to as a *bill*. Bills may originate in either the House of Representatives or the Senate, except that, per Article 1 of the Constitution, all bills for raising revenue must originate in the House of Representatives. A bill must be passed (approved) by both chambers before it is sent to the president. If the president vetoes a bill, Congress may override the veto by approving the bill again with at least a two-thirds majority vote in both the House and the Senate. The bill then becomes a law, despite the president's veto. The process for enacting laws within the state legislatures is similar, and most governors have veto power over state legislation.

1.2.3 Agency Regulations

The executive branch of the U.S. government is charged with implementing the laws passed by Congress. The administrative bodies (agencies) in the executive branch issue regulations (rules) and make adjudications that apply the regulations. They also provide opinions and guidelines to follow. Federal regulations are issued under statutory authority granted to the agencies by Congress; state agencies issue regulations under authority granted to them by the state legislature. Regulations have the force of law, and federal regulations preempt state laws as well as state regulations.

In addition, the president has the power to issue executive orders. Executive orders are presidential directives governing actions by other federal officials and agencies. Executive orders do not have to be approved by Congress.

1.2.4 International Treaties

Article II, Section 2, Clause 2 of the U.S. Constitution grants the president power to enter into treaties with other countries, with the "advice and consent" of two-thirds of the Senate. Once signed, treaties become part of U.S. federal law. As a result, Congress can modify or repeal treaties by subsequent legislative action, even if this amounts to a violation of the treaty under international law. The changes will be enforced by U.S. courts despite the fact that the international community considers the United States to be bound by the original treaty obligations.

States are forbidden to make treaties with other countries. Furthermore, the Supreme Court has ruled that the power to make treaties is separate from the federal government's other enumerated powers, and the federal government can use treaties to legislate in areas that would otherwise fall within the exclusive authority of the states.

1.2.5 Appellate Court Opinions

An appellate court is a court that hears appeals from lower-level courts. Usually, when an appellate court makes a decision, it not only decides who wins that specific case but also provides a written opinion that explains the basis for the decision as a guide to lower courts in handling future cases. When a case in a lower court is similar to a dispute that has already been resolved by a higher court in the jurisdiction, the court is bound to follow the reasoning used in the prior decision. Appellate court opinions are also referred to as *common law, case law*, or *judicially-created law*.

1.3 THE AMERICAN JUDICIAL SYSTEM

The role of the courts in America is to decide cases and controversies between adversarial parties. The American judicial system comprises two court systems— federal and state—that exist in parallel to one another. Although every state has its own court system, there are also federal courts in every state. However, federal courts have limited jurisdiction. *Jurisdiction* means the court has authority to hear a case and impose a remedy; the court must have jurisdiction over both the parties and the subject matter of the dispute in order to impose a remedy.

A case can only be brought in federal court if the dispute involves the U.S. Constitution or a federal statute, or is between citizens of different states and involves an aggregate claim of more than $75,000. A suit involving citizens of different states is referred to as a *diversity suit*; the "citizens" can be legal entities such as partnerships and corporations as well as individuals. Some claims involving the Constitution or a federal statute can be brought in either state court or federal court; this is referred to as *concurrent jurisdiction*. However, certain matters such as bankruptcy, patents and copyrights, actions involving the United States, and violations of federal criminal statutes can only be brought in federal court.

Only federal courts have the power to interpret the U.S. Constitution, federal laws, and federal agency regulations. Federal courts also have the power to review federal agency actions and determine the constitutionality of both federal and state laws. State courts have the power to interpret the state constitution, state laws, and state agency regulations.

1.3.1 Structure of the Court Systems

Both the state and federal court systems are multi-tiered. Cases are initially brought in a trial court; the trial can be either a jury or a bench (nonjury) trial. In a bench trial, the presiding judge delivers the verdict; in a jury trial, the jury delivers the verdict. Either party can appeal any part of the verdict to a first-level appeals court. In the federal system and the majority of the states, the ruling in the first-level appeals court can be appealed to a second-level appeals court. Courts of appeals do not use juries or witnesses, and no new evidence is submitted; appellate courts base their decisions on a review of lower-court records.

1.3.2 Federal Trial and Appeals Courts

In the federal system, most of the trial courts are district courts. Each state has at least one federal district case; more populous states can have three or four. In addition to the district courts, there is the Court of Federal Claims, a trial court that hears claims against the U.S. government. The district courts have concurrent jurisdiction with the Court of Federal Claims for claims under $10,000. When the claim involves a contract with a government agency, the Court of Federal Claims has concurrent jurisdiction with the applicable Board of Contract Appeals. Federal district courts are bound by legal precedents established by the decisions of the Supreme Court and the court of appeals for their respective circuit.

There are 13 federal courts of appeals. The U.S. Court of Appeals for the Federal Circuit hears appeals of decisions in cases involving patents, contract claims against the federal government, federal employment claims, and international trade. The Court of Appeals for the District of Columbia hears appeals from the DC District Court; the other 11 courts are circuit courts and hear appeals from the district courts in several states, called a *circuit*. For example, the Court of Appeals for the Eleventh Circuit hears appeals from the district courts in Florida, Alabama, and Georgia.

Although decisions from the federal courts of appeals can be appealed to the Supreme Court, the Supreme Court is not required to hear the appeal. In general, the Supreme Court will not accept a petition to review a lower-court ruling unless the case presents an important legal issue or there is a conflict in the rulings of the circuit courts with respect to the issue. In certain circumstances, the ruling of a state supreme court can be appealed to the U.S. Supreme Court; this usually occurs when the case involves a constitutional right that has been denied in the state courts.

1.3.3 State Trial and Appeals Courts

Although the states vary in the way they have structured their court systems, many states have a court of general jurisdiction that hears all types of cases. The court of general jurisdiction may also review challenges to rulings by administrative agencies such as those involving zoning and licensing. Some states have courts with specialized jurisdictions—for example, family courts that have jurisdiction over divorce and child custody disputes. In addition to these specialized trial courts, there may be less formal trial courts, such as magistrate courts, municipal courts, and justice of the peace courts that handle minor cases such as traffic offenses. Generally, the rulings in these courts can be appealed to a court of general jurisdiction.

Although some states have only one appeals court, most states have both an intermediate (first-level) appeals court and a second-level appeals court. In most states the second-level appeals court is called the *supreme court* of that state. While there is always the right of an appeal from a trial court decision, the state supreme courts are generally not required to hear an appeal of an intermediate appeals court decision.

1.4 COMMON LAW

There are two basic types of legal systems in the United States: common law and civil law. Louisiana has a civil law system that is derived from the French civil law system. Every other state has a common-law system; the federal legal system is also a common-law system. Common-law courts give great weight to previous court decisions, on the principle that it is unfair to treat similar facts differently on different occasions. The body of previous decisions (precedent) is referred to as *common law*.

Judges establish common law through written opinions that are binding on subsequent decisions of lower courts in the same jurisdiction. A federal district court is thus bound by the decisions of both its circuit court and the Supreme Court. A state trial court is bound by the appellate courts of that state. The reasoning and holdings of the courts in one state are not binding on the courts of any other states, but a decision in one state may influence or persuade the court of another state to reach a similar decision on an issue.

Common law is mostly state law. Broad areas of the law, including contracts, property, and torts, have traditionally been governed by the common law but these areas of the law are primarily within the jurisdiction of the states. Federal common law is relatively narrow in scope and is primarily limited to issues that are clearly federal and that have not been addressed by a statute.

1.4.1 Stare Decisis

The policy of adhering to principles established by decisions in earlier cases is known as *stare decisis*, which is Latin for "let the decision stand." Under stare decisis, once a court has addressed a legal question, the question must be addressed the same way in other cases that come before that court or lower courts in that jurisdiction. Decisions can be overturned by a higher court, however. For example, the decision of a federal district court can be overturned by the court of appeals for that circuit. A court of appeals decision can be overturned by the Supreme Court.

Courts sometimes overrule their own precedents by issuing an opinion that contradicts a previous ruling, but they generally only do so for a good reason. A ruling that does not follow precedent will almost certainly be appealed and may be overturned by the appeals court. The U.S. Supreme Court rarely overrules one of its precedents, but when it does, the new ruling usually signifies a radically different way of looking at an important legal issue.

Civil law systems, such as Louisiana's, do not follow stare decisis. In a civil law system, the primary source of law is the law code, which is a systematic collection of interrelated articles that explain the principles of law, rights, and entitlements. Civil law judges do not interpret the law but instead follow predetermined legal rules to arrive at their decisions. Civil law is the dominant legal tradition in most of Europe, all of Central and South America, and parts of Asia and Africa.

1.4.2 Restatements of the Law

Appellate court decisions are considered primary (binding) authority on lower courts. There are also a number of sources of secondary (nonbinding) authority. The secondary authorities that are cited most often in legal decisions are the Restatements of the Law, a series of treatises published by the American Law Institute (ALI). The ALI, a private organization composed of judges, lawyers, legal scholars, and law professors, was founded in 1923 with the objective of improving the law by gathering, studying, and synthesizing the common law of the states.

The Restatements attempt to organize the case law on a topic and present the rules or principles distilled from the cases. They are divided into sections, with each section containing a rule of law, comments and illustrations that clarify the rule, and major exceptions to the rule. Most of the original Restatements have been reissued in an updated Restatement 2nd series, and some have been reissued in a Restatement 3rd series. The Restatements cited most often in construction industry cases are the Restatement (2nd) of Contracts and the Restatement (2nd) of Torts.

Although the Restatements are not binding precedent in any jurisdiction, they reflect the consensus of the American legal community on what the law is and, in some cases, what it should be. As a result, they are typically granted considerable deference by judges. If a trial court finds that a dispute is fundamentally different from all previous cases heard in that state ("a matter of first impression"), the judge will often look to the relevant Restatement section to understand how other states have addressed the issue. In some cases, judges have explicitly adopted a section of the Restatement as the common law of the state.

1.5   LEGAL CODES

A *code* is a compilation of related statutes. The compilation of permanent federal laws is referred to as the *United States Code* (U.S.C.). The U.S.C. is divided into 50 titles by subject matter; Title 41, for example, encompasses statutes related to federal government contracts. A new edition of the U.S.C. is published every six years, and annual supplements are published between editions. Each annual supplement includes all new laws and all changes to existing laws since the previous edition. Various subsets of the U.S.C. are also identified as codes. Some codes collect and organize statutes that have been adopted over the years on a particular subject matter. Other codes, such as the federal Bankruptcy Code, consist of a group of statutes that were drafted and adopted by a legislature as a unified whole.

1.5.1   Uniform Codes

State laws are often based on uniform codes. Uniform codes are not in themselves statutes but are a set of model statutes related to a particular subject that can be adopted by the states. Once adopted by a state, the uniform code becomes the law in that state. A state may adopt all or part of a uniform code; it may also add its own amendments to the code to reflect local concerns or local approaches to particular issues.

The International Building Code (IBC) is an example of a uniform code. The IBC is published by the International Code Council (ICC) and does not become the law in any state until it is explicitly adopted by that state. The IBC has now been adopted by all of the states, but virtually every state has adopted amendments that add to, vary, or delete particular sections of the IBC.

1.5.2 The Uniform Commercial Code

The National Conference of Commissioners on Uniform State Laws (NCCUSL) has published a number of uniform codes. These include the Uniform Partnership Act (UPA), the Uniform Arbitration Act of 1956 (UAA), and its successor, the Revised Uniform Arbitration Act of 2000 (RUAA). The uniform code that is most applicable to the construction industry is the Uniform Commercial Code (UCC). The UCC is a collection of laws aimed at furthering uniformity and fair dealing in business and commercial transactions. It has been adopted, at least in part, by all of the states. As with building codes, the law of any particular state is not the UCC but whatever parts of the UCC that the state has adopted, along with any amendments it has adopted.

Although the UCC consists of 13 sections (referred to as Articles), the only sections that are significant to construction are Article 1, General Provisions, and Article 2, Sales. Article 2 applies to transactions in goods, where "goods" are things that are tangible and movable. Thus, Article 2 does not apply to real estate; it also does not apply to services like design or construction. However, it does apply to the contracts to purchase the materials used in construction.

It should be noted that the UCC generally supplies default terms; it does not override any terms in a contract. For example, Article 2 provides a remedy for breach of a sales contract where the parties have not specifically agreed to a remedy in their contract. This is different from the IBC, which sets building code requirements.

As judicial decisions in each state have interpreted and applied sections of that state's UCC, they have established a common-law commercial code that supplements the explicit language of the code. Moreover, even if a dispute is not covered by the UCC (for example, a dispute involving an employment contract), a court may apply a section of the UCC by analogy if it believes the rule expressed by the code section is appropriate to adopt as a more general common-law rule.

1.6 LEGAL DOCTRINES

A legal doctrine is a framework or set of rules established by precedent in the common law, through which judgments can be determined on a particular issue. A doctrine comes about when a judge makes a ruling and outlines a process in a way that allows the process to be applied in subsequent cases. When enough judges make use of the process, it becomes established as the de facto method of deciding that issue and is considered a doctrine.

Many of the legal doctrines used in the construction industry have evolved from cases involving federal government contracts. While the holding in the case is only applicable to cases brought in federal court, state courts often adopt the doctrine as the law of the state. The doctrine cited most often in both state and federal courts is the Spearin doctrine, from the case *United States v. Spearin.*[1] Under the Spearin doctrine, the owner is liable for any delays or cost increases due to defects in the plans and specifications. Doctrines may also evolve over time from a series of cases in both federal and state courts. An example of such a doctrine is the economic loss doctrine, which imposes limits on a party's ability to recover damages for a tort claim such as negligence.

Doctrines are not necessarily interpreted the same way in every state, however. A state may create exceptions such that the doctrine does not apply in specific circumstances. Likewise, a state may extend the doctrine to cover circumstances not included in the original holdings. The economic loss doctrine, for example, is interpreted very differently by different states.

1.7 CHOICE-OF-LAW CLAUSES

Construction contracts and design agreements typically include a "choice-of-law" clause that indicates which state's law will govern any disputes. For example, §13.1 of AIA A201 states:

> *The Contract shall be governed by the law of the place where the Project is located, except, that if the parties have selected arbitration as the method of binding dispute resolution, the Federal Arbitration Act shall govern Section 15.4. [Section 15.4 specifies the procedure to be used for arbitration.]*

The choice of law can be significant, as the law that applies to construction projects is primarily state law, and the law on a particular issue can be very different in the different states.

The state chosen must have some connection with the parties or the project. Generally, it must be either the state in which the project is located (the project's *situs state*), the state in which at least one of the parties has its principal place of business, or the state in which at least one of the parties is incorporated. When these are all the same state, that state is the only choice for governing law. When these are different states, the parties may prefer one state over another. For example, an Illinois architect working on a project in Wisconsin would probably want Illinois law to apply to the design agreement, because Illinois strictly applies the economic loss doctrine to prevent negligence claims for defective architectural design services. The owner would probably prefer that Wisconsin law apply, because Wisconsin does allow such claims.

---

[1] *United States v. Spearin*, 248 U.S. 132, 39 S.Ct. 59, 63 L.Ed. 166 (1918).

If the parties want to make their choice of law apply to tort claims as well as contract claims the contract would state that the chosen state's law:

> *. . . governs all matters arising from, related to, or connected with, the contract or the work, regardless of how remotely and regardless of whether sounding in contract, tort, arising under a statute, or some other body of law.*

Some states have mandatory choice-of-law statutes. Under these statutes, the law of that state governs all projects within the state, regardless of the contract language. When federal courts have to decide a matter involving state law in a diversity case, they will use the law of the state in which the court is located, unless the parties have specified that the law of another state applies.

1.8   CRIMINAL LAW VERSUS CIVIL LAW

There are two broad categories of law: civil law and criminal law. Civil law deals with disputes between individuals, organizations, or government agencies, in which compensation or some other remedy may be awarded to the injured party. In a civil lawsuit, the party that brings the case (the plaintiff) is typically awarded money damages if it prevails on its claim against the other party (the defendant).

In contrast, criminal law comprises rules prohibiting conduct that threatens, harms, or otherwise endangers the safety and welfare of the public, and sets out the punishment to be imposed on those who break these rules. Criminal lawsuits are filed by the government against individuals or organizations that have violated criminal statutes. If the defendants in a criminal case are found guilty, they may be punished by incarceration or a fine paid to the government. Victims of crimes must usually bring a civil case in order to be compensated for the injuries they suffered as a result of the crimes.

The vast majority of the legal issues arising in construction are civil. For instance, if an owner felt its roof was leaking because of defective construction, it could bring a breach-of-contract case against the contractor and, if successful, would probably be awarded the cost of repair. Criminal cases do occur, however. The federal government has brought criminal complaints on construction projects because of serious violations of environmental statutes, particularly when the violations were intentional or grossly negligent.

1.9   CAUSE OF ACTION

The legal theory upon which a plaintiff brings a lawsuit is referred to as the *cause of action*. The most common cause of action in the construction industry is breach of contract, but other causes of action include professional negligence, negligent misrepresentation, unjust enrichment, and *quantum meruit*.

The plaintiff initiates a lawsuit by filing a complaint with the appropriate court. The complaint must state both the cause of action for the injury that the plaintiff claims to have suffered and the legal remedy it is seeking (the relief that the court is asked to grant). Often, the facts or events that entitle a person to seek judicial relief may create more than one cause of action; in the interest of judicial efficiency, all causes of action arising out of a set of facts or events must typically be brought in the same lawsuit.

The defendant must file an answer to the complaint within a certain number of days. In the answer, the plaintiff's allegations can be admitted, denied, or neither admitted nor denied, on the basis that the defendant has insufficient information to form a response. The answer may also include counterclaims whereby the defendant states its own causes of action against the plaintiff. Finally, the answer may contain affirmative defenses. An affirmative defense does not consider whether the facts alleged are true; instead, it presents facts that attempt to justify or excuse the behavior on which the lawsuit is based. For example, self-defense might be raised as a defense to an assault claim.

A cause of action can arise from either a failure to perform a legal obligation or a violation of a right. The importance of the failure or violation lies in its legal effect, in other words, how the facts and circumstances, considered as a whole, relate to applicable law. An act might give rise to a cause of action in one set of circumstances but not in another. For example, an individual may be privileged to trespass on the property of another if the individual was in danger. In such a case, the property owner would not have a cause of action for trespass. However, the trespasser would need to compensate the property owner for any property damage.

The points that a plaintiff must prove for a given cause of action are called the *elements* of that cause of action. For example, the elements of a negligence claim are the existence of a duty, breach of that duty, a connection between the breach and the plaintiff's injury, and damages as result of the breach. If a complaint does not allege facts sufficient to support every element of a claim, the court may dismiss the complaint.

1.10 SUMMARY JUDGMENT

Summary judgment is a procedural device used to dispose of a case without a trial. It is applicable when there is no dispute about the material facts of the case, and one of the parties is entitled to judgment as a matter of law. Either party may move for summary judgment, and it is not uncommon for both parties to seek it. A judge may also determine *sua sponte* (on its own initiative) that summary judgment is appropriate. A partial summary judgment can be used to dispose of certain issues or claims. For example, a court might grant partial summary judgment and find that the defendant is liable for the plaintiff's injuries, but a trial would still be necessary to determine the amount of damages.

A motion for summary judgment is usually based on information obtained during discovery. Any evidence that would be admissible at trial can be used to support a motion for summary judgment. Summary judgment does not mean that the judge has decided which side would prevail at trial. Rather, it means there are no factual questions for a judge or jury to decide.

Summary judgment is properly granted only when two conditions are met: (1) There is no genuine issues of material fact, and (2) the moving party is entitled to judgment as a matter of law. A genuine issue of material fact requires there to be a legitimate dispute over facts that are central to the case; minor factual disputes will not defeat a motion for summary judgment. In addition, the law as applied to the undisputed facts of the case must require judgment for the moving party.

The moving party has the burden of proving that summary judgment is proper; the court examines the evidence presented with the motion in the light most favorable to the nonmoving party. The nonmoving party must generally cite to evidence that contradicts the moving party's version of the facts. When the nonmoving party will bear the burden of proof at trial, the moving party may obtain summary judgment by showing that the nonmoving party has no evidence or that its evidence is insufficient to meet its burden at trial.

2

BASIC LEGAL PRINCIPLES

2.1   LEGAL ISSUES IN CONSTRUCTION

Although construction is not as regulated as many other industries, law is still
an integral part of the construction process. Most of the legal issues that arise in
the construction industry involve contract law. Contract law governs the enforcement of voluntary agreements between parties and the resolution of disputes
that arise under such agreements. Contract disputes on construction projects
may also include issues related to agency law, as the owner is often represented
by an agent such as an architect or engineer (A/E). Likewise, the contractor's
project superintendent is an agent for the contractor. Often the issue that arises
is whether the agent had authority for its actions. Contract disputes may also
include issues related to insurance law, such as whether a specific loss is covered
under the terms of an insurance policy.

Tort claims are not as common as contract claims but may arise between parties that do not have a contract. For example, the contractor may want to bring
a negligence claim against the A/E because the A/E improperly rejected work.
Tort claims may also be brought by third parties that are not involved in the
construction project, such as adjacent landowners that have suffered property
damage.

Certain aspects of property law, such as easements and zoning regulations,
can have a significant impact on a construction project. Such issues are typically
governed by city or county ordinances. Property law also encompasses issues
related to the transfer of title to land and buildings. When a project runs into
financial problems, the relative priority of those who have claims on the title to
the property may determine who gets paid.

2.2   PRINCIPLES OF CONTRACT LAW

In legal terms, a contract is a promise that the law will enforce. The primary purpose of a contract is to state each party's obligations and inform each party of

its rights if the other party does not perform its obligations in accordance with the contract. An executed contract is one that has been signed by the parties; the parties that have signed the contract are said to be in *privity of contract*.

A contract is not formed unless there is a "meeting of the minds" such that both parties are agreeing to the same terms. One party (the *offeror*) must make an offer, and the other party (the *offeree*) must accept that offer. If the offeree does not accept the offer but instead makes a counteroffer, the original offer is no longer valid and there is no contract unless the original offeror accepts the counteroffer. In addition, a contract is not valid unless each party provides the other party with *consideration*. The legal meaning of the word consideration has nothing to do with its ordinary meaning. Legal consideration simply means something of legal value.

2.2.1 Unilateral Contracts versus Bilateral Contracts

Contracts can be unilateral or bilateral. In a bilateral contract, each party's consideration is a promise. It can be either a promise to do something that the party has no legal obligation to do, or a promise to refrain from doing something it has the legal right to do. For example, a promise to refrain from suing when one honestly believes that one has a valid claim would qualify as consideration. In a typical business contract, one party promises to provide merchandise or a service; the other party promises to pay for the merchandise or service. In addition to the promises that define the exchange, each party typically makes a number of other promises with respect to the quality of the merchandise or service and the timing of performance and payment.

In a unilateral contract, only one party makes a promise; the other party's consideration is an action. The most common type of unilateral contract is when one party promises to pay for a service. The other party does not promise to perform the service, but a contract exists once the service is performed. An example would be promising to pay the first person who hauls away trash from a construction site. The offer can be made to several trash removal companies; the contract is not formed until someone actually performs the requested service. Although most contracts are bilateral, unilateral contracts are sometimes made for services or commodity goods like lumber or fill dirt.

It should be noted that contracts seldom use the word *promise* to express the parties' commitments to future performance. Contractual obligations are typically phrased using the words *shall, shall not, will, must, is obligated to, covenants*, or *agrees to*.

2.2.2 Oral Contracts

Most contracts on construction projects are written; the written document provides evidence of the parties' agreement. However, with the exception of contracts that are required by law to be in writing, oral contracts are valid as long as a meeting of the minds can be inferred from the parties' conduct.

Every state has what is known as a *statute of frauds* that requires certain types of contracts to be in writing and signed by the parties. Although these statutes vary somewhat from state to state, all states require that a contract be in writing if the terms of the contract are such that it cannot be completed within a year. This does not mean that the contract will probably take more than a year to complete; it means that there is a contractual obligation that cannot be satisfied within a year of the contract execution. As an example, a contract that included performance testing a year after substantial completion of the project could not be completed within a year.

In addition, all state statutes of fraud require that a contract be in writing when it involves the sale of real estate. Many states have other statutes that require written contracts for certain types of transactions. For example, under California law, architects and engineers must use a written contract when contracting to provide professional services to a client.

It should be noted that even if a written contract is required, an oral contract is not void or illegal, and the parties can choose to comply with it. Nevertheless, the contract is voidable, which means that if either party chooses not to comply with it, a court will not enforce it.

2.2.3   Third-Party Beneficiaries

A third-party beneficiary is a person or entity that is entitled to benefit from a contract, even though it is not a party to the contract. The benefit may be intended as a gift or to satisfy a legal obligation. In either case, the third party acquires rights under the contract and may sue to enforce the parties' contractual obligations.

A party claiming third-party beneficiary status must establish that the contracting parties intended to afford the third party some benefit. In particular, the third party must show that it was an intentional, rather than incidental, beneficiary of the contract. An example of an incidental beneficiary is someone whose property values would increase because of construction on an adjacent property. Absent a specific agreement, the adjacent property owner would have no claim if the owner decided to abandon the project.

2.2.4   Contract Interpretation

When a dispute over contract requirements ends up in court and cannot be resolved under the terms of the contract, the court typically resorts to standard rules of contract interpretation that have developed through case law. The goal of contract interpretation is to carry out the intent of the parties as it existed at the time of contracting. However, the courts do not look at what the parties meant to say (their subjective intent) but to the meaning of what they did say, as expressed by the language of the contract.

If the court finds that the contract is unambiguous, the parties' differing interpretations are immaterial; an ambiguity does not arise merely because the parties disagree on the interpretation of their contract. Courts enforce unambiguous contracts according to what they consider the plain meaning of the words.

CASE STUDY—CONTRACT INTERPRETATION

An owner/general contractor hired a subcontractor to do plumbing work on a condominium project. The contract stated: "Owner to carry fire, tornado, and other necessary insurance." During construction, the subcontractor's negligence resulted in a fire that caused $120,000 in damages. When the owner sued the subcontractor to recover these damages, the subcontractor said it should be covered by the owner's insurance.

The court noted that the owner had the right to insure its own property without the consent or agreement of the subcontractor. Therefore, the only reasonable explanation for a contract provision requiring the owner to carry insurance was to protect the subcontractor from risk of the insured loss. The court held that, based on the contract language, it was the parties' intent to shift the risk of fire damage to the owner's insurance company. Thus, the subcontractor was not liable for the loss; the owner had to recover its damages from its insurance company.

Berger v. Teton Shadows Incorporated,
820 P.2d 176 (Wyo. 1991)

2.2.4.1 Integration Clauses and Parol Evidence

Before the parties sign the contract, there are often preliminary negotiations and discussions. When the written contract is finally signed, it may not include some of the issues that were discussed in preliminary negotiations, or it may deal with various issues differently than in the preliminary discussions. Evidence of the parties' discussions (oral or written) before and at the time the contract was signed is referred to as *parol evidence*.

If there is a dispute over the meaning of the contract but the written document appears to be an integration (a complete and final expression of the parties' agreement), courts will not permit either party to present parol evidence that alters or contradicts the written document. This is known as the *parol evidence rule*; the rationale is that the purpose of creating a written agreement is to memorialize the contract terms and exclude all understandings to the contrary.

In determining whether a document is an integration, courts look at both the circumstances under which the agreement was reached and the actual words of the contract. Construction contracts often contain an integration clause, which states that the contract represents "the entire and integrated agreement between the parties." Integration clauses may expressly state that the contract supersedes all prior negotiations, proposals, bids, and agreements, whether written or oral. Even without an integration clause, courts only allow the parties to present evidence of contradictory terms and agreements if it is clear that the contract was not intended to encompass the parties' entire agreement.

The parol evidence rule only applies to communications that occurred before or at the time the contract was executed, however. The parties may modify or supplement a written contract after its execution, and evidence of such later agreements would be allowed in a dispute over the contract requirements. There are also a number of exceptions to the parol evidence rule. For example, a party may introduce parol evidence to show that a contract was never formed because its formation was based on a condition that was never met. Likewise, a party may introduce parol evidence to show that the contract is unenforceable because it was procured by fraud or duress. Parol evidence is also admissible to show that the original writing contains a mistake or has been altered.

CASE STUDY—EXTRINSIC EVIDENCE

An owner entered into a contract with a contractor to build a grain storage building. The building was not completed on time, and the contractor stated it would reduce the price if the owner did not sue because of the late completion. The owner agreed and signed a release discharging the contractor from all current and future claims concerning the contract.

The owner subsequently discovered that the building had structural defects and did not hold the amount of grain contracted for. The owner attempted to bring a claim against the contractor, arguing that in signing the release, the owner only intended to discharge the delay claims. The court dismissed the owner's claims, holding that the plain language of the release discharged the contractor from all claims. Since the wording of the release was unambiguous, the court did not allow extrinsic evidence.

Grimm v. F. D. Borkholder Co., Inc.,
454 N.E.2d 84 (Ind. App. 1983)

2.2.4.2 *Ambiguities*

Even when the parties agree that the contract is the complete statement of their intentions, they may have different interpretations as to what the contract requires. If the contract has been put into writing, courts will attempt to determine the parties' intent from the writing alone if possible. If the words of a written contract can be given a definite or certain legal meaning, the contract is unambiguous. Courts will not allow the parties to introduce extrinsic evidence (evidence external to the contract) that alters or varies an unambiguous contract. Courts must enforce an unambiguous contract according to its terms, regardless of its apparent unreasonableness. Whether a contract is ambiguous is a question of law that the court decides by looking at the contract as a whole in light of the circumstances under which the contract was formed.

If the language of the contract is subject to two or more reasonable interpreta-tions, the contract is ambiguous. Courts then consider both parties' interpretations and allow the parties to present evidence explaining the ambiguity. For example, if the contract uses the term *affiliated entities* but does not define the term, the court may allow extrinsic evidence showing whether the parties meant only the contracting party and its wholly owned subsidiaries, or whether they also meant to include independent subcontractors.

Extrinsic evidence may include the parties' conduct over the course of the contract to date (course of performance), prior dealings, and industry custom, as well as evidence of the parties' negotiations. In such cases, the evidence of the negotiations (parol evidence) is not being used to contradict the terms of the contract but to explain an ambiguity.

2.2.4.3   Reasonable Interpretation of the Entire Contract

When interpreting contract documents, courts view the contract as would a reasonably intelligent third person who is acquainted with the trade usage of the words. They consider both the expressed intent of the parties and the circumstances surrounding the contract formation. Although courts typi-cally try to avoid an interpretation that is inequitable or oppressive, they will not rewrite a contract simply because one of the parties has made a bad bargain.

Courts interpret the contract as a whole. When the parties disagree on the interpretation of a particular provision, the court will consider the entire contract to determine the meaning of that provision. Likewise, when vari-ous provisions in an agreement appear to be in conflict, the court will try to reconcile the conflicting provisions to the remainder of the contract. All interpretations must be reasonable and logical, and courts presume that the parties intended every word in the contract to have some purpose. Thus, they will favor an interpretation that does not make any part of the docu-ment meaningless.

2.2.4.4   Trade Custom and Usage

Contracts are generally governed by the customs of the industry in which the parties conduct their business. If the contract is ambiguous and a cus-tom is so well known that it is reasonable to assume the parties contracted with reference to it, the custom is considered when interpreting the contract. Industry customs are not used to vary or contradict an unambiguous con-tract, however.

Words, terms, and phrases in the contract are given their ordinary mean-ings unless it is clear that the parties intended them to have different meanings. Technical terms are given the meanings they usually have within the industry, unless it is clear that the parties intended to use different meanings.

2.2.4.5   *Course of Performance and Prior Dealings*

The parties themselves have the best understanding of what they meant by specific terms, and their actions typically reflect this understanding. When a contract is deemed ambiguous, the court usually considers the parties' performance of the contract (*course of performance*) as the best evidence of their intentions when contracting.

The court may also look at the parties' prior dealings under other contracts. *Prior dealing* is defined as previous conduct between the parties that establishes a common basis for interpreting other conduct. Because course of performance and prior dealings reflect the actions of the disputing parties, courts tend to give them more weight than trade custom and usage.

2.3   PRINCIPLES OF AGENCY LAW

An agency relationship is a contractual relationship between an individual or business (the principal) and another individual (the agent) under which the principal authorizes the agent to act for it. The contract between the parties defines the nature and scope of the actions that the agent is authorized to undertake on behalf of the principal.

Agency relationships are common in businesses, as corporations and partnerships can take action only through an agent; the directors, officers, and even the employees of a business are all agents for the business. The agents of a business do not necessarily have the same authority, however. Officers such as the president and secretary of a business are usually general agents with a wide range of powers. Other employees are typically special (limited) agents whose authority is limited to certain acts. For example, the office manager might be authorized to make purchases of up to $200 without getting approval from the company president.

The authority explicitly delegated by the terms of the agency contract is referred to as *express authority*. In addition to express authority, the agent will have implied authority for certain acts. *Implied authority* is the authority to perform actions that are not specifically authorized but are reasonably necessary if the agent is to accomplish the tasks that are expressly authorized. For example, when a testing company is hired to test concrete for air content, it will have the implied authority to reject any loads that are not within the allowable tolerances.

2.3.1   Apparent Authority

In addition to the actual (explicit and implicit) authority delegated by the contract, the agent may also have *apparent authority*. Apparent authority exists when the principal acted in such a way that a third party (a person or entity other than the agent and principal) reasonably believed that the principal authorized the agent to take the action in question. Out of fairness to the third party, the law holds the principal liable for the agent's acts in such circumstances.

To create apparent authority, there must have been some act or knowing omission on the principal's part; the principal is not bound when it is the agent that has given the third party this false impression. However, the principal will be bound if the agent says or does something while the principal is present, and the principal does nothing to prevent the third party from believing that the agent has the authority to bind the principal with respect to the decisions or instructions in question. Apparent authority can also arise when the principal has terminated the agent's authority but did not inform the third party of this termination.

2.3.2   The Principal's Liability for the Agent's Acts

An agent is considered a fiduciary to the principal. This means that the agent has implicitly promised to act in the best interests of the principal. The agent must act in good faith and must disclose any information that is relevant to the agency relationship. For example, an architect or engineer (A/E) that is assisting the owner by reviewing bids would be required to disclose the fact that a close relative was a principal in one of the companies that was bidding.

An agent that acts within the scope of its authority may legally bind the principal to contracts or other commitments to third parties. Those third parties, in turn, expect that the agent is acting on behalf of the principal and conduct their affairs in reliance on the actions and commitments of the agent. As an example, when the president of a contracting company signs a lease for a piece of equipment, he is acting as an agent of the company, and, as such, his signature is enough to bind the company to the terms of the lease.

When the agent acted within the scope of its agency, the principal is liable for the agent's acts, even if the agent acted contrary to the principal's instructions. If the contract documents state that the A/E may authorize additional work, the owner is liable for the cost of such work, even if what the A/E directed the contractor to do was not what the owner wanted. The A/E may be liable to the owner for breach of contract, but as long as the contractor's reliance on the A/E's direction was reasonable, the owner is bound by the A/E's acts and must pay for the work.

A principal is generally not liable for contracts or commitments made on its behalf if the agent acted outside the scope of its authority. Thus, the owner has no obligation to pay for additional work if the contractor performed the work at the direction of the A/E but the construction contract required the owner's approval for additional work.

2.3.3   Ratification

If an agent acts outside its scope of authority but the principal affirms the unauthorized action, the principal is bound by the action. This is referred to as *ratification*. Ratification can be based on either the principal's express approval of the action or implied approval. An example of implied approval is the principal's failure to return an item that it knew was bought without proper authorization.

2.4 PRINCIPLES OF TORT LAW

In contrast to contract law, which rests on obligations that the parties have bargained for through the terms of their contract, tort law is based on legal obligations created by statute or through judicial opinions. The goal of tort law is to protect people from unexpected and overwhelming misfortunes through the fault of others and to compensate them when such misfortunes occur.

Relatively few tort claims arise as a result of federal law; tort claims generally arise out of state common law or state statutes. The only common federal tort claim is the 42 U.S.C. §1983 remedy for violation of an individual's civil rights, which can be used to sue for anything from a free speech claim to use of excessive force by the police.

2.4.1 Intentional Torts

There are three categories of torts: intentional torts, unintentional torts, and strict liability torts. An *intentional tort* is a tort that results from an intentional act on the part of the tortfeasor (wrongdoer). An individual can be liable for an intentional tort even if he or she did not intend to cause any harm; it is enough that the act which resulted in the injury was intentional. Courts generally allow both compensatory and punitive damages for an intentional tort. *Compensatory damages* attempt to make the victim whole by placing a monetary value on the harm done. *Punitive damages*, also called *exemplary damages*, are designed to punish malicious wrongdoers and deter others from behaving in a similar fashion. In many states, intentional torts are uninsurable as a matter of public policy, so individuals found guilty of such torts must pay damages out of their own pockets.

Intentional torts include assault, false imprisonment, trespass to land, fraud, and the so-called dignitary torts that arise when the injury is to an individual's reputation or privacy. Dignitary torts include defamation (libel and slander), intentional infliction of emotional distress, and invasion of privacy. However, the only intentional tort that arises with any frequency in the context of a construction project is fraud (intentional misrepresentation).

2.4.2 Unintentional Torts (Negligence)

Negligence involves carelessness rather than an intentional act; the harm results from the tortfeasor's failure to take sufficient care in fulfilling a duty.

Failure to take sufficient care can mean either doing something that a reasonably prudent person would not do under similar circumstances or failing to do something that a reasonably prudent person would do. The elements of a negligence claim are defined by common law as well as statutory standards. Statutes are often intended to codify principles embodied in common law, but a statute can also be a reaction to a judicial opinion that the legislature thinks is contrary to public policy. In such cases, the statute overrules or modifies the common law.

Tort law imposes minimum standards of behavior on all members of society; these standards include the duty to take reasonable steps to protect others from being injured or having their possessions damaged. In order not to breach this duty of care, a defendant must generally meet the standard of a "reasonable person." This is an objective standard; it does not require perfection, and it takes into account that an average person does not foresee every risk. The average person is not assumed to be perfect, just ordinarily careful and prudent. The test of an ordinary average person would not be appropriate for professionals such as architects and engineers who hold themselves out as possessing certain skills, however. In order not to breach its duty of care, a professional must meet the standard of a "reasonable professional."

2.4.2.1 Elements of Negligence

The tort of negligence has four basic elements: The defendant must owe the claimant a duty of care, the defendant must have breached that duty of care, the claimant must have suffered actual injuries, and the defendant's breach must have been the cause of the injuries. There can be no liability in negligence unless the claimant establishes both that it was owed a duty of care by the defendant and that there has been a breach of that duty.

Having established that it was owed a duty of care, the claimant must prove that the defendant failed to do what the reasonable person or reasonable professional would have done under similar circumstances. The defendant has breached its duty toward the claimant if its conduct fell short of the standard expected under the circumstances.

Because negligence is based on state law, the circumstances under which a defendant will be found liable for negligence can vary from state to state. State law may differ as to whether there was a duty in a particular case or, if there was a duty, whether the defendant's actions amounted to a breach of that duty. If a breach of duty is found, tort law requires that the injured party be compensated, provided the injury was both actually and proximately caused by the defendant's wrongdoing.

Actual causation, also referred to as *cause in fact*, means that the injury would not have happened "but for" the defendant's action. Proximate (legal) causation means that the injury is sufficiently related to the defendant's conduct that liability should attach. *Proximate causation* is thus a legal limitation on cause in fact; it prevents recovery when the relationship between the defendant's conduct and the claimant's injury is so tenuous that it does not justify imposing tort liability.

In most states, proximate cause is based on foreseeability. In other words, the injury must have been at least a reasonably foreseeable result of the defendant's action. As an example, if a contractor left a piece of equipment in an unlocked shed with the keys easily accessible, it is foreseeable that the equipment might be stolen. The contractor could be held liable if the equipment was, in fact, stolen and was subsequently involved in an accident where people were injured. The contractor is less likely to be held liable if the shed had been locked, there was an alarm system, and the keys had been removed.

2.4.2.2 Simple Negligence versus Gross Negligence

Negligence can be categorized as simple negligence or gross negligence. *Simple negligence*, also referred to as *ordinary negligence*, is failure to exercise the degree of care expected of a person of ordinary prudence under like circumstances to protect others from a foreseeable risk of harm. In contrast, *gross negligence* is marked by a failure to exercise even the slightest care in protecting others from harm; it is conduct that presents an unreasonably high degree of risk to others.

Although there is no bright line between ordinary and gross negligence, gross negligence is often considered to involve such a conscious indifference to the welfare of another that it is the close equivalent of a willingness that the harm will occur. Gross negligence does not require proof of a motive, but if a motive such as profit or personal fame can be shown, it is easier to prove.

Negligence that is both offensive and of a type that a juror would consider reckless, without the help of expert testimony, may be found to be gross negligence. For example, if a contractor knowingly used a piece of defective equipment, and the equipment subsequently malfunctioned and caused a serious injury, the contractor could be found liable for gross negligence. In contrast, if the injury occurred because the contractor had not tested the equipment properly before use, the contractor is more likely to be found liable for simple negligence.

2.4.2.3 Proof of Damages

Compensatory damages for negligence claims include special damages and general damages. *Special damages* are quantifiable dollar losses; they include lost wages, medical bills, and property damage. *General damages* are damages for things that are not easily quantified, such as pain and suffering. Punitive damages typically are not allowed for an ordinary negligence claim. However, if the defendant is found guilty of gross negligence, the court will often allow both compensatory and punitive damages.

CASE STUDY—PUNITIVE DAMAGES

The general contractor on a motel construction project built three long free-standing fire walls. Two of the walls fell over during a windstorm; the third remained standing and was partially braced, but a few weeks later the bracing was removed and the wall fell over, injuring a subcontractor. The court held that the danger of the wall collapsing was not so obvious that the subcontractor assumed the risk of injury simply by going in its vicinity; the subcontractor was thus entitled to recover for its actual damages.

However, the contractor was not liable for punitive damages, as it had not demonstrated any willful misconduct or malice. Although the contractor was negligent in constructing a freestanding wall of such length, simple negligence does not give rise to punitive damages. In order to be liable for punitive damages, the contractor must have demonstrated such an entire lack of care that it could be presumed to be consciously indifferent to the consequences of its actions.

BLI Construction Company, Inc., v. L. J. Debari et al.
217 S.E.2d 426 (Ga. App. 1975)

2.4.2.4 Defenses to a Negligence Claim

Historically, contributory negligence was allowed as a defense to a negligence claim. Under the doctrine of *contributory negligence*, if the injured party's negligence contributed to the injury, the injured party was not allowed any recovery. Most states now follow the doctrine of comparative negligence, however. Under *comparative negligence*, damages are determined by reference to the proportionate fault of the claimant and the defendant. For example, a claimant awarded $100,000 in damages might have been found 30 percent responsible for the injury. The recoverable damages would therefore be reduced to $70,000.

2.4.2.5 Negligence per se

Negligence per se (statutory negligence) entails violation of a statute designed to protect the public safety. *Per se* means without regard for the circumstances. Something that is negligent per se is considered negligence as a matter of law; the plaintiff does not need to prove there was a breach of duty. However, the plaintiff must still prove that the defendant's act was both the actual and proximate cause of its injuries. In addition, the plaintiff can only recover on a theory of negligence per se if the injury is of the type that the statute is designed to prevent, the injured party is a member of the class of persons sought to be protected by the statute, and the violation is the proximate cause of the injury.

As an example, local ordinances typically restrict the hours during which construction can take place, to minimize the inconvenience to those living nearby. If an accident took place while the contractor was working after hours, the fact that the contractor was working in violation of the ordinance would not make the contractor negligent per se. In contrast, parking restrictions typically designate certain areas as noparking zones because of safety concerns. If the contractor parked its truck in a noparking zone and there was an accident involving the truck, the contractor would likely be held negligent per se.

A few states define violation of a statute to be evidence of negligence rather than negligence per se. The evidence is presented to the jury or the judge to consider along with the other evidence.

2.4.2.6 Res Ipsa Loquitur

Generally, the plaintiff has the burden of proving that the defendant has not met the standard of a reasonable person. In certain situations, it may be difficult for the plaintiff to make this proof, even though it is unlikely that a certain event could have taken place without the defendant's negligence. In such cases, it may be possible to shift the evidentiary burden to the defendant under the theory of *res ipsa loquitur* ("the thing speaks for itself"). The defendant must then show that the injury did not result from its negligence.

The evidentiary burden can only be shifted to the defendant if the following criteria are satisfied:

- The incident occurred in an unexplainable fashion;
- The incident would not have occurred in the ordinary course of events if not for the defendant's negligence; and
- The defendant had control of the object that caused the injury.

As an example, a fire could have started in an area where a subcontractor stored its materials and equipment. Although it might be impossible to prove that the subcontractor was responsible for the fire, if no one else had access to the area, the subcontractor would be required to show that the fire was not started by one of its employees.

2.4.3 Strict Liability

Strict liability refers to situations where a party is liable for injuries no matter what precautions were taken. Strict liability often applies to product liability claims; in addition, some statutory torts, including many environmental torts, constitute strict liability. The term *strict liability* refers to the fact that the tortfeasor's liability is based strictly on the result of its conduct; it does not matter that the tortfeasor may have done all that was possible to prevent injuries.

In the context of a construction project, strict liability claims are typically brought for injuries resulting from ultra-hazardous activities such as blasting. The contractor will be held liable for any injuries that result from blasting, even if it was not negligent.

2.4.4 Misrepresentation

The tort that arises most often in the construction industry is misrepresentation. Misrepresentation involves either a misrepresentation of a material (significant) fact or a failure to provide material information. The party alleging injury must have relied on the misrepresentation, the reliance must have been reasonable, and the party must have suffered its injury as a result of this reliance. Misrepresentation can be either negligent or intentional; intentional misrepresentation is referred to as *fraud*.

Fraud claims often involve complicated financial transactions conducted by business professionals with specialized knowledge and criminal intent. Although fraud claims occasionally arise on construction projects, they are difficult to prove. To prevail on a fraud claim, the claimant must prove that the defendant either knew the representation at issue was false or made it recklessly as a positive assertion, without any knowledge of its truth. In addition, the claimant must prove that the defendant intended to induce the claimant to act upon the representation.

Claims of negligent misrepresentation are more common than fraud claims. They are most often asserted against design professionals and allege either negligent supervision or defective plans and specifications. To prove negligent misrepresentation in a claim against the design professional, the claimant must show that:

- The design professional misrepresented a material fact;
- The design professional did not exercise reasonable care or competence in verifying that the representation was correct;
- The claimant's reliance on the misrepresentation was reasonable; and
- Reliance on the misrepresentation was the cause of the claimant's damages.

Claimants cannot recover damages for either intentional or negligent misrepresentation unless they actually suffered an injury, however. As an example, the claimants may have purchased a house for $500,000, based on the seller's representation that there was no termite damage. After the sale closed, the claimants found that there actually was termite damage, and it would cost $50,000 to remove the termites. Nevertheless, if the court found that the fair market value of the house was $600,000, the claimants would not have suffered an injury, because their total cost was still less than the value of the house. Since the claimants had not suffered an injury, they would not be entitled to recover damages.

3

PROJECT PARTICIPANTS

To understand the legal issues that arise during a construction project, one must look at the roles of the various participants. On all projects there will be an owner and a contractor. On most projects there will also be a design professional (A/E). On many projects, the owner, contractor, and A/E are separate entities. On some projects, however, the same entity may be both the A/E and the contractor. Alternatively, the owner may also be the contractor or A/E, or both the contractor and the A/E. Despite the resulting differences in contractual relationships, the basic legal issues are similar on all projects.

3.1 THE OWNER

The owner is responsible for providing the project site and arranging for the project financing. In addition, the owner is ultimately responsible for ensuring that the project complies with all applicable regulations, both during construction and once the project is complete. Various characteristics of the owner affect the legal issues that can arise.

All projects must comply with federal and state regulations designed to protect the health and safety of the public. However, projects constructed for public owners such as federal, state, and local agencies must also comply with regulations designed both to promote specific public policies and ensure proper use of public funds. Although private owners may be limited by restrictions imposed by their lender, or by their own business policies, such restrictions are rarely as demanding as those imposed by law on public owners.

On many projects, the owner is a somewhat nebulous presence, as its participation is often through a third party such as the A/E. Nevertheless, the owner is the entity that the work is being done for, and the project must be designed and constructed in accordance with the owner's requirements. Often, the owner owns the property that the project is being built on. However, in the context of a construction project, the "owner" may also be a tenant doing fit-out of a leased property.

The owner's knowledge and experience in construction may affect its level of participation in the project. Owners who have been involved in previous construction projects may want to play an active role in the design and construction process. Inexperienced owners are likely to delegate more responsibility and control to third parties.

The owner's reason for undertaking the project can also have a significant effect on the project. Cost concerns are a priority for many owners, particularly if the project will be sold once it is finished. However, if there are critical schedule requirements, the owner may be willing to accept increased costs to ensure that these requirements are met. An owner who intends to occupy the project may view it from a long-term perspective. As such, the owner may be as concerned about the project's performance and maintenance aspects as the cost. If the project is being built as a rental investment, the owner may be constrained by the requirements of the future tenant.

3.1.1 Access to the Building Site

The owner has an implied obligation to provide the contractor with unencumbered site access throughout construction, even if the contract does not explicitly address this issue. If the contractor is prevented from accessing the site, the owner may be liable to the contractor for delay damages. The obligation to provide access can be breached even if the owner is not directly responsible for the problem—for example, if access to the project is blocked because of roadwork.

Ensuring adequate site access may require agreements with adjacent landowners to allow use of their properties during construction. A short-term agreement that allows use of someone else's property is called a *license*. If there is a need for long-term access rights—for example, to perform maintenance once the building is in service—the owner generally obtains a permanent easement that covers access during construction as well.

Easements are considered a property interest and are often recorded as part of the deeds to the properties. Easements that are recorded can be enforced against subsequent owners of the adjacent property and transferred to subsequent owners of the property requiring access. In contrast, a license does not convey an interest in the property; it is simply a contractual agreement between the parties that conveys certain rights. The most common type of license is the purchase of the right to park a vehicle on someone else's property such as in a parking garage.

Most jurisdictions provide landowners limited air rights (rights to the space over their property). Thus, an owner typically does not have to obtain easements from adjacent landowners for the swing of the crane jib. Nevertheless, an owner may obtain an easement to avoid claims that its crane interfered with the adjacent landowners' construction plans. Under such an easement, the owner is generally required to indemnify the adjacent landowners, their tenants, and their mortgage holders from any losses due to the construction work; the owner may also be required to maintain a stated amount of liability insurance. The easement typically specifies that a minimum clearance must be maintained between any materials transported by the crane and any structures on the adjacent property. In lieu of any payment, the easement may give the adjacent landowners reciprocal rights over the owner's property.

The owner may need to obtain permission for an encroachment at a lower height, such as for scaffolding. However, permission cannot be unreasonably denied, provided the owner has sufficient insurance and the adjacent landowners are indemnified for any damage to their property. The owner will need to get a permit to encroach on public space—for example, if it is necessary to close a sidewalk to allow for construction traffic.

3.1.2 Restrictions on Use of the Property

Often, the title to a property contains easements that grant rights in the property to others for utilities or public access; construction cannot infringe upon these rights. There may also be restrictions such as homeowner association rules (covenants) that limit both what can be constructed and the means of construction. Before purchasing property, the owner typically obtains a title report and survey to determine whether easements or other restrictions exist. Any restrictions that have been recorded as part of the deed to the property will be found by a title search. Such restrictions are generally enforceable unless they violate public policy. Under the doctrine of constructive notice, an individual is assumed to know of any restrictions that have been recorded, whether or not the individual had actual knowledge. A court may also enforce unrecorded restrictions if the owner knew, or should have known, about the restrictions at the time the owner purchased the property.

Most industry standard form contracts require the owner to provide both the A/E and the contractor with a survey that describes the physical characteristics of the site and any legal limitations. The survey should show the property lines, adjoining properties and structures, the location of utilities, rights-of-way, easements, designated wetlands, and any other potential impediments to construction.

3.2 THE DESIGN PROFESSIONAL TEAM

Although some owners have in-house design capability, most owners hire a third-party design professional to prepare the plans and specifications for the project. When the project involves structures that will be occupied by people—office buildings, hospitals, restaurants, and hotels—the lead design professional is usually an architect. Under many design agreements, the architect must also provide the required structural, mechanical, and electrical engineering services.

Larger architectural firms often have engineers on staff, but most architects subcontract these services to an engineering firm. The architect may either retain several different engineering specialists as its own subcontractors or one engineer who subcontracts to other engineers as necessary. In addition, the architect may retain various architectural consultants such as lighting and acoustical specialists, security consultants, and green building experts.

On civil construction projects—water treatment plants, bridges, oil refineries, tunnels, railways, roads, and dams—the lead design professional is typically an engineer. The engineer will retain an architect for any portions of the project that require an architect's stamp on the drawings. Because civil construction projects often involve highly specialized equipment or machinery, the equipment manufacturers and suppliers may have a significant role on the design team for such projects.

It typically makes little difference to the owner whether the lead design professional is an engineer or an architect. The relationship between the owner and the lead A/E is established by the terms of the design agreement, not the licensing of the A/E. Even when portions of the work are subcontracted out, the lead A/E retains overall responsibility for the design and is responsible for the work of its subconsultants. One potential difference is that architects are likely to suggest that American Institute of Architects (AIA) contract forms be used, while engineers are likely to suggest Engineers Joint Contract Documents Committee (EJCDC) or ConsensusDOCS forms. The owner ultimately decides which forms to use, but in most cases, the owner follows the A/E's recommendation.

Although the A/E's primary responsibility is to prepare the plans and specifications for the project, the A/E often assists the owner in administering the construction contract. Contract administration services are intended to assure the owner that the project is constructed in accordance with the plans and specifications.

3.2.1 Site Evaluation Consultants

Before design begins on a project, the owner typically engages various consultants to investigate site development issues such as soil conditions, easements, the availability of utilities, and whether there are any zoning restrictions or covenants that limit what can be built. Environmental consultants may be asked to assess both the potential environmental impacts of a proposed development and whether previous development has created any environmental concerns. Transportation engineers may be asked to evaluate traffic patterns and projected traffic flow to ensure that transportation capacity is sufficient for the development.

If the A/E firm that the owner intends to retain for design provides comprehensive evaluation and planning services, the owner may contract with the A/E to provide such services. In most cases, however, these services are provided by firms that specialize in site development. Because the owner may not be able to obtain financing for the project without a site evaluation, the owner may contract for such services even before acquiring the property.

3.2.2 The Geotechnical Consultant

In some parts of the country, it is customary for owners to contract directly with the structural, mechanical, and electrical engineers, rather than have A/Es contract with them as subconsultants. Owners may also contract directly with specialty designers such as security consultants. The A/E coordinates its work with the work of these design professionals.

Geotechnical engineers are almost always retained directly by owners. A/Es typically do not take even an administrative role with respect to geotechnical engineers and their investigation of subsurface conditions, however. This is partly because an A/E seldom has the training required to understand geotechnical information, so its role would simply be to provide the information to the owner. More important, there is considerable liability associated with the geotechnical investigation.

Most of the industry standard form contracts state that the owner is responsible for obtaining the services of a geotechnical engineer to do test borings, test pits, determinations of soil bearing values, percolation tests, evaluations of hazardous materials, and seismic evaluations, as necessary and required by the prevailing code. Obtaining soil borings and doing soil testing can be extremely expensive, particularly if the site is large. In deciding how much money to spend on the geotechnical investigation, owners consider the geotechnical engineer's recommendations and their own willingness to accept the risk of unforeseen problems. Even with an extensive investigation, there is still the possibility of unforeseen problems. Most of the industry standard form contracts contain a "differing site conditions" clause that makes owners liable for any cost increases resulting from subsurface conditions that were not detected during the geotechnical investigation.

If the geotechnical engineer determines that the proposed construction is feasible, it typically provides a foundation design. When the owner has hired the geotechnical engineer directly, the owner is responsible for any additional design and construction costs if there are problems with the foundation.

3.3 THE CONSTRUCTION TEAM

A contractor that contracts directly with the owner is referred to as a *prime contractor*. On a traditional design-bid-build project, the owner contracts with a single contractor, referred to as a *general contractor* (GC). The GC usually assumes overall responsibility for the project. This means that the GC is responsible for site security, debris removal, coordinating delivery and storage of materials, and temporary water, heat, and utilities.

Most construction contracts and design agreements state that the GC is solely responsible for construction means, methods, techniques, sequences, and procedures. This is partly because the GC will have certain preferences for how to approach the project. Owners and A/Es want to avoid allegations that they interfered with the GC's decisions and adversely affected the GC's costs or its ability to satisfy its contractual obligations. Even more important, owners and A/Es want to avoid any liability for the safety of the construction workers. The contract typically states that the GC is responsible for maintaining all safety precautions and programs.

3.3.1 Subcontractors and Suppliers

Although GCs usually perform some of the construction work with their own employees, few GCs have employees capable of performing work in all trades. In many cases, the GC performs the work of only one trade, such as carpentry or concrete work; the other work is done by subcontractors. A subcontractor may in turn retain a sub-subcontractor to perform some of the work of its subcontract, particularly if there is work that requires a specialized skill. In such cases, the subcontractor is referred to as a *first-tier* subcontractor; the sub-subcontractor is referred to as a *second-tier* subcontractor.

The GC is contractually liable to the owner for all work within the scope of its contract, regardless of whether the work is performed by its own employees or by subcontractors. Likewise, subcontractors are contractually liable to the contractor for all work within the scope of their subcontracts and are responsible for the performance of their second-tier subcontractors.

3.4 CONSTRUCTION LENDERS

Most owners do not have enough cash to finance large projects by themselves. Even those owners with sufficient funds often find it advantageous, for both business and tax reasons, to borrow money rather than have their money tied up during construction. Thus, virtually all construction projects other than residential remodeling and repair projects are financed, usually by construction loans. Construction loans can be risky, however, and lenders seldom make loans unless the owners have a certain amount of their own money (equity) invested in the project.

The biggest risk for a construction lender is that the security for the loan is typically the land and building under construction. The design, permitting, and construction process may take several years, and a lot can happen between the time the construction loan is obtained and the time the project is completed. Problems during construction, such as unforeseen site conditions or design errors, may jeopardize completion; a change in building or zoning requirements may jeopardize occupancy. If the owner runs into financial problems, third parties holding mechanic's liens may have priority over the lender in the proceeds of a foreclosure sale. Even if the project is completed successfully, it may be unmarketable because of a poor economy, or because it failed to anticipate a change in what potential purchasers or tenants would want.

3.4.1 Collateral Assignment to Lender

To protect their investment, construction lenders normally reserve the right to approve the owner's contracts with both the contractor and the A/E. Furthermore, they often require a collateral assignment of the owner's rights under the construction contract as security for the loan. Under such an assignment, if the lender declares the construction loan in default and forecloses on the project, the lender can either complete construction with the existing contractor or terminate the construction contract and engage another contractor.

The lender usually requires both the owner and the contractor to execute assignment agreements. However, most construction lenders would prefer not to have to take over a partially completed project. Lenders thus require various contractual provisions and project controls to ensure that the contractor completes the project in accordance with the plans and specifications.

3.4.2 Other Lender Requirements

The lender may require the contractor to provide a performance bond, a payment bond, or both. A performance bond ensures that funds will be available to complete the project if the contractor defaults or goes bankrupt; a payment bond ensures that funds will be available to pay subcontractors and suppliers if the contractor fails to do so. The lender may also require the contractor to obtain lien waivers from its subcontractors and suppliers, as proof they are being paid.

Even when the loan agreement states that the lender has priority over the owner's other creditors, some states give contractors and suppliers with mechanic's liens priority over the lender, at least to the extent the contractor or supplier has increased the value of the property. The lender may ask the owner to obtain the contractor's agreement to subordinate its lien rights to the lender's rights but contractors will often refuse to sign such subordination agreements, as a mechanic's lien may be their only security for payment. Furthermore, to be truly effective, subordination agreements would have to be obtained from any subcontractors or suppliers that had lien rights on the project.

Liability for an accident resulting in personal injury or property damage can bankrupt an uninsured contractor and put the entire project at risk. As a result, lenders typically require project participants to carry insurance that is sufficient to ensure their financial stability in case of an accident. They typically also require that the project itself be insured. In addition, the lender will require that the loan remain "in balance," such that the undisbursed loan balance is always greater than the cost to complete the project. When change orders increase the contract sum, the A/E is typically asked to certify that the loan is still in balance. If the cost to complete the project exceeds the undisbursed loan balance, the owner may be required to provide funds to make up the difference.

On many projects, the lender plays a key role, as it will increase the interest rate if it considers the project to be high risk; the viability of the project may depend on the owner's ability to obtain financing at a favorable rate. Sometimes the owner is a *single-purpose vehicle* (SPV)—an entity specifically created for the purpose of developing the project. Often, the project is the SPV's only asset; thus, the lender has nothing else to attach if the SPV defaults on the loan. In such cases, the lender will usually require the individual project owners to personally guarantee the loan.

3.4.3 Construction Loans

Most construction loans are interest-only loans. Money is drawn from the loan account as construction proceeds, and the owner either pays interest on the amount it has drawn or the interest is added to the loan balance. Construction loans are not intended to be long-term loans, however; the lender expects to be repaid once construction is complete, either from the money the owner receives when the project is sold or from the money the owner receives from a permanent loan.

Because of the risks involved in construction, the interest rate charged on a construction loan is high and may fluctuate. The owner thus has an incentive to ensure that the project is completed on schedule so that the loan can be refinanced. The permanent financing used to repay the construction loan is called a *take-out loan*—the funds are taken out by the owner in a lump sum at the completion of construction. Lenders sometimes refuse to make construction loans unless a commitment for the take-out loan is in place; as a result, owners often try to get a take-out commitment even before applying for a construction loan.

The amount of the permanent loan is generally based on the project's estimated value, not its actual or estimated construction cost. One method of estimating the value of an office or apartment building is to back-calculate from its expected annual income and the lender's desired rate of return. This is referred to as the *capitalized income stream* approach. As an example, if the project was expected to generate $1 million of income per year and the lender wanted a 10 percent rate of return on the its loan, the building would be valued at $10 million. (If the lender invested $10 million at 10 percent, it would earn $1 million a year.) The lender typically does not lend more than a certain percentage of the capitalized income stream value, however, even if the actual design and construction costs for the project are considerably more than the calculated value.

Despite a take-out commitment, the permanent loan may fall through if the owner does not meet the conditions established for the financing—for example, if there was a significant delay in completion or there was a significant change in the design. Thus, even a take-out commitment is not an absolute guarantee for the construction lender.

3.4.4 Bond Financing

Although construction loans are the most common form of financing, public agencies sometimes finance capital improvement projects by selling long-term bonds. In addition, private entities such as corporations occasionally use bonds to finance large projects. The bond's interest rate depends on a number of factors, including the bond's rating and whether the interest is tax exempt.

Unlike lenders, bondholders typically have no control over the provisions of the construction contract. However, the bond's rating depends on the perceived risk to the bondholders, which depends in part on the terms of the contract. If potential investors do not think they will be able to protect their investment, the bonds may be difficult to sell.

4

PROJECT DELIVERY
SYSTEMS

The term *project delivery system* refers to the system by which the design, procurement, and construction of a project is managed. The choice of project delivery system can have a significant impact on the project costs and schedule. In addition, it can have a significant impact on the owner's rights and responsibilities during construction.

The terminology used to describe project delivery systems is somewhat imprecise, and there is no universal agreement on what actually distinguishes one project delivery system from another. Nevertheless, broad categories can be established based on the contractual relationships between the project participants. These relationships determine how the responsibilities for design, procurement, and construction are allocated and thus establish the legal framework for the project.

4.1 DESIGN-BID-BUILD

Historically, construction projects were overseen by a master builder who was in charge of both design and construction. By the mid-1800s, advances in technology and increases in project complexity created a need for engineering and architecture specialists. The emergence of architecture and engineering as separate professions prompted the development of the *design-bid-build* (DBB) project delivery system. Also referred to as *design-bid-construct* and *design-award-construct*, DBB is a three-party arrangement that involves two principal contracts. The owner contracts with an architect or engineer (A/E) to design the project and enters into a separate contract with a general contractor (GC) for construction. The A/E and GC do not have a direct contractual relationship, and construction usually does not begin until the A/E has completed a detailed set of plans and specifications.

DBB is attractive to owners for a number of reasons. The design and construction industries are familiar with the process, and the roles of the A/E and GC are well defined. Likewise, the owner's role is well defined but can be adjusted to match the owner's interest and expertise. Many of the provisions of the industry standard-form DBB contracts have been subjected to litigation, and while holdings have not always been consistent, there is considerable case law to use as guidance in determining how a particular provision will be interpreted in court.

Because the owner has a direct contractual relationship with the A/E, it can select an A/E with particular qualifications and can monitor the design process. In addition, because the plans and specifications are well developed when the construction contract is put out for bid, bidders can usually compete on a fixed-price basis for the work. Cost is a key consideration on most projects, and many owners believe that competitive fixed-price bidding provides the best price.

There are also inherent checks and balances in the system. On most projects, the A/E is retained to provide contract administration. The A/E acts as the owner's agent to ensure that construction proceeds in accordance with the plans and specifications. At the same time, the GC has an incentive to identify any errors in the plans or specifications so that it is not held liable for defective construction.

There are a number of drawbacks to the DBB approach, however. Since the A/E produces relatively finished plans and specifications before construction begins, the contractor cannot provide input on the availability and pricing of materials during design. The contractor can sometimes provide such insight through value engineering during construction, but changes after construction have started are not as cost effective and may delay project completion.

In addition, the owner may be drawn into disputes between the A/E and the GC, particularly with a fixed-price construction contract. Often, such disputes arise from a legitimate difference of opinion over whether certain work is within the original scope of work. Regardless of whose interpretation is more reasonable, the owner may be forced to agree to a change order and price increase to ensure that the project is completed on schedule.

Likewise, the GC may allege that defects in the plans and specifications have caused delays or an increase in costs. Under the Spearin doctrine, the owner warrants the plans and specifications and is thus liable for such delays or cost increases. Because the A/E is acting as the owner's agent, the owner may also be liable for delays or cost increases if the A/E improperly rejects work or fails to review shop drawings in a timely manner.

Another consideration with the DBB approach is that because construction does not start until the design is complete, the project may take longer than if the design, procurement, and construction phases overlapped. A longer schedule means increased financing costs. Furthermore, many projects are intended to generate revenue through rental income, producing items for sale, or sale of the completed project. A longer schedule means that the project's ability to generate revenue is delayed. Although DBB remains the most widely used project delivery system in the United States, the use of alternative project delivery systems has increased in recent years.

4.2 MULTIPLE PRIMES

If the owner acts as the general contractor and contracts directly with the trade contractors, the project is referred to as a *multiple prime* project. A multiple prime project gives the owner control over the trade contracts and thus allows the owner to set the bidding parameters. Some states require that multiple prime contracts be used for public projects on the theory that they allow more contractors to participate in the bidding and reduce the potential for exclusionary practices.

In the private sector, multiple prime construction is used by owners who either want more control over the project or want to reduce costs by eliminating the GC's markup on the trade contracts. Multiple prime construction can often reduce the overall project schedule, since contracts for work such as site clearing and excavation can generally start before the design is finished. The increased control over the bidding can also reduce the owner's liability for delays. If one aspect of the work—for example, foundation construction—is delayed, the owner can postpone the bidding on subsequent work packages.

There are a number of disadvantages to multiple prime construction, however. On a project with multiple primes, no contractor has overall responsibility for managing the project. Because few owners have the required project management capability in-house, the owner must typically retain a construction manager to coordinate the work of the trade contractors. On small projects, the owner may hire the A/E to perform construction management as an additional service. However, an A/E lacking considerable field experience may not be well suited for the work.

Even with an effective construction manager, the owner's administration burden is likely to be greater than on a DBB project. As the GC, the owner is responsible for site security, materials storage, and debris removal. The actual work may be subcontracted out, but the owner retains overall responsibility for the site. In addition, the owner will be directly exposed to delay claims from the trade contractors.

4.3 CONSTRUCTION MANAGEMENT

On a DBB project, the owner relies on the contractor to control costs and manage the project schedule. Although the A/E may provide oversight during the construction phase, its obligations are generally limited to verifying that the contractor's costs and schedule appear reasonable. An owner who wants a more proactive role in project management generally retains a third-party construction manager (CM) to provide expertise in scheduling, estimating, and cost control.

Often, the owner retains the CM during, or even before the start of, design; the CM then works with the A/E to evaluate alternative materials, systems, and equipment. This provides the owner with construction-related advice on costs, quality, and constructability as the plans and specifications evolve.

Construction management is a relatively new project delivery system, and, as such, there are no universally accepted standards for the parties' rights and responsibilities. The Construction Management Association of America (CMAA) has developed form contracts, but the body of case law available to interpret these contracts is limited. In addition, most contracts are customized to the project, based on lengthy negotiations.

Sureties may refuse to bond construction management services, because there is no standard for determining whether construction managers have provided the services they contracted for. Likewise, it may not be clear what kind of insurance is appropriate for these services. Some states require that CMs on public projects be licensed, but the licensing requirements vary from state to state. In California, for example, a CM on a public project must be a licensed architect, engineer, or contractor. In Idaho, there is a separate license for construction managers, based on an exam administered by the Construction Manager Certification Institute (CMCI), which is an independent administrative body of the CMAA.

4.3.1 Agency Construction Management

A construction management contract can be structured as either agency construction management or construction management at-risk (CMAR). Under an agency construction management contract, the CM is paid a fee to provide project management services to the owner. Strictly speaking, agency construction management is not a project delivery system. Rather, it is a management system that is used with various project delivery systems, most commonly multiple prime projects. On multiple prime projects, the CM is typically responsible for coordination and contract administration. The CM's obligations can vary greatly, however, depending on the project and the owner's requirements.

The notable feature of agency construction management is that the CM's only involvement with the project is as a consultant to the owner. Its interests are thus aligned with those of the owner, and it can provide impartial advice with respect to trade-offs between project costs, schedule, and quality. The disadvantage of agency construction management is that it does not provide a single point of responsibility for construction. The CM may contract with trade contractors as the owner's agent but does not guarantee costs or time of completion. Likewise, the CM may coordinate the work of the trade contractors but does not assume any liability for safety or quality.

4.3.2 Construction Management At-Risk (CMAR)

In contrast to agency construction management, construction management at-risk is typically considered a distinct project delivery system. A construction manager at-risk does not act as the owner's agent during the construction phase of the project. Instead, the CM assumes the obligations customarily assumed by a GC, including responsibility for the quality, cost, and timely completion of construction. The CM does not do any of the work, but the trade contractors are subcontractors of the CM and are not in contractual privity with the owner.

Having the CM at-risk involved during design facilitates the use of fast-track construction, as construction can generally start before the design is finalized. However, if the CM at-risk is retained during the design phase, there is no project design for it to bid on. CMAR contracts are thus usually procured through negotiation rather than competitive bidding.

Often, the owner asks the CM to provide a guaranteed maximum price (GMP) for the work, but the CM typically does not do so until the plans and specifications are complete enough that the CM understands what is required to complete the work. Depending on the type of project, this might be at any point from 50 to 90 percent completion. Even so, there may be issues with respect to the accuracy and reliability of the GMP, as the CM typically makes various assumptions and qualifications and there may be disputes about what design features could have been reasonably anticipated. The CM's assumptions and qualifications may not always be explicitly stated, but to the extent they are reasonable, they will generally be upheld in court and the owner will be liable for the costs of any changes. In addition, the GMP will likely include a contingency commensurate with the risk the CM thinks it is taking.

Once construction begins, the CM's role converts from that of the owner's adviser to that of the general contractor. If the CM has provided a GMP, the CM's interests are not entirely aligned with those of the owner during the construction phase. Because the CM's ability to earn a profit on the project depends on construction proceeding in accordance with its assumptions, it may resist any change that might adversely affect the project cost or schedule. Even during preconstruction services, CMs at-risk may recommend materials and systems that they are familiar with, even if other materials and systems are better suited to the owner's requirements.

Like the GC on a DBB project, the CM provides the owner with a single point of responsibility for overall construction of the project. However, as with a DBB project, the division of responsibility between the A/E and the CM can result in an adversarial relationship. To reduce tensions with the A/E, the CM may agree to assume some responsibility for design errors, particularly if the CM was involved in reviewing the design before providing the GMP.

4.4 DESIGN-BUILD

The *design-build* approach is essentially a return to the traditional master builder concept. On a design-build project, the owner contracts with a single entity that is responsible for both design and construction. There are thus only two principal participants: the owner and the design-build firm.

Design-build firms are typically general contractors that either have the required design expertise in-house or subcontract the design work to an A/E. A/Es rarely act as design-builders because most A/Es aren't comfortable with the risks involved in construction. A/Es sometimes form joint ventures with contractors, however. When the design-build firm is structured as a joint venture, all of the construction is typically subcontracted; even the contractor partner is engaged as a subcontractor to the joint venture partnership.

4.4.1 Design-Build Proposals

An owner contemplating a design-build project often requests proposals from several design-build firms. The owner provides the firms with basic performance criteria and schedule requirements; each firm then proposes a design approach that meets these criteria. After reviewing the different design approaches and estimated costs, the owner selects a firm to negotiate with.

Because the overall design is determined by the owner's performance criteria, the owner must ensure that these criteria define the project requirements accurately and completely. The owner may retain a design consultant to help define the scope of work. Performance criteria are most effective when they describe requirements that can be measured, such as occupancy requirements and HVAC loads. The owner's expectations with respect to the aesthetic qualities of the project are typically addressed through more detailed design specifications.

Design-build proposals can be problematic for both the owner and the design-build firms. Often, the proposals contain very different design approaches, and it is difficult for the owner to compare them. In addition, the pricing data provided with a design-build proposal is based on a very rudimentary design and, therefore, may not be very reliable. Since much of the design will be done after the proposal is accepted, if the design-build firm is required to commit to a budget, it may simply adjust the quality and features of the project to meet the budget.

For its part, the design-build firm must determine how much time to invest in preparing the proposal. Putting minimal effort into preparing a proposal is risky, even if only basic design information is required. If the resulting proposal is not responsive to the owner's needs, the effort is wasted. It can be even worse if the owner accepts the proposal and the design-build firm has not verified that its approach is valid and its costs are reasonable. In such cases, the design-build firm may have committed itself to a project that it will be unable to complete for the proposal price, no matter what adjustments it makes to features and quality.

Alternatively, the design-build firm can develop the design to the point where it understands what will be necessary to complete the project and can make reasonable projections about costs, time of completion, and performance characteristics. Such an effort can be costly, though, and the design-build firm will not recover those costs if the project is abandoned or another firm is awarded the contract.

4.4.2   Advantages and Disadvantages of Design-Build

Nevertheless, there are several advantages to the design-build approach. For many owners, the key advantage is that there is a single point of responsibility for the entire project. The owner thus avoids being drawn into disputes between the contractor and the A/E. In addition, because the design-build firm is responsible for both design and construction, the design, procurement, and construction phases can overlap. As a result, the overall project schedule can often be significantly shortened. Another advantage is that the contractor can be involved in the design. This facilitates the involvement of specialty trade contractors and product manufacturers that may have valuable insight into the types of building equipment and systems that are best for a particular project, which ones are readily available, and how a given system can be modified to meet any special needs.

While owners typically cannot control the makeup of the design-build team when soliciting proposals, they can require that team members possess certain qualifications with respect to design expertise, financial capability, and construction experience. They can also require that the team members have worked together successfully on similar projects. At some point in the design process, the design-build firm usually provides the owner with a guaranteed maximum price to complete the design and construction. At that point, the owner knows what the costs will be, and the risks of delay and cost overruns due to design errors are transferred to the design-builder.

There are also disadvantages to using the design-build approach, however. Because the A/E works for the design-builder rather than the owner, the owner will not have the independent advice of the A/E during the construction phase. Unless it hires a third-party consultant, the owner may not be able to gauge the contractor's performance. Once the design-builder has provided a GMP, the owner gives up much of the control over the project, and any design changes put the owner at risk in terms of costs and delays.

Because the distinction between design services and construction work is not always clear on a design-build project, obtaining bonds or insurance can sometimes be difficult. When the design-build team is composed of different entities, the team members' roles, responsibilities, and liabilities must be clearly defined. A breakdown of the costs and fees between design and construction may be required for licensing and insurance purposes. Although sureties are accustomed to underwriting construction work, design services are generally not bondable. Similarly, the insurance carried by most contractors excludes any liability for design work.

The fact that the owner cannot select the A/E and has no contractual relationship with the A/E means the owner has less control over the design process. Thus, design-build generally is not appropriate when aesthetics are an important concern. Likewise, it generally is not appropriate if the owner has specialized program needs. Design-build often works best on conventional projects whose requirements can be clearly defined, such as office buildings or small strip malls. In most projects of this type, the owner does not assume excessive risk by giving up some control over the project.

4.4.3 Bridging Consultants

An owner who wants more control over design may retain an A/E to prepare a preliminary design; the preliminary design is subsequently provided to the design-build firm for completion. By retaining its own A/E—a process known as *bridging*—the owner has greater assurance that the completed project will conform to its aesthetic and functional goals. However, the owner must balance the desire to control the project design with the fact that doing so, it limits the options available to the design-builder and thus reduces the potential for innovation and efficiencies.

The owner's A/E is often referred to as a *design criteria consultant* (DCC). The DCC may specify the project's aesthetic requirements in considerable detail but typically uses performance specifications for the technical aspects of the construction. The DCC typically develops the project through the schematic design phase (approximately 30 percent of the design work) but in some cases may take the project through design development (approximately 50 percent of the design work). The design-builder is then responsible for completing the design in accordance with the specifications.

The DCC generally prepares the scope-of-work documents that form the basis of the contract between the owner and the design-builder. Often, the DCC remains associated with the project through the construction phase to observe the work, review pay applications, and certify substantial completion.

4.5 ENGINEER-PROCURE-CONSTRUCT (EPC)

Industrial facilities such as refineries and processing plants often include specialized equipment that must be custom designed and fabricated; the facilities are usually designed to optimize the performance of this equipment. Some of the larger design-build firms have begun to specialize in the design and construction of such facilities. Because of the emphasis on engineering and equipment on such projects, the project delivery system is typically referred to as *engineer-procure-construct* (EPC). EPC projects are generally high-risk propositions, and the contracts are usually heavily negotiated. Most EPC projects include a detailed completion/acceptance protocol, as well as damages for both delays and failure to achieve the agreed-upon performance.

When the equipment required for the facility must be custom-fabricated, the fabricator often requires payment in advance. In such cases, there may be significant expenses before construction even starts at the site. On many EPC projects, the lender is relying on anticipated project revenue as security for the construction loan. Because the lender has limited recourse if the construction is defective or there are significant delays, the lender may hire its own A/E to perform inspections and review the contractor's applications for payment.

4.6 TURNKEY CONSTRUCTION

Turnkey construction refers to an arrangement under which the owner contracts to purchase a completed project. The contractor is responsible for all aspects of the project, including purchasing the land, obtaining any necessary permits, and engaging the design professional. In many cases, the owner makes no payment until the building is ready for occupancy. The contractor thus assumes all financial risk of delay, unforeseen site conditions, and price increases. Although the contractor will increase its price to cover these risks, this option may be attractive to an owner lacking in-house project development expertise. Government-owned public housing projects are often developed as turnkey projects.

In some cases, the contractor may retain ownership of the project and enter into a long-term lease with the owner. This type of project is typically referred to as *build-to-suit*.

4.7 INTEGRATED PROJECT DELIVERY (IPD)

In recent years, various project delivery systems that emphasize collaboration among the principal participants have been developed. These approaches attempt to eliminate aspects of other project delivery systems that produce adversarial relationships and impair coordination. One such approach is *integrated project delivery* (IPD), which is premised on the project participants' agreeing to place the interests of the project before their own interests. The stated goal of IPD is to harness the talents of all participants to optimize project results, increase value to the owner, and maximize efficiency through all phases of the project. Collaborative tools such as building information modeling (BIM) are a key feature of IPD.

IPD has been actively promoted by the AIA but has not yet caught on in the United States. A similar project delivery system known as *Alliance* has been used in Australia, however. In the alliance approach, all of the primary participants are signatories to the same contract. The overall project goals are in an appendix to the contract, and the project is managed by a team with representatives from all of the principal participants. Project personnel are drawn as necessary from the project participants, and staffing assignments are made on the basis of qualifications, without regard to which firm the individual works for.

4.8 FAST-TRACK CONSTRUCTION

A typical fixed-price design-bid-build project proceeds sequentially. The project is not put out for bid until the plans and specifications are finalized; construction does not start until the contract between the owner and the general contractor has been signed. Often, the overall project schedule can be shortened by using fast-track construction, which allows the design, procurement, and construction phases to overlap. Shortening the project schedule can reduce the construction financing debt and allow the project to begin generating revenue sooner.

Fast-track construction is almost always used in design-build construction, as the ability to start construction before the design is complete is one of the key advantages of design-build. Fast-track construction can also be used on multiple prime projects, construction management projects, and design-bid-build projects that are being performed on a time and materials basis.

Nevertheless, fast-track construction is only advantageous if the benefits of early completion outweigh the potential problems and additional costs that can result. In particular, the owner must weigh the benefits of starting construction before the design is finalized. Once the owner has let the contracts for site work and excavation, it has committed to the project. If the total price comes in so high that the project is not viable, the owner must choose between abandoning the work and attempting to reduce costs by redesigning the project.

In addition, fast-track construction generally creates pricing uncertainty. When the contractor is bidding on a complete set of plans and specifications, it can usually provide the owner with a fixed price for the work. The owner can thus be reasonably confident of what the project will cost before construction starts. In contrast, a contractor bidding on incomplete drawings will seldom agree to a fixed price. The contractor may be willing to provide a guaranteed maximum price before the design is final, but the price will be subject to numerous assumptions and qualifications. Fast-track construction works best on fairly routine projects, where design requirements can be clearly defined and the likelihood of design changes is small.

4.9 PUBLIC-PRIVATE PARTNERSHIPS

Public-private partnerships (PPPs) are long-term contractual agreements between a public agency (federal, state, or local) and one or more private-sector entities. Despite the name, PPPs are not legally binding business partnerships. Rather, they are contractual arrangements that try to improve public services and infrastructure by capturing the benefits of private-sector involvement.

PPPs must be distinguished from privatization. Privatization occurs when the government divests itself of a traditionally public function or facility by transferring ownership and control to the private sector. This sometimes involves the government selling a facility to a private entity and then leasing it back. In contrast, the private-sector entities in a PPP do not get title to the assets. Instead, they are granted a long-term lease, sometimes referred to as a *concession*.

4.9.1 History of Public-Private Partnerships

Public-private partnerships have been used for numerous projects in Europe and Australia. They were also crucial in the westward expansion of railroads and canals in the United States during the 1800s. Unfortunately, many of the early ventures in the United States were unsuccessful, and the governments that invested in them lost significant amounts of money. As a result, many states enacted constitutional amendments that limited the ability of their state and local governments to extend credit to private entities.

Over time, the political and economic climate in the United States shifted such that by the late 1970s PPPs began to reemerge as an attractive alternative to the standard model of public procurement. In recent years, the most significant use of PPPs has been in road construction and modernization of existing roadways. When the project involves construction of a new road, the private-sector partners typically agree to design, construct, and operate the roadway for a specific term of years, in exchange for the toll revenues. With an existing roadway, the private-sector partners usually pay an upfront fee to the government for the contract and agree to maintain the road. In exchange, they are entitled to the toll revenues for the length of the contract. Examples of PPP highway projects include the construction of the South Bay Expressway in San Diego, California; the Dulles Greenway in Virginia; and the concessions for the Chicago Skyway and the Indiana Toll Road. PPPs have also been used in construction of rail and airport facilities, water and wastewater plants, and schools.

As of 2010, approximately half of the states had passed statutes to authorize public-private initiatives. While the statutes vary considerably, most allow the public entity to solicit PPP proposals for specific infrastructure projects. Some statutes also authorize the public agency to accept unsolicited proposals. Unsolicited proposals allow the private sector to propose a project that the agency might not have considered or might have decided was not a priority for funding.

4.9.2 Constraints on Public-Private Partnerships

One of the potential advantages of PPPs is that they allow the public and private sectors to jointly take on projects that neither would be willing or able to attempt alone. In addition, PPPs allow public agencies to undertake projects that would not be otherwise viable because of funding limitations. However, statutory constraints still pose an obstacle to PPPs. For example, the federal Antideficiency Act limits the ability of federal agencies to enter into long-term partnerships, absent express authorization or appropriation.

PPPs are rarely used for small projects because the cost of structuring and managing them can be prohibitive. Thus, most PPP agreements have involved complex, long-term projects. As the financial risks can be considerable, PPP proposals must usually include a financing plan with well-documented projections for the long-term income stream.

5

CONSTRUCTION CONTRACTS

5.1 THE CONSTRUCTION CONTRACT

In legal terms, a contract is a promise that the law will enforce. A typical construction contract contains at least two reciprocal promises: the contractor promises to perform the work specified in the contract, and the owner promises to pay the contractor for that work. In addition, the contract generally contains a number of other promises related to the parties' obligations. The contract should establish the five key components of the legal relationship between the owner and the contractor:

- The scope of work
- The quality of the work
- The project schedule
- The project budget
- Each party's rights and remedies if the other party breaches its obligations

Unless the project involves the sale of land or will take more than a year to complete, the contract is not required to be in writing. However, because of the complexity involved in a construction project, contracts are typically written and executed (signed) by both parties.

5.1.1 Prebid Conferences

Owners will often conduct a prebid conference with prospective bidders. Such conferences allow owners to answer questions and ensure that all bidders are provided the same information. Some owners require attendance at these conferences; failure to attend a mandatory prebid conference may preclude the bidder from submitting a bid. The prebid conference may be done in conjunction with a project walk-through, particularly if the project involves renovation of an existing building.

5.1.2 Right to Reject Bids

It is important to understand that an owner's request for bids or request for proposals is not an offer or an invitation to form a contract. Thus, submitting a bid or proposal does not create a contract. The contractor's bid is the offer; a contract is not formed unless the owner accepts the bid. On private construction projects, the owner has no obligation to the bidders—the owner may reject any or all bids without giving a reason. On public projects, the owner's right to reject bids may be limited by the applicable procurement regulations, but public owners can typically reject bids if there is a compelling reason to do so.

5.2 THE CONTRACT DOCUMENTS (OWNER-CONTRACTOR)

On most construction projects, the construction contract consists of a set of documents. The *contract documents* describe the work that is to be performed by the contractor and the contractual relationship between the owner and the contractor in connection with that work. The contract documents typically include the following.

The owner-contractor agreement: This is the actual agreement signed by the owner and the contractor. The agreement defines the essential parameters of the owner-contractor relationship, such as the identity of the parties, the legal address of the project, the time for commencement and completion, the price, and procedures for payment. In addition, the agreement usually includes a list of the documents making up the contract.

General conditions of the contract for construction: The general conditions provide more complete contract terms and define the services that the contractor will provide. They typically include insurance and bonding requirements, procedures for addressing changes in the work, payment procedures, site safety, and termination procedures. Although the A/E is not a party to the owner-contractor agreement, the general conditions usually describe the services that the A/E will provide during construction. This provides the contractor with notice of the A/E's scope of authority as the owner's agent.

Supplementary (special) conditions of the contract for construction: The general conditions are often a standard industry form. Since construction practices may vary by locality and project type, supplementary conditions may be added to modify or supplement portions of the general conditions as necessary for project.

Other conditions: The contract documents may also include other documents that indicate conditions relevant to the project such as restrictions on access or requirements to protect adjacent property. Contracts for public projects may include affirmative action or minimum wage requirements.

Drawings prepared by the design professionals: The drawings are the graphic expressions of the work to be performed. They show the design, location, and dimensions of the work, and typically include plans, elevations, sections, details, and various schedules. In addition to the drawings issued for bidding, drawings may also be found in addenda, change orders, construction change directives, and in responses to the contractor's requests for information.

Specifications prepared by the design professionals: The specifications are the technical requirements for the materials, equipment, and systems, as well as the standards for the work. Specifications are usually organized according to divisions set out in the MasterFormat, a format developed by the Construction Specifications Institute. The MasterFormat divisions are further divided into sections, with each section describing the scope, materials, and execution of a particular work item, such as cast-in-place concrete. Guide specifications have been developed for a wide variety of MasterFormat sections. The most widely used library of guide specifications is the AIA's MasterSpec system.

Addenda: Addenda are additions or corrections to the drawings or specifications that are issued before the construction contract is executed. Like the other materials contained in the bid package, addenda are binding on the prospective bidders. Bidders are usually required to formally acknowledge receipt of all addenda when they submit their bids.

Modifications: Modifications are changes to the contract that are issued after the construction contract is executed. These may include construction change directives, change orders, or other modifications.

When the general conditions of the contract are written as a stand-alone document, they can be provided to other parties without disclosing the business terms of the owner-contractor agreement. The general conditions are often incorporated by reference into the owner-A/E agreement, the contractor-subcontractor agreements, and the A/E's contracts with its consultants. The supplementary and other conditions are typically incorporated by reference into these contracts as well. This helps to ensure that the contracts are consistent with respect to the various parties' obligations.

5.2.1 The Contractor's Bid

The contractor may request that its bid, including any qualifications, be made a contract document and that the bid govern over other contract documents. Making the bid a contract document protects the basis upon which the contractor has agreed to the price, the schedule, and other contractual matters. Allowing the bid to be a contract document can create inconsistencies among the documents, however. If the contractor included qualifications with respect to the work, these qualifications may contradict requirements stated in other documents. Contractors may also request that approved shop drawings and other submittals be made a part of the contract documents. Owners are typically reluctant to agree to this request, however, since a court may hold that the owner has assumed liability for any errors in approved shop drawings.

5.3 CONFLICTS BETWEEN THE DOCUMENTS

Given the number of documents included in the contract, inconsistencies are almost inevitable. Some contracts address this issue by specifying a hierarchy for the contract documents. A typical hierarchy might be that modifications and change orders have the highest priority, the supplementary conditions govern over the general conditions, the drawings govern over the specifications, and large-scale drawings govern over small-scale drawings. The contract may also state that if there are inconsistencies within a particular document, the contractor must provide the better quality or greater quantity of work and must comply with the more stringent requirement, in accordance with the owner's interpretation.

A preset document hierarchy may generate unintended results, however, as the error may be in the document with higher priority. Thus, some construction contracts require the documents to be read as a whole and reconciled in accordance with the standard rules of contract interpretation. For example, §1.2.1 of AIA A201 states: "The Contract Documents are complementary, and what is required by one shall be as binding as if required by all."

5.4 ERRORS IN THE DOCUMENTS

On most projects, the bidding instructions require bidders to request clarification of patent (obvious) discrepancies in the bid materials before submitting their bids. Even without such a requirement, courts will typically hold that a bidder has an obligation to notify the owner of any obvious discrepancies. This is referred to as the *patent ambiguity rule*.

Under the patent ambiguity rule, a contractor that makes erroneous assumptions about a patent discrepancy will be held responsible for any extra costs that result. Thus, a contractor that fails to notify the owner of a patent discrepancy is generally not entitled to an increase in the contract price if the owner's interpretation of the work is more costly than what the contractor included in its bid. Depending on the language of the contract, the owner may not have to prove that the contractor actually knew of the discrepancy; the contractor may be assumed to know of a discrepancy if a reasonable and prudent contractor would have known. However, when the bidding documents indicate a contract hierarchy, some courts have held that bidders are entitled to rely on the stated hierarchy to resolve patent ambiguities.

CASE STUDY—PATENT AMBIGUITY

The contractor was awarded a contract to construct a medical clinic on an army base. Plans for the work showed two conflicting details for rebar laps. The contractor did not ask for clarification but exercised its own judgment as to which detail it should use. Since the detail used did not comply with local standards and practices, the owner required the contractor to demolish the work and reconstruct it in accordance with the other detail. The Armed Services Board of Contract Appeals denied the contractor's request for an equitable adjustment for the additional work, and the contractor appealed.

The Court of Appeals upheld the Board's denial. Because the plans were patently ambiguous as to which detail should be used, the contractor had a duty to obtain clarification. Because the contractor did not obtain clarification, it was appropriate to consider local trade standards and practices when determining the correct meaning of the ambiguity. A contractor is expected to know such standards and practices.

Fortec Constructors v. United States,
760 F.2d 1288 (Fed. Cir. 1985)

5.4.1 Latent Discrepancies

In many cases, errors or discrepancies in the documents do not become apparent until construction has started. Such discrepancies are referred to as *latent ambiguities*. The contract documents usually require the contractor to promptly notify the A/E of such discrepancies, so that they can be resolved before the work affected by the discrepancy is performed. A contractor that proceeds without notifying the A/E of a latent discrepancy may be liable for the cost of any corrections that are necessary. However, unless it is specifically stated in the contract, the contractor is not required to review the contract documents for the specific purpose of finding discrepancies. The contractor is only required to report the discrepancies that it does find.

Likewise, although most contracts do not require the contractor to ensure that the documents comply with applicable laws and codes, if the contractor discovers or is made aware of a possible code or statutory violation, it must notify the A/E before starting the work in question. If the contractor performs work it knows is not in compliance with either statutory or code requirements, it may be liable for the cost of any corrections.

5.5 SPECIFIC OVER GENERAL; WRITTEN OVER PRINTED

When interpreting a contract, a specific clause will prevail over a general one. For example, the general conditions typically require the work to meet applicable building codes, but the plans and specifications may set higher standards for various aspects of the work. The specific provisions of the plans and specifications would supersede the general provision. Specific terms may also have a limiting effect, because it will be assumed that work that is not specified is not required. For example, if the painting schedule calls for certain surfaces to be primed before painting, there is a presumption that these are the only surfaces that need to be primed.

Terms that the parties have specifically negotiated have precedence over those contained in a preprinted form. If the contract contains handwritten and typewritten language as well as preprinted language, the handwritten language controls over the typewritten language, and both the handwritten and typewritten language control over the preprinted form.

5.6 INTERPRETATION AGAINST DRAFTER

If ambiguities in the contract cannot be resolved with the standard rules of contract interpretation, the contract will be interpreted against the party that drafted it. This rule is known as *contra proferentem* (against the drafter) and

CASE STUDY—CONTRACT INTERPRETATION

A government contractor was awarded a contract to install heating and air-conditioning equipment for three buildings on an army base. The contract was ambiguous as to whether conventional motor starters or more expensive variable-speed fan power controllers were required, as both were referenced at various points in the specifications. After the contractor's proposal to use conventional motor starters was rejected, it requested an equitable adjustment for the extra cost of the variable-speed controllers.

The contractor argued that under the rule of *contra proferentum*, the ambiguities in the contract should be resolved against the government because the government drafted the contract. However, the court held that the contractor was not entitled to an equitable adjustment, even though the contract was confusing and internally inconsistent. There is an exception to the rule of *contra proferentum* when an ambiguity is patent: the contractor has a duty to inquire about the ambiguity and obtain clarification before submitting its bid.

Interstate General Government Contractors, Inc., v. Stone,
980 F.2d 1433 (Fed. Cir. 1992)

is particularly likely to be applied when the party that drafted the agreement alleges that the agreement relieves it of liability for its acts.

Most construction contracts are drafted by the A/E, acting as an agent for the owner. Thus, ambiguities will be resolved in favor of the contractor, provided the contractor's interpretation is reasonable.

5.7 SPECIFICATIONS

Project specifications are classified as either design specifications or performance specifications. *Design specifications*, also referred to as prescriptive specifications, set forth detailed and precise requirements for materials, equipment, tolerances, and finishes. If the contractor deviates from these requirements, it could be considered a breach of contract.

In contrast, *performance specifications* merely indicate the results to be obtained; the contractor determines how to achieve those results. As an example, a design specification might call out three models of pumps from which the contractor must choose. A performance specification might simply specify the pump capacity and warranty requirements; the contractor can supply any model that meets these requirements. Performance criteria are often used in industrial facilities such as processing plants. If the owner does not have a preference for a particular equipment model, allowing the contractor to select the equipment can result in considerable cost savings. It also puts the burden on the contractor to make sure the required performance is achieved.

The distinction between design and performance specifications has considerable legal significance. In particular, the distinction is significant for claims related to defective specifications. Under the Spearin doctrine, the owner implicitly warrants the accuracy of design specifications. In contrast, performance specifications do not carry any implied warranty of accuracy or adequacy. Performance specifications simply set forth an objective or standard to be achieved; the contractor decides how to achieve that objective and assumes responsibility for the decision.

When distinguishing between design and performance specifications, courts generally look at how much discretion the contractor is given. Under a design specification, the contractor typically has little or no discretion in carrying out its contractual obligations.

5.8 DESCRIPTION OF THE WORK UNDER
A CONSTRUCTION CONTRACT

Construction contracts often contain clauses stating that the intent of the contract documents is to include all items necessary for the proper execution and completion of the work. Under such language, the contractor is required to perform not only the work described in the contract documents, but also the work reasonably inferable as necessary to produce the results indicated by the contract documents. When the documents show drywall partitions, for example, the contractor should infer that the drywall is to be attached to the studs and that the method used to attach the drywall must comply with applicable code requirements.

Any work not indicated by the plans and specifications must be incidental to the work that is indicated, however. When work not indicated in the plans and specifications involves considerable extra cost or involves design work that requires a submittal, it is generally not considered reasonably inferable from the work shown. In addition, the contractor's performance is required only to the extent reasonably inferable to produce the indicated results; the indicated results are not always the intended results.

5.9   THIRD-PARTY BENEFICIARIES

Although the construction contract is between the owner and the contractor, the contract documents typically contain references to the A/E and the lender as well as subcontractors and suppliers. Such references recognize the role of these other parties in the project and ensure that the construction contract is consistent with these parties' rights and obligations under their separate agreements with the owner or contractor. Most construction contracts specifically prohibit a third party (someone other than the owner or contractor) from claiming rights under the contract as a third-party beneficiary, however.

In particular, neither the owner nor the contractor wants the A/E to be a third-party beneficiary of the construction contract because this would allow the A/E to enforce the provisions of the contract against them. For example, the A/E could prevent the owner from terminating the construction contract for convenience if the owner also intended to cancel the design agreement.

A supplier that has not been paid by a subcontractor may claim it is a third-party beneficiary of the contractor-subcontractor agreement and is thus entitled to any funds the contractor owes to the subcontractor. Courts tend to reject such claims unless the supplier's position as a third-party beneficiary is clearly stated in the subcontract, however.

5.10   INDUSTRY STANDARD FORMS VERSUS CUSTOM FORMS

In selecting a construction contract, the parties must decide whether to draft a custom (manuscript) document or use an industry standard form. There are a number of industry standard forms available. The documents developed by the AIA are commonly used for general building construction in the United

States; the ConsensusDOCS and documents developed by the Engineers Joint Contract Documents Committee (EJCDC) are commonly used for heavy construction and industrial projects. The industry standard forms are typically published as families that harmonize the various legal relationships that arise under a particular project delivery system. Within each family, the requirements of the construction contract are coordinated with those of the design agreement and the subcontracts to ensure that the allocation of risk and responsibility is consistent.

One of the main advantages of using an industry standard form, particularly one that is familiar to both parties, is that contract negotiations can often be concluded very quickly. This can save both parties money and may allow construction to begin sooner. Even if one of the parties is not familiar with the form, the fact that it is an industry standard form provides some assurance that both parties' rights, responsibilities, and risks will be adequately defined. Some of the provisions of the commonly used forms have been extensively litigated; thus, the parties have guidance as to how a particular provision may be interpreted by the courts. Although the industry standard forms are not intended to conform to the law of any one state, they are generally drafted so that they are enforceable under the laws in force at the time they are published.

There are disadvantages to using industry standard forms, however. Standard forms may not address the requirements of a particular state adequately. Likewise, even though most standard forms are updated regularly, they may not reflect current law or practices. Standard forms are generally not appropriate for highly specialized projects, as they may not deal with important issues raised by the project requirements. In addition, the industry standard forms have all been drafted by particular design- or construction-related trade associations. Although the associations attempt to be fair and balanced in the allocation of risk, there is typically a bias in favor of their own members.

5.10.1 Drafting Custom Forms

A custom contract may be drafted for a particular project, or may be drafted by one of the parties as a standard form for all of its projects. Custom contracts are often used by residential developers with in-house construction divisions; they may also be used by large commercial developers and commercial contractors whose volume justifies drafting a form that can be used with little or no modification on any project.

A party that drafts a custom form will typically start with one of the industry standard forms and then makes changes as necessary. Often, the basic format of the standard form is retained, and applicable provisions from the standard form are incorporated verbatim. The major advantage of custom forms is that they can address the parties' priorities and define the relationship between the parties with precision. In addition, the perceived biases found in the industry standard forms can be eliminated.

The disadvantages of using a custom form drafted by one of the parties arise from the other party's lack of familiarity with the terms of the document; the other party will need to determine which provisions of the industry standard form have been omitted or substantially modified. A custom form may thus require significantly more time to negotiate, which can be an issue if there is a deadline for the start of construction. If the contract has been drafted by the owner, the contractor may increase its bid to cover both the perceived risks and the increased legal fees it will incur to negotiate the agreement.

Even when standard forms are used, the parties may need to retain legal counsel to ensure that the forms are consistent with the parties' actual intent. In addition, any changes to the standard forms should be reviewed by legal counsel to ensure that the changes do not conflict with other contract documents or contracts between other project participants. Many of the industry standard form documents are available in electronic format and will automatically generate an additions and deletions report that lists the alterations to the form document.

5.10.2 AIA Contract Documents

The AIA has been publishing form contracts for the construction industry since 1888. The first AIA General Conditions for Construction was published in 1911; the 2007 edition of AIA A201 is the sixteenth edition of that document. This history has given the AIA a considerable advantage over other organizations that publish standard forms. A significant percentage of the case law concerning contracts for private construction is based on the language of the AIA standard forms.

The AIA currently publishes more than 100 contract documents and administrative forms. The documents are developed by a committee of practicing architects who are selected on the basis of their experience, regional diversity, and variety of practices. The AIA also solicits feedback from owners, general contractors, engineers, subcontractors, sureties, lawyers, and insurers.

The AIA regularly revises and adds to its documents to ensure that they remain current with developments in the construction industry. The most commonly used AIA forms are revised every ten years, with the last revision in 2007. The 2007 revision generated considerable controversy, however; the Associated General Contractors (AGC), which had endorsed previous versions of A201, voted not to endorse the 2007 version. In an October 2007 press release, the AGC stated that the 2007 version of A201 did not balance risk among all parties fairly and shifted significant risk to parties outside the design profession, including general contractors. The AGC also objected to the fact that the AIA documents give the A/E a major role in contract administration. The AGC subsequently published a commentary for AGC members bidding on projects that require the use of A201-2007. The commentary includes suggested additions, deletions, and modifications to the form document.

5.10.2.1 AIA Document Families

The AIA contract documents are grouped by family, with the documents in a family covering the various relationships that occur with a particular type of project or project delivery method. There are currently eight families:

- Conventional
- Construction Manager as Adviser (CMa)
- Construction Manager as Constructor (CMc)
- Design-Build
- Integrated Project Delivery (IPD)
- Interiors
- International
- Small Projects

The documents in the conventional family are intended for use on design-bid-build projects and are by far the most commonly used AIA documents. The conventional family is also called the A201 family, because the A201 General Conditions document is adopted by reference in the Owner-Contractor, Owner-Architect, and Contractor-Subcontractor documents in this family. A503, *Guide for Supplementary Conditions*, provides model language to modify A201 or create supplementary conditions for use with A201.

The AIA documents are also divided into six letter-designated series, with each series pertaining to a particular type of form or use. The six document series are:

- A-Series: Owner-Contractor Agreements
- B-Series: Owner-Architect Agreements
- C-Series: Other Agreements
- D-Series: Miscellaneous Documents
- E-Series: Exhibits
- G-Series: Contract Administration and Project Management Forms

The A-Series comprises the Owner-Contractor Agreements for the different project delivery systems and the corresponding general conditions. There are different forms of the agreements for the various pricing mechanisms (fixed-fee, cost-plus, unit-pricing). Similarly, the various Owner-Architect Agreements in the B-Series allow for the different roles the architect can have on different types of projects. The C-Series documents govern the relationship between the architect and its consultants (typically, either engineers or other architects). These documents are drafted such that the architect's obligations to the owner with respect to basic and additional services, insurance coverage, and indemnification flow down to the architect's consultants.

The E-Series documents are for projects that use digital data transmission and building information modeling (BIM). The documents provide a licensing agreement for transmission of digital data and protocols for managing digital data and BIM. The G-Series documents include a number of forms commonly used in project administration, including insurance specifications, requests for information, change orders, applications for payment, and certificates for substantial completion.

5.10.3 Engineers Joint Contract Documents Committee (EJCDC)

The Engineers Joint Contract Documents Committee (EJCDC) develops and publishes a variety of standard forms of agreement for professional engineering services, as well as other contract documents and related forms for various types of construction projects. The EJCDC was formed in 1975, in response to a perceived increase in professional liability for engineers. It is now a joint venture of the Associated General Contractors of America (AGC), the National Society of Professional Engineers/Professional Engineers in Private Practice (NSPE/PEPP), the American Council of Engineering Companies (ACEC), and the American Society of Civil Engineers–Construction Institute (ASCE–CI). It thus represents a major portion of the professional groups engaged in providing engineering and construction services. Representatives of various other segments of the construction industry, including owner groups, risk managers, surety and insurance experts, and construction lawyers, also participate in drafting and reviewing the EJCDC documents.

The EJCDC contract documents are primarily intended for use on projects designed by engineers. Sometimes referred to as *horizontal* or *civil construction*, such projects include water treatment plants, waste handling and disposal facilities, production and processing facilities, site development and utility work, environmental remediation projects, roads and bridges, and tunneling and excavation projects. The EJCDC documents are updated approximately every five years to reflect industry trends, court decisions, and changes in applicable laws and regulations.

5.10.3.1 *EJCDC Document Families*

The EJCDC documents are published as five families:

- E-series: Engineering (includes Owner-Engineer Agreements and Engineer-Consultant agreements)
- C-series: Construction (Owner-Contractor)
- D-series: Design/Build
- R-series: Environmental Remediation
- P-series: Procurement (for Engineer-designed or specified equipment)

The Construction series (C-series) is the most comprehensive of the document families and consists of integrated documents plus a narrative guide. The principal documents in the C-series are the Standard General Conditions (C-700), Suggested Owner-Contractor Agreement Forms (Stipulated price C-520; Cost-plus C-525), and Suggested Instructions to Bidders (C-200). The C-series documents are coordinated with the E-series documents and assume that the A/E will be engaged as the owner's agent during construction.

The C-series documents were last revised in 2007; a number of the 2007 revisions related to the allocation of risk among the project participants. For example, under the 2007 revision, the contractor is responsible for both its actual knowledge of site conditions and information generally known about the site conditions. In previous versions, the contractor only had to consider site information furnished by the owner. Additionally, under the 2007 revisions, the owner must provide the contractor with all known reports and drawings of site conditions. In the previous versions, the owner had to provide only the reports and drawings relied on by the A/E.

The 2007 revisions also increase the contractor's responsibility for safety monitoring and compliance. The previous document versions merely stated that the contractor was responsible for initiating, maintaining, and supervising all safety programs in connection with the work. The 2007 revisions require the contractor to inform the owner and engineer of any specific safety requirements that must be followed at the site; the owner and engineer have a corresponding obligation to comply with such requirements. In addition, the 2007 documents require the contractor to comply with all applicable owner-instituted safety programs.

The 2007 revisions reduced the contractor's liability for failing to report discrepancies in the contract documents, however. Under the previous versions, the contractor could be liable for failing to report discrepancies it knew about or reasonably should have known about. The 2007 series revisions limit the contractor's reporting duty to discrepancies it had actual knowledge of.

Another change in the 2007 revisions is that the Suggested Bid Form (C-410) and the Owner-Contractor Agreements now require contractors to certify that they have not engaged in corrupt, fraudulent, collusive, or coercive practices in obtaining the contract.

5.10.4 ConsensusDOCS

The ConsensusDOCS are a relatively new set of documents, with the first 72 documents released in September 2007; additional documents have been released on a rolling basis since then. The ConsensusDOCS are grouped into six series:

- 200 Series: General Contracting
- 300 Series: Collaborative Agreements
- 400 Series: Design-Build
- 500 Series: Construction Management
- 700 Series: Subcontracting
- 800 Series: Program Management

The initial documents were developed over a period of three years by 23 construction-related associations, led by the AGC. The goal was to develop standard form construction documents that represented a consensus within a broad spectrum of the construction industry, including designers, owners, contractors, subcontractors, sureties, and other stakeholders (DOCS).

Nevertheless, most of the associations involved in developing the documents are primarily contractor-focused. While some of the associations include representation of design professionals, such representation is typically incidental to the primary interests of the association. In addition, many of the documents released in 2007 were based on forms originally developed by the AGC. For example, CD 200, *ConsensusDOCS 200: Agreement and General Conditions Between Owner and Contractor (Lump Sum)*, is almost identical to the AGC 200 document.

5.10.5 Comparing the AIA, EJCDC, and ConsensusDOCS Documents

While the AIA, EJCDC, and ConsensusDOCS all include documents for general construction, including owner-contractor and owner-A/E agreements, each set of documents emphasizes certain relationships and topics, and minimizes or omits others. The AIA documents include a large number of contract and administrative forms related to architectural services. The EJCDC documents include a significant number of forms dealing with environmental remediation, procurement, and agency funding. The ConsensusDOCS documents include a number of forms that deal with program management. Because of differences in the parties' roles in each set of documents, documents from one set of industry standard form documents may not be compatible with documents from another set without substantial modifications.

Each set of documents is represented as being "fair to all parties." The perception of being fair is critical to the documents' acceptance by the ultimate decision maker—the owner. The AIA documents have the advantage of more than 120 years of development, with contract provisions being refined in response to court cases and changes in the construction industry. As a result, they have a huge lead in the marketplace. The EJCDC documents, while newer, have also evolved since their introduction in 1975, based on industry feedback and interpretation by the courts. The AGC documents that have been republished as part of the ConsensusDOCS documents are substantially newer, and most have not been tested in court.

5.10.5.1 The ConsensusDOCS Compared to the AIA and EJCDC Documents

The ConsensusDOCS agreements differ from both the AIA and the EJCDC documents in several respects. One significant difference is that the ConsensusDOCS agreements provide the A/E with a much smaller role in contract administration. Under the AIA and EJCDC documents, the owner and the contractor communicate with each other through the A/E. In contrast, the ConsensusDOCS agreements anticipate direct communication between the owner and the contractor; the contractor only communicates with the A/E when directed to do so by the owner.

The A/E has very few formal responsibilities in the owner-contractor legal relationship under the ConsensusDOCS. The A/E's only direct approval authority is certification of the contractor's pay applications. The owner is responsible for reviewing the schedule, the submittals, and requests for information (RFIs); the A/E merely assists and advises the owner. Another difference is that, unlike the AIA and EJCDC forms, which separate the general conditions of the contract from the owner-contractor agreement, the two are combined in the ConsensusDOCS forms, including CD 200.

5.10.6   AGC Forms

The majority of the documents previously published as AGC documents were incorporated into the ConsensusDOCS forms. However, as of 2011, there were a few specialty documents that were still available only as AGC documents. AGC also publishes an online State Law Matrix that provides information on state laws affecting construction. Among the laws covered are those addressing procurement, bidding, bond requirements, alternative delivery systems, subcontracting, payment clauses, lien laws, trust fund statutes, statutes of repose, and immigration.

5.10.7   Other Industry Standard Forms

A number of other organizations, including the Design-Build Institute of America (DBIA) and the Construction Management Association of America (CMAA), publish contract forms. The DBIA is an association of firms that provide design-build construction services; the contracts it publishes are specifically for use on design-build projects.

CMAA is a national organization that promotes the use of construction management. CMAA publishes two sets of documents, one for agency construction management and one for construction management at-risk CMAR. Within each set, there are standard form agreements between the owner and the CM, and the owner and the A/E. In the agency construction management set, there is also a standard form agreement between the owner and the contractor, and general conditions for the owner-contractor agreement. In the CMAR set, there is a standard form agreement between the CM and the contractor, and general conditions for the CM-contractor agreement.

5.11   COMMENCEMENT OF WORK PRIOR TO CONTRACT

On large or particularly complex projects, the construction contract may take months to negotiate and draft. If the project requires items that must be custom-fabricated, the delay in starting construction can have an adverse effect on both the project's schedule and its cost, as custom-fabricated items typically have long lead times. To avoid project delays, the owner may want to ensure that these items are ordered, even though the construction contract is still being negotiated. Likewise, an owner concerned about volatility in materials costs or labor shortages may want to guarantee materials prices and subcontractor availability prior to finalizing the construction contract. In addition, loan agreements often have deadlines, with financial penalties if construction is not started by a specific date.

An owner who wants to start construction before the construction contract is finalized may provide the contractor with an early-start letter. Such letters typically provide for a limited scope of work for a specific price and with a specific timetable. If the parties cannot come to an agreement on the construction contract, the letter allows the owner-contractor relationship to be terminated, with either assignment of the subcontracts and purchase orders from the contractor to the owner, or termination of the subcontracts and purchase orders. If the parties do enter into a contract, the contract will supersede the letter.

5.11.1   Letters of Intent

Letters of intent are sometimes used in other countries, particularly England, to allow limited construction to take place before the contract documents are finalized. In the United States, however, letters of intent are typically only used to express the parties' good-faith intention to enter into a construction contract when the plans and specifications are finalized. Such letters have no legal force, but the contractor can show the letter to potential subcontractors and suppliers when soliciting bids. A letter of intent may also be used to create a confidentiality agreement when the parties are discussing a joint venture project.

6

THE DESIGN PROCESS

To understand the legal issues related to design, one must look at the contractual obligations of the parties involved in a construction project. Although government regulations such as zoning and building codes can have a significant impact on the design of a project, the rights and responsibilities of the parties are determined by their contracts.

6.1 DESIGN RESPONSIBILITIES

The owner's primary responsibilities with respect to design are to communicate its choices, requirements, and budget to the A/E. The owner's choices may be based on a variety of factors including functional requirements, financial considerations, schedule constraints, and aesthetics.

The A/E's responsibility is to produce plans and specifications that implement the owner's choices and govern the contractor's work. On a design-bid-build project, the A/E works under contract with the owner and has no contractual relationship with the contractor. Nevertheless, on most projects there is regular communication between the contractor and the A/E throughout construction. As a result, the contractor's input can have a significant impact on the final design.

6.1.1 Contractor's Responsibility for Design

In some cases, the construction contract may explicitly allocate certain portions of the design to the contractor. This often occurs with specialized systems such as sophisticated lighting and sound systems, because the expertise required for these systems is such that the same subcontractor may do both the design and installation. Likewise, certain aspects of the project may involve proprietary products or systems and may require knowledge that is unique to these products or systems. These design details may be delegated to the contractor through requirements for shop drawings or the use of performance specifications.

The specifications for a project may also state that a product or system must be a certain brand name "or equal." If the contractor proposes an alternate product or system, it has the burden of showing that the alternate is equal to the specified brand.

6.1.2 Value Engineering

The construction contract may permit the contractor to propose design changes through *value engineering*. Value engineering allows the contractor to use its knowledge of construction materials and methods to suggest how equivalent quality can be obtained at a lower cost. Typically, the contractor is entitled to a percentage of any cost savings. Although value engineering is an attractive concept, it may create a problem with respect to the contractor's insurance coverage if any design work is required–the liability insurance carried by most contractors explicitly exempts coverage for design work.

6.2 THE OWNER'S PROGRAM

Before the start of design, the owner typically prepares a summary of major objectives and constraints for the project. This summary, referred to as the *owner's program*, generally includes the owner's aesthetic preferences, schedule requirements, and budget constraints, as well as site limitations, spatial considerations, and functional parameters.

Under most industry standard form contracts, the owner is responsible for furnishing the A/E with a written program. The A/E will review the program and prepare a preliminary design based on its understanding. Developing a program can be extremely complicated and time consuming, however, and many owners do not have the ability to develop effective programs in-house. As a result, owners often hire the A/E to develop the program as an additional service. There are also firms that specialize in providing architectural programming services.

6.3 THE DESIGN AGREEMENT (OWNER-A/E)

The contract between the owner and the lead A/E is referred to as the *design agreement*. Most design agreements consist of a single document that states the terms of the agreement, and various exhibits or attachments. The exhibits may include a schedule for the A/E's work, a list of required insurance coverage, an index of key personnel and consultants, and other terms or conditions that supplement the underlying agreement. Although some states have laws requiring agreements for design services to be in writing, most states allow oral agreements. Nevertheless, both design agreements and agreements for related consulting work are typically written and signed by both parties.

AIA B101, *Standard Form of Agreement Between Owner and Architect*, is typical of many design agreements. B101 anticipates that the contract will comprise five phases: the schematic design phase, the design development phase, the construction documents phase, the bid or negotiation phase, and the construction phase. The agreement describes the five phases, the deliverables that will be furnished to the owner during each phase, and the contract administration activities that will be provided. Under AIA terminology, the design professional provides "services" to the owner. B101 includes a list of the basic services that are included in each phase and a list of additional services that may either be contracted for at the time the agreement is signed or at a later time.

6.3.1 Schematic Design Phase

During the schematic design phase, the A/E performs a preliminary evaluation of the owner's program, the site, and the proposed project delivery system. The A/E then prepares a preliminary design illustrating the scale and relationship of the project components based on its understanding of the owner's project requirements.

If the owner approves the preliminary design, the A/E prepares schematic design documents and an estimate of the cost of the work. The schematic design documents may include a site plan, preliminary drawings, study models, and preliminary selections of major building systems and construction materials.

6.3.2 Design Development Phase

Once the owner approves the schematic design documents, the A/E prepares design development documents. The design development documents incorporate any adjustments the owner has made to the project requirements or budget, and usually include plans, sections, elevations, and typical construction details. In addition, the design development documents usually include layouts that describe the architectural, structural, mechanical, and electrical systems, and outline specifications for the major materials and systems. The outline specifications establish the overall quality of the project; the A/E refines its estimate for the cost of the work based on these specifications and the updated plans.

6.3.3 Construction Documents Phase

Once the owner approves the design development documents, the A/E prepares the plans and specifications that will be used for construction. The construction documents set forth the appearance, dimensions, and layout of the structure; the quality of the materials and systems; and other requirements for construction. The documents must have enough information and detail that the contractor can estimate the cost of construction and subsequently build the structure. The owner generally cannot get a building permit until the construction documents are complete, as most building departments reject applications that include drawings marked "Not for Construction."

Once the construction documents are complete, the A/E will typically compile a project manual that includes the drawings, the specifications, the conditions of the contract, the bidding requirements, and bid or proposal forms. The A/E may assist the owner in preparing bid documents that describe the time, place, and conditions of bidding. The A/E may also assist the owner in preparing the construction contract and the conditions of the contract, but any proposed changes to industry standard form contracts should be reviewed by the owner's legal counsel.

6.3.4   Bidding or Negotiation Phase Services

During the bid or negotiation phase, the A/E acts as a limited agent for the owner, with the scope of its authority defined by the design agreement. The A/E usually answers questions from bidders and may provide addenda that clarify the bid documents. If the bid documents allow substitutions, the A/E will consider any proposed substitutes.

The A/E often assists the owner in establishing a list of prospective bidders and may assist the owner in selecting a contractor. The A/E is not a party to the contract between the owner and the contractor, however, and the owner must ultimately make the selection. Specific questions regarding the responsiveness of a bid or the responsibility of a bidder on a public project may need to be addressed by the owner's legal counsel.

6.3.5   Construction Phase Services

During the construction phase, the A/E again acts as a limited agent for the owner. The nature and scope of the A/E's role during construction can vary considerably, however, depending on the project and the owner. On small projects, the A/E's role may be limited to administrative functions, such as reviewing the contractor's applications for payment. On complex projects, the A/E may be extensively involved in answering requests for information (RFIs), approving shop drawings, and preparing change orders.

Under AIA B101, the A/E has a central role in contract administration. The A/E is responsible for providing interpretations of the plans and specifications, reviewing and coordinating submittals, approving applications for payment, and preparing change orders for the owner's approval. The A/E is also responsible for determining when substantial and final completion are achieved. Unless the design agreement specifies an alternate initial decision maker, the A/E is responsible for attempting to resolve any disputes between the owner and the contractor.

6.3.6 Basic Services versus Additional Services

On many projects, the A/E needs to perform services beyond those classified as basic services in most of the industry standard design agreements. For example, the owner may want the project to qualify for Leadership in Energy and Environmental Design (LEED) certification. Alternatively, the owner may want the design agreement to include landscape design or civil engineering services that are not typically provided as basic services. Certain types of projects almost always require additional services. For example, renovation projects usually require analysis of the existing structure.

If the need for these additional services is known before the design agreement is executed, the agreement can be modified to include these services. However, the need for additional services often arises unexpectedly during construction because of defective work or unforeseen site conditions. Since it is difficult to predict the extent of such work in advance, additional services are typically paid for on a time and materials basis, using an hourly rate stipulated in the contract.

The need for additional services sometimes arises because the owner has requested a design change. The A/E typically develops the design in phases; at the end of each phase, the owner reviews and approves the documents. If the owner requests changes to documents that have already been approved, the A/E must spend additional time modifying the documents to implement the changes. Unless this time was accounted for in the design fee, the A/E is entitled to compensation for this work as an additional service.

6.3.7 The A/E's Compensation

The A/E's fee for basic services is generally either a lump-sum amount or a percentage of the construction costs. AIA B101 anticipates that the fee will be allocated between the various phases of work in accordance with percentages agreed upon in the design agreement. Anything not designated as a basic service is billed as an additional service.

Most design agreements state that the A/E is allowed to bill for expenses such as renderings, printing, and postage as well as permit fees, out-of-town travel, and site office expenses. Often, the A/E will include a markup on these expenses, to cover administrative costs.

6.4 STANDARD OF CARE APPLICABLE TO DESIGN SERVICES

If problems arise during construction, or the owner is not satisfied with the design, the owner may allege that the A/E has been negligent. In determining whether there is liability for negligence, tort law typically uses the standard of what a reasonable, prudent person would do. A reasonable, prudent person has a duty to take reasonable steps to protect others from being injured or having their possessions damaged. However, because professional work such as design requires expertise that is outside the realm of knowledge of an ordinary person, the standard for such work is what a reasonable, prudent A/E within the community would do. For purposes of professional negligence liability, the A/E is thus held to a standard of care defined as "the ordinary and reasonable degree of care required of a prudent professional under the circumstances."

By its contract with the owner, the A/E implies that it possesses the skill and ability required for the work. The A/E's duty of care is similar to that of any professional entity claiming to possess skill and ability in some type of employment and offering its services to the public on the basis of its aptitude for that employment. Designs are not expected to be flawless, however. Unless the design agreement contains special guarantees or warranties, there is no assurance that the plans and specifications are free from errors. Courts only allow the owner to recover damages when the A/E has been negligent, where *negligence* means failure to exercise reasonable care and skill.

6.4.1 Contractual Standard of Care

Because the courts have established a standard of care for design work, it is not necessary for the design agreement to include a standard of care. Nevertheless, many design agreements explicitly state the standard of care required of the design professional. Usually, the standard is the same as the "reasonable degree of care" standard established by the courts for negligence claims. However, including an explicit standard of care in the contract means that if an A/E is charged with violating the required standard of care, it will be a breach-of-contract claim rather than a tort claim. This may limit the damages that the A/E is liable for.

The AIA added the following standard of care to AIA B201 in 2007:

2.2 The Architect shall perform its services consistent with the professional skill and care ordinarily provided by architects practicing in the same or similar community under the same or similar circumstances.

The AIA included this statement of the standard of care because users of the previous versions of the AIA documents were adding standard-of-care language to the documents themselves and, in doing so, were often misstating the standard and potentially increasing the A/E's liability.

The EJCDC documents contain a similar provision in §6.01 of EJCDC E-500, *Standard Form of Agreement Between Owner and Engineer for Professional Services*. The EJCDC document limits the standard of care such that the A/E's liability cannot be expanded by implied warranties.

6.4.2 Proving Violation of the Standard of Care

As a general rule, professional negligence must be proven through the testimony of an expert qualified in the same field as the individual accused of negligence. The expert must establish both the standard of care and that the defendant failed to meet this standard. For example, if the plaintiff alleges that the A/E's decision to use a particular material was the cause of the plaintiff's injury, an expert must testify that use of the material was a deviation from the A/E's obligation to use reasonable care. The expert witness testimony is intended to help the fact finder (the judge or jury) understand the terminology and technical aspects of the issue. The requirement of expert testimony acknowledges that the fact finder may have trouble understanding an issue related to architecture or engineering.

Most states hold that an A/E's failure to comply with an obvious building code requirement is negligence per se. Under negligence per se, it is not necessary to prove the standard of care or that the standard has been violated. The owner simply must prove that the negligent act (failure to comply with the building code) was committed and was the cause of the owner's damages.

The mere fact that the design did not pass an inspection does not necessarily mean the A/E was negligent, however. Provisions from different sections of the building code may be in conflict, but the conflict might arise only in very unusual circumstances such that the A/E would have no reason to know of it. Alternatively, it might not be clear how a code provision should be interpreted, and the inspector's interpretation might be different from the A/E's. The A/E is generally not considered negligent if its interpretation was reasonable.

Even though the building department typically reviews the plans prior to issuing a building permit, it does not assume any liability for the correctness of the plans. If the A/E is not sure whether some aspect of the design complies with the building code, it may be possible to schedule a special review of the design and get written confirmation that the design complies with applicable code requirements.

6.4.3 Implied Warranties

Under the Spearin doctrine, the owner provides the contractor with an implied warranty that the plans and specifications are satisfactory for construction of the proposed work. Implied warranties are generally disfavored, however, and courts typically do not find an implied warranty unless there is a clear reason to do so. Although it might seem inconsistent, courts typically do not find that the A/E provides the owner with an implied warranty that the plans and specifications are suitable for construction.

Courts are most likely to find that the A/E created an implied warranty of fitness if the A/E held itself out as having some particular skill or expertise, such as expertise in design of medical facilities. When the A/E holds itself out as specially qualified to perform work of a particular character, the court may find that the A/E has implicitly warranted that the work will be of reasonable fitness for its intended use.

6.4.4   Designing to the Owner's Budget

Under most design agreements, the owner is required to establish a budget prior to the start of design and must periodically update the budget throughout the design process. In establishing its budget, the owner should consider the design fee, the fees of other consultants, and permit fees, as well as the cost of construction. Owners who significantly increase or decrease their budgets during the design process must notify the A/E. The owner and the A/E can then work out a corresponding change in the scope and/or quality of the project.

It is important for an A/E to be able to design to the owner's budget. If the cost of construction is more than what the owner can obtain financing for, the project may not be viable. In addition to losing what was spent on fees and permits, the owner may also be liable for commitments made to third parties such as prospective tenants.

AIA B101 requires the A/E to evaluate the owner's budget as part of its preliminary review and verify that the budget is reasonable in light of the proposed schedule and scope of construction. The A/E is also required to develop its own cost estimate during the schematic design phase and update it during the design development and construction document phases. In developing its cost estimate, the A/E is allowed to select the materials, equipment, component systems, and types of construction, within the constraints imposed by the owner's program. The A/E is also allowed to include reasonable contingencies in its estimate.

6.4.5   The A/E's Liability for its Estimate

Estimating construction costs can be difficult, particularly when a design is unique or the site presents challenges for the proposed construction. Unless the A/E specifically guarantees its estimate, the owner typically cannot recover damages if the construction ultimately costs much more than the A/E's estimate, even if the A/E was negligent in providing the estimate. The resulting structure is presumed to be worth what the owner paid for it; thus, the owner has not been damaged.

A court sometimes allows damages when the project involves a commercial building and the more expensive building does not result in additional income for the owner. Courts are most likely to find damages if the owner is a tenant that will have no claim on the improvement once its lease expires. Even in such cases, courts allow a broad margin of error in construction cost estimating. If the owner alleges the A/E has been negligent, an expert in cost estimating must generally identify the specific acts or omissions that were negligent. Courts have awarded damages for breach of contract when the A/E failed to make any attempt to determine expected construction costs or knew that bids would come in well above the owner's budget and made no attempt to notify the owner.

Under AIA B101, the parties acknowledge that the A/E does not control the costs of labor or materials and that the A/E's estimate is not a guarantee. If all legitimate bids exceed the owner's budget, the owner can require the A/E to modify the construction documents to meet the budget, for no additional compensation. This is the extent of the A/E's obligation, however. In addition, the A/E's estimate is good only if bidding begins within 90 days after the A/E submits the construction documents to the owner. After 90 days, the owner must revise the budget to reflect market prices.

6.5 OWNERSHIP OF THE DESIGN DOCUMENTS

Absent a contractual provision to the contrary, the A/E holds the copyright to the plans and specifications that it prepares for a project. The legal basis for this right is the Copyright Act of 1976, which granted copyright owners the exclusive right to authorize reproduction of their work, prepare derivative works, and display the work publicly. The Copyright Act provided complete protection to architectural plans and drawings but protection of actual structures was limited to decorative elements and nonfunctional structures such as monuments. A builder that built a structure substantially similar to an existing building was not liable for copyright infringement unless it used copyrighted drawings without authorization.

This changed in 1990, when the Architectural Works Copyright Protection Act (AWCPA) established that an architectural work was an original work of authorship eligible for copyright protection. The AWCPA defines an architectural work as "the design of a building as embodied in any tangible medium of expression, including a building, architectural plans, or drawings." Under the AWCPA, a copyright owner can claim infringement of both the architectural plans and the structure based on such plans. Infringement is most commonly claimed by home builders; courts have found that residential homes possess the minimal amount of originality that copyright law requires for protection.

In addition to the protection that designers have under copyright law, most industry standard form design agreements expressly provide that all ownership rights in the design documents remain with the party that prepared the documents (i.e., the A/E or its subconsultant). The AIA contract documents refer to the drawings, specifications, and other documents prepared by the A/E and its subconsultants as "instruments of service." The owner is granted a nonexclusive license to use these instruments solely for the project that is the subject of the design agreement. The license is revocable and contingent on the owner's substantial compliance with all of its obligations in the agreement, including prompt payment to the A/E.

6.5.1 Use of the Plans and Specifications

Issues may arise if the agreement between the owner and the A/E is terminated and the owner attempts to complete the project with another A/E, or the owner wants to use the plans and specifications for another project. Owners often feel that because they have paid for the documents, they are entitled to use them however they see fit. However, completing the project without the A/E or reusing the documents on another project creates a potential liability for the A/E; the A/E may not have contemplated this liability when setting its fee for the work.

Older standard form agreements gave the A/E broad rights to prevent the owner from using the plans and specifications without the A/E's involvement. More recent versions of these agreements attempt to balance the expectations of the owner and the concerns of the A/E. Under some agreements, if the owner uses plans and specifications on another project without hiring the A/E to work on the project, the owner is deemed to release the A/E and its subconsultants from any claims arising out of such use. The owner may also be required to pay an additional fee.

6.6   TERMINATION OF THE DESIGN AGREEMENT

There may be times when termination of the design agreement is necessary or appropriate; for example, if the owner is unable to obtain the necessary financing or its needs have changed. Additionally, if the relationship between the owner and the A/E has deteriorated such that it has become unworkable, it may be better for the owner to terminate the agreement and retain another A/E.

Most standard form agreements allow the owner to terminate the design agreement for convenience, without cause. They vary with respect to the termination expenses that the A/E is entitled to, however. The AIA documents provide that the A/E will be compensated for any expenses directly attributable to the termination that it is not otherwise compensated for, plus the anticipated profit on services not performed. Because the profit on unperformed work is difficult to prove, the parties may agree to a set fee or a percentage of the contract balance.

In addition to the owner's right to terminate for convenience, design agreements typically allow both parties to terminate "for cause" if the other party has materially breached its obligations. The A/E's right to terminate for cause is generally limited to situations where the owner has failed to make payment in accordance with the agreement or has suspended the project for an extended period of time, through no fault of the A/E. Under the AIA documents, the A/E can also suspend work if the owner has failed to make payment as required. The A/E should carefully consider a decision to either terminate the agreement or suspend work. Both a termination and a suspension of services can have drastic financial implications for the owner, and if the A/E's actions are found to be unjustified, the A/E may be liable for the owner's damages.

7

THE PROCUREMENT PROCESS

The most significant difference between public and private construction is in the area of procurement of design and construction services, in particular, the selection of the contractor. On public projects, procurement is often extensively regulated, and contractors must usually be selected through a publicly announced, competitive bidding process. In contrast, private owners have considerable freedom when procuring design and construction services.

Although the increased use of public-private partnerships and privatization has blurred the distinction between public and private projects, projects that receive significant public funding and privately funded projects that will be controlled or owned by the government are typically subject to public procurement regulations. Some public contracts are exempt from the standard procurement regulations, however. These include contracts for emergency work and contracts involving proprietary technology or restricted materials, where it would be impossible to obtain full and open competition. Contracts for amounts below the simplified acquisition threshold (currently $150,000) and contracts that have been set aside for small businesses are also exempt from standard procurement regulations.

7.1 SELECTION OF CONTRACTORS FOR PUBLIC PROJECTS

Public procurement regulations often require public owners such as government agencies to use the design-bid-build project delivery system and award the contract to the lowest responsive, responsible bidder under a sealed, competitive bid process. A competitive procurement typically begins with the owner's advertisement for bids, also referred to as an *invitation for bids* (IFB). The advertisement provides prospective bidders with a description of the project and instructions on how to obtain the project plans and specifications, as well as the time and place for the bid submission and opening. The advertisement may include other information, such as bid security and bonding requirements, the length of time that bids must be held "firm," and any requirements affecting subcontractor hiring. Advertisements for bids must usually be published in a newspaper having general circulation in the geographic area where the project is located.

7.1.1 The Bid Package

To ensure that all bidders are bidding on the same information, the owner generally provides bidders with a standardized *bid package*. Also referred to as the *project manual*, the bid package typically includes the plans and specifications, the proposed contractual terms, the general conditions, and any special or supplementary conditions. The owner may also provide potential bidders with the geotechnical report and any other engineering reports it has for the project site. Bidders who want to obtain a bid package must typically put up a nominal deposit that is refunded if the drawings and plans are returned in good condition within a certain amount of time after the bid opening. Often, the bid package can be examined for free at a local plan room. In addition, public owners are increasingly making plans and specifications available for free download by registered bidders.

Sometimes an owner needs to put a project out for bid before making a final decision on the work that will be included. Likewise, until the bids are received, the owner may not know whether its budget will cover all the work that it wants to include. In such cases, the owner may ask bidders to submit a base bid that covers the work that will definitely be included and separate bids for various alternates. Using alternates on a competitively bid public project may lead to a bid protest, however, as the lowest bidder on the base work may not be the lowest bidder when some of the alternates are considered. Thus, the low bidder may ultimately be determined by what work is included in the contract.

7.1.2 Duty to Award to the Lowest Bidder

Most public owners are required to use an *open bidding* process; the bids are opened simultaneously and publicly at a predetermined time, and the project is awarded to the lowest bidder. If the low bid is more than the amount authorized for the project, the agency is typically allowed to readvertise the project. In addition, some states allow the agency to negotiate with the lowest bidder and reduce the project costs by reducing the quantity or quality of the work. The agency cannot engage in negotiations to drive down the price of the advertised project, however.

7.1.3 Bid Responsiveness

Before awarding a contract, public owners must verify that the bidder is responsible and that its bid is responsive. A material deviation that would give the bidder a substantial advantage or benefit over other bidders will make the bid nonresponsive. Material deviations from the requirements of the invitation prevent the owner from comparing the bids competitively; considering such bids would violate the public policy objective of allowing all bidders an equal right to compete. Examples of such material deviations include bids that are incomplete or late and bids that propose work or materials that do not conform to the requirements.

A bid that is not responsive to the owner's solicitation may be rejected, even if it is the lowest bid. To be responsive, the bid must strictly comply with all mandatory requirements in the invitation and substantially comply with all nonmandatory requirements. A bid that does not conform precisely to the requirements of the IFB may still be considered if the deviation is nonmaterial. A nonmaterial deviation is one that has no more than a negligible effect on the price, quantity, quality, or time of completion of the work. Nonmaterial bid deviations are usually administrative issues such as failing to initial changes or corrections. Public agencies typically have broad discretion in deciding whether a bid is responsive, and courts will set aside these decisions only if they are arbitrary, capricious, or an abuse of discretion.

Public procurement statutes routinely grant agencies the right to reject a bid for compelling reasons and may even allow an agency to cancel an IFB if it is determined to be in the agency's best interests. Often, the bid advertisement explicitly states that the owner reserves both the right to reject any and all bids, and the right to waive any informality in the bids if it is in the agency's best interests. However, if an agency rejects a bid, it is typically required to show that its actions were not arbitrary and were not designed to evade public procurement regulations.

7.1.4 Responsible Bidder

To be awarded the contract, the bidder with the lowest responsive bid must also qualify as responsible. Agencies have broad discretion in making decisions regarding bidder responsibility. These decisions may be based on any evidence reasonably likely to establish whether the contract, if awarded to that bidder, would be completed in accordance with its terms. The agency may consider such factors as the bidder's past performance, technical and managerial capability, financial stability, bonding capacity, and safety record. The agency may also consider the bidder's character and reputation, including allegations of fraud or unfairness in previous dealings.

The low bidder does not have to be the *most* responsible of the bidders; it must simply be deemed responsible. To prevent their decision from being overturned as arbitrary and capricious, public agencies often include the criteria they will use to determine responsibility in the bid invitation. An agency that does not strictly follow the published criteria may still be given deference by courts, as long as its decision is reasonable and rationally based.

Traditionally, responsibility is determined after the bids are reviewed for responsiveness. In recent years, however, agencies have begun prequalifying bidders by making an initial determination of responsibility before soliciting bids.

Under some state procurement laws, the initial screening does not consider all of the attributes used in the responsibility determination. Thus, while bids are accepted only from prequalified bidders, passing the initial screening does not guarantee that the bidder will ultimately be deemed responsible.

7.1.5 Bid Protests

An unsuccessful bidder may think that the low bidder should have been rejected as nonresponsive or non-responsible. Alternatively, a bidder rejected as non-responsive or non-responsible may believe that the determination was unfair. In such cases, the bidder may challenge the procurement through a bid protest. At the federal level, only an "interested party" can protest an award; an *interested party* is defined as an actual or prospective bidder whose direct economic interest would be affected by the award. Some states allow any bidder, actual or prospective, who is adversely affect by the solicitation or award to file a protest; other states only allow bid protests to be asserted by taxpayers.

Protests involving federal projects can be brought before the contracting agency, the U.S. General Accounting Office (GAO), or the U.S. Court of Federal Claims. The process for bringing a bid protest at the state or local level varies from state to state. Some states have a centralized agency or board of contract appeals that hears all bid protests. Other states have a decentralized system whereby each agency is responsible for hearing its own protests, with different procedures depending upon the type of project. If the initial decision is unfavorable, the protestor can typically appeal to the state court system. In the absence of formal protest procedures at the state or local level, bid protests are typically heard in state court.

Protestors who want to challenge contract awards must assert their claims in a timely manner. Failure to file a protest within the required time limits typically results in a waiver of the right to protest the award. For federal projects, protests of an award must be made within ten days of the award and must set forth both the grounds for the protest and the relief requested. State and local requirements vary according to the applicable statutes and the nature of the protest.

7.1.5.1 Filing for an Injunction

If the contract has already been executed, a protestor's remedies are typically limited to recovering its bid preparation costs; agencies are rarely required to pay an unsuccessful bidder its lost profits. As a result, many protestors seek an injunction to enjoin (prevent) the agency from proceeding with the award, so that it can have another chance at the contract. Injunctive relief is difficult to obtain, however, because the protester must show that it will suffer irreparable injury if the agency proceeds with the award. The protestor must also show that it is likely to succeed on the merits of its protest, that the harm to the protestor if the award is made outweighs the harm to the agency if the award is not made, and that it would be in the public interest to enjoin the agency.

CASE STUDY—BID PROTEST

Immediately after the bid opening for a school project, the low bidder notified the owner that it had omitted a subcontractor's bid for roofing. The bidder was allowed to amend its bid to include the $613,000 bid; since it was still the low bidder, it was awarded the contract. The next-lowest bidder filed a protest seeking an injunction, alleging that allowing the bid to be amended was improper and the bidder should be disqualified.

The court held that the low bidder was entitled to correct its bid. The relevant procurement code allowed such corrections when it was clear that there had been an error and the error would cause the bidder a substantial loss. As the low bidder was low both before and after the correction, allowing the correction was not prejudicial to the interests of either the school district or fair competition. In contrast, disqualifying the low bidder would be prejudicial to the school district, as the protestor's bid was several hundred thousand dollars higher.

Martin Engineering, Inc., v. Lexington County School District One,
365 S.C. 1, 615 S.E.2d 110 (2005)

Some states require anyone seeking an injunction to post a bond that may be forfeited if the protest is rejected. If it is subsequently determined that the protest was unlawful or fraudulent, a bidder who loses a contract as a result of a protest may bring a fraud claim against the protestor.

7.1.6 Bid Security

On competitively bid public projects, bidders are typically required to submit firm bids. A firm bid is irrevocable and must remain in force for a specified amount of time after the bid opening while the owner determines the lowest responsible and responsive bidder.

Unless there is a bid protest, the owner's selection of the lowest responsible and responsive bidder typically results in a contract with that bidder. To ensure that the bidder honors its bid, most public bid solicitations require bidders to provide some form of bid guarantee, generally a cash deposit or bid bond of at least 5 percent of the total bid price. Requiring a bid guarantee discourages contractors from submitting a bid unless they are prepared to honor it. If the selected contractor refuses to enter into a contract, the owner can use the bid guarantee to cover the costs of rebidding the project.

7.1.7 "Best Value" Awards

Competitive "lowest-price" bidding on public projects is generally considered to encourage competition among bidders and provide taxpayers with the lowest possible construction costs. It is also considered the best way to provide all qualified contractors an opportunity to compete for government contracts and avoid favoritism or fraud. Given the complexity of modern construction projects, however, it is not always appropriate to award contracts solely on the basis of price.

Value-based contracting ("best value" awards) allows the owner to consider factors other than initial construction costs when awarding the bid. Often, those considerations are the life-cycle costs associated with owning the building, such as operating and maintenance costs, repair costs, and renovation costs. Life-cycle costing can result in savings over the life of the project, even though the initial construction costs may be higher than under the lowest-bidder method of contracting. Some value-based contracts require the contractor to guarantee that the owner will have a positive return from anticipated maintenance and operational savings. Other types of value-based contracting include sustainable design, which emphasizes "green" technology, and qualifications-based selection, where selection is based on the builder's competence and expertise.

Value-based contracting raises a number of concerns, however. It typically includes a subjective assessment, which may lead to allegations of favoritism. In addition, considering factors such as a builder's capabilities and previous performance may create an anti-competitive bias in favor of larger, more established builders. To address this concern, a few states require agencies to consider the equitable distribution of contracts when making best-value awards.

When the award is based on life-cycle costing, there may be a problem with the long-term accountability of both the design professional and the contractor. General construction warranties typically only run for a year from the date of substantial completion, and liability for defective construction is limited by the applicable statute of limitation and statute of repose. To hold the design professional and contractor liable for long-term costs, the owner would need to negotiate additional guarantees and keep detailed performance records. Design professionals and contractors faced with long-term liabilities would need longer-term insurance, which could make the project considerably more costly.

7.2 SELECTION OF DESIGN PROFESSIONALS

It is generally acknowledged that the price-based procurement policies used for awarding construction contracts are not well suited for selecting design professionals. Because design work requires skill, expertise, and technical training, the lowest bidder is likely to be the least capable and most inexperienced. In recognition of this fact, the federal government and many state governments have enacted laws specifically governing the selection of design professionals. These laws attempt to balance the goal of securing design professionals who have the required abilities with the goals of containing costs and limiting favoritism.

On federal projects, selection of design professionals is governed by the Brooks Act, 40 U.S.C. §§1101–1104. The Brooks Act requires the government to negotiate contracts for architectural and engineering services at fair and reasonable prices, on the basis of demonstrated competence and qualification for the type of professional services required. Federal agencies must publicly announce all requirements for architectural and engineering services and must encourage design professionals to submit qualification and performance data for the agency's consideration.

Agencies are required to conduct discussions with at least three firms and compare the firms' proposals for furnishing the required services. The agency must then attempt to negotiate a fair and reasonable contract with the firm that it considers the most qualified for the job. If these negotiations are not successful, the agency must attempt to negotiate with the next-most-qualified firm and then the next, until an agreement for the design services is reached.

Many of the states have similar acts, referred to as "Baby Brooks Acts." These states typically follow the federal practice of advertising design projects and may require that a minimum number of design firms be considered. Other states do not require public agencies to consider a specific number of firms; they only require the agencies to begin negotiations with the "best qualified" firm.

When evaluating design firms, many states specify criteria other than cost, and some states base designer selection solely on the designer's competence and qualifications. Other states consider factors such as the design professional's previous performance, location, and current workloads. A number of states have increased oversight of the selection process by requiring that agencies go through an independent selection or negotiation committee or by requiring that design agreements be approved by the state purchasing director. Although some states have statutorily limited the design professional's fee to a fixed percentage of the total project cost, in many states the only limit on these agreements is that the price must be "fair and reasonable."

7.3 ALTERNATIVES TO DESIGN-BID-BUILD IN THE PUBLIC SECTOR

Although design-bid-build is by far the most common project delivery system in the public sector, construction management agreements have become increasingly popular with public owners, and a number states have expressly authorized construction management at-risk agreements for public projects. Construction management contracts are usually not exempt from public procurement laws, but in most states the construction manager is selected under regulations similar to those that govern selection of design professionals. On a construction management at-risk project, the CM is typically required to put the work out for bid and must award its subcontracts to the lowest responsible, responsive bidder.

7.3.1 Design-Build Construction in the Public Sector

Design-build has been heavily promoted by the Design Build Institute of America, and its use has increased significantly in the public sector in recent years. Federal procurement statutes have been amended to allow design-build construction under certain circumstances, and a number of states and local agencies allow design-build construction on certain types of projects.

Because design-build contracts do not allow owners to make the comparisons that are required for competitive bidding, the procedures for awarding design-build contracts on public projects are typically similar to those used for awarding contracts for design agreements. Agencies identify the key parameters of the project, advertise those parameters, invite proposals, and then evaluate both the proposals and the expertise of the various bidders. Common criteria for evaluating proposals include initial cost, features, functions, time for completion, and life-cycle costs. Agencies often include the relative weights of the evaluation criteria in their invitations for bid so bidders can tailor their proposals accordingly.

CASE STUDY—AWARD OF CONSTRUCTION MANAGEMENT CONTRACT

A school board awarded a contract to manage and coordinate renovations to several buildings; the contract did not require the construction manager to perform any physical work. A taxpayer sought to enjoin execution of the contract, alleging that the applicable procurement code required competitive bidding. The court held that the contract was not subject to competitive bidding requirements. The basis for the holding was long-standing state court decisions that contracts for professional-skill services were exempt from the competitive bidding process.

The court defined professional-skill contracts as contracts that involved quality as the paramount concern and required a recognized professional and special expertise. The court concluded that the construction manager's duty was to ensure that the quality and workmanship of the project complied with the requirements of the contract and that this required specialized judgment and skills.

Malloy v. Boyertown Area School Board,
540 Pa. 308, 657 A.2d 915 (Pa. 1995)

7.4 THE FEDERAL ACQUISITION REGULATION (FAR)

The process by which the federal government acquires goods and services is governed by a set of regulations collectively referred to as the *Federal Acquisition Regulation System*. These regulations implement the laws passed by Congress to govern acquisition planning, contract formation, and contract administration. The principal set of regulations is the Federal Acquisition Regulation (FAR).

The original purpose of the FAR was to consolidate all of the individual agency acquisition regulations into one comprehensive set of regulations that would apply government-wide. However, almost every major cabinet-level department (and many of the lower agencies) has issued supplemental regulations. As an example, the Defense Federal Acquisition Regulation Supplement (DFARS) is the Department of Defense supplement. A handful of federal agencies including the U.S. Postal Service and the Federal Aviation Administration are exempt from the FAR and have their own specific procurement rules. All other agencies are required to comply with the FAR. The FAR and its supplements comprise Title 48 of the U.S. Code of Federal Regulations (CFR).[1]

The FAR is divided into 53 parts. The most heavily regulated aspect of acquisition is contract pricing, which is addressed throughout the FAR, but especially in Parts 30 and 31, and Subparts 15.4, 42.7, 42.8, and 42.17. The largest single part of the FAR is Part 52, which contains standard contract clauses and solicitation provisions. For example, FAR §52.249-10 provides examples of delays that are considered to be beyond either party's control. When a government agency issues an invitation for bid, it specifies a list of FAR provisions that apply to that contract. To be awarded the contract, a bidder must either comply with the requirements of these provisions, show that it will be able to comply with them at the time of award, or claim an exemption. Bidders that meet Small Business Administration (SBA) criteria for a small business are exempt from certain FAR provisions.

If the FAR requires that a clause be included in a government contract and the government's acquisition personnel omit the clause without authorization, the contract will be interpreted as though the clause was included. This is known as the *Christian doctrine*, from the case *G. L. Christian and Assoc. v. United States*.[2] The principle underlying the Christian doctrine is that government regulations have the force and effect of law, and government personnel may not deviate from the law without proper authorization. Contractors are expected to know what the law requires, as well as the limitations of the authority of government acquisition personnel.

7.5 PROCUREMENT ON PRIVATE PROJECTS

Procurement of construction services on private projects is significantly less structured than on public projects, and private owners select contractors in a variety of ways. Private owners often send a request for proposals to several contractors, review the written submissions, and then meet with two or three

---

[1] The Code of Federal Regulations (CFR) is the codification of the general and permanent rules published in the *Federal Register* by the executive departments and agencies of the federal government. It is divided into 50 titles that represent broad areas subject to federal regulation.

[2] *G. L. Christian and Associates v. United States*, 312 F.2d 418, 160 Ct.Cl. 1 (1963).

contractors before making their final selection. In some cases, the proposals may be based on incomplete project plans and specifications; the plans and specifications may not be finalized until after the contractor is selected.

Price is an important factor for most owners, but private owners often negotiate trade-offs between price, time for completion, and project scope. Although private owners often require fixed-price bids, they are free to use cost-plus or unit pricing unless prohibited from doing so by their lender. Even when private owners solicit competitive fixed-price bids, it is typically "closed bidding," as opposed to the "open bidding" required in the public sector. Under closed bidding, owners specify a time and place for bid submission, but the bids are opened in private and the owners can negotiate privately with each bidder before deciding which bid to accept. Owners are not required to accept the low bid and may base their selection on whatever criteria they choose.

Nevertheless, there are many similarities between competitive bidding in the public and the private sectors. Even though private owners do not have to formally ensure that the bidders are responsible and responsive, they typically require firm bids so they have time to evaluate the bidders and review their bids. Prior to awarding the contract, an owner usually verifies that the contractor has appropriate insurance and otherwise complies with the contract requirements.

8

PRICING CONSTRUCTION PROJECTS

The mechanism by which a construction project is priced determines how economic risks are allocated between the owner and the contractor. The most common pricing mechanisms are fixed price, cost of the work plus a fee (cost-plus), and unit pricing.

8.1 FIXED-PRICE CONTRACTS

Fixed price, also referred to as *stipulated sum* or *lump sum*, is the traditional mechanism for pricing construction work. Under a fixed-price contract, the contractor agrees to perform all of the work for a fixed price, subject to any additions or deductions from change orders.

Fixed-price contracts are often used with the design-bid-build (DBB) project delivery system. On a DBB project, the owner provides plans and specifications prepared by the A/E to a group of contractors. The owner reviews the bids that are submitted and selects a contractor, who then agrees to construct the project for a fixed price. The wording in a fixed-price agreement is usually quite straightforward, for example:

> *The Owner shall pay the Contractor the Contract Sum for the Contractor's performance of the Contract. The Contract Sum shall be $_____, subject to additions and deductions as provided in the Contract Documents.*

8.1.1 Fundamental Characteristic of a Fixed-Price Contract

The fundamental characteristic of a fixed-price contract is that the contractor bears the risk associated with the cost of performance. The contractor is required to perform the work identified in the contract, in the manner identified in the contract, for the agreed-upon price. If there are unforeseen price increases for labor or materials, the contractor may incur a loss on the project.

Contractors are willing to take this risk because the likelihood that prices will increase enough that contractor incurs a loss is generally small, at least on short-term contracts. In addition, if the contractor works very efficiently or materials cost less than expected, the contractor's profit can be considerably higher than expected. The contractor can reduce the risk of price increases by purchasing materials in advance or by entering into fixed-price subcontracts.

When the owner, or circumstances attributable to the owner, change the work in a manner that increases the contractor's costs, the contractor is generally entitled to an increase in the contract price. For example, if the owner requires the project to be completed earlier than the date specified in the contract, the contractor may need to expedite materials deliveries and schedule overtime work. The contractor is entitled to recover any costs it incurs because the owner has changed the completion date.

The contractor is also generally entitled to an increase in the contract price if the owner requests work that is outside the scope of the contract. Because the contractor has committed to doing the contract work for a fixed price, it has something of an incentive to identify work as falling outside the scope of the contract. As a result, there may be disputes over the parties' interpretation of the scope of the work required by the contract.

8.1.2 Allowances

Often, the owner has not made its final selections for various finishes and fixtures at the time a project is put out for bid. Under a fixed-price contract, the owner will typically ask bidders to include allowances for these items in their bids. An allowance is essentially a placeholder for the cost of a particular item—the contract amount includes a stated amount for a particular item, with a provision that the contract price will be adjusted if the actual price varies from the stated amount. As an example, the contract may include an allowance of $8,000 for floor finishes, based on an estimate of $5 per square foot. Depending on the carpet or flooring the owner chooses for the various rooms, the actual cost may be higher or lower, and the contract price will be adjusted accordingly.

Including an allowance for an item means that the item is considered part of the original contract and does not have to be negotiated as a change order. Allowances are often used for items such as floor coverings and lighting fixtures whose costs can vary considerably, depending on the particular items selected.

8.1.3 Material Price Escalation Clauses

At any given time during a construction project, some materials will be more expensive than usual, while others will be less expensive. Under a fixed-price contract, the contractor bears the risk of these price fluctuations; the contractor is expected to use its experience and knowledge of the market to obtain materials at a reasonable price.

Sometimes, however, there may be significant price increases due to events that are completely outside the reasonable expectation of the parties. For

example, a natural disaster such as a hurricane may cause a shortage of a particular construction material. A contractor that wants to avoid bearing the risk of
a significant (material) price increase in response to an unanticipated event may
request that the contract include a *material price escalation* clause, also referred
to as a *price adjustment* clause. The clause allows the contract price to increase
if there is a significant unanticipated price increase and thus shifts the risk of
unforeseen conditions or events to the owner.

An escalation clause must indicate what materials it applies to, how the clause
will be triggered, and how the price adjustment will be done. An example of
such a clause might be:

> *If the price of _____ significantly increases during the performance
> of this contract, through no fault of the Contractor, the contract amount
> shall be equitably adjusted by the amount reasonably necessary to cover the
> price increase. A significant price increase shall mean any increase in price
> exceeding ___ percent experienced by Contractor from the date the contract
> is signed. Price increases shall be documented through quotes, invoices, or
> receipts.*

Federal Acquisition Regulation (FAR) §16.203-2 allows an agency to use
a fixed-price contract with economic price adjustment when there is serious
doubt concerning the stability of market or labor conditions during the contract
performance.

8.1.4   Index Pricing

Index-pricing clauses are another way to allocate the risk of fluctuating materials
prices. When the cost of a particular material is likely to fluctuate unpredictably,
the contract can specify that the cost charged to the owner will be determined
by reference to a published index. The index does not have to be directly related
to the material; the parties are free to select any index they want. The clause
allocates the cost risk to the owner according to the index price, without regard
to the actual cost of the materials purchased by the contractor. As with a price
escalation clause, an index-pricing clause must state which materials are covered
and how the clause will be triggered.

8.2   COST-PLUS CONTRACTS

A cost-plus contract, also referred to as a *cost-reimbursable* contract, is one in
which the contract sum is the "cost of the work" plus a fee that covers the contractor's overhead and profit. In contrast to a fixed-price contract, a cost-plus
contract allocates the risks and benefits associated with changes in material and
labor costs to the owner. It also allocates the risk and benefit of the contractor's
efficiency or inefficiency to the owner.

The key pricing term in a cost-plus contract is the term that sets out which costs are to be reimbursed to the contractor and which costs are included in the contractor's fee. Under most contracts, on-site overhead costs such as the job trailer, temporary utilities, and water are included in the cost of the work and are thus reimbursable. Home office costs are typically considered to be included in the contractor's fee, however. Depending on the terms of the contract, supervisory personnel may be considered either a recoverable (reimbursable) cost or a component of the contractor's fee. Under the AIA contract documents, supervisory and administrative personnel costs are recoverable when the individuals are stationed at the site with the owner's prior approval.

The AIA contract documents define the reimbursable cost of the work to include labor costs, subcontract costs, costs of the material and equipment incorporated in the completion of construction, costs of other materials and equipment, temporary facilities, and miscellaneous costs. Miscellaneous costs include premiums for insurance or bonds required for the project, testing and permit fees, licenses, and inspections. Miscellaneous costs can also include legal costs incurred by the contractor for disputes related to the project, other than disputes between the owner and the contractor.

8.2.1 Labor

In addition to paying their employees' hourly wages or salary, contractors must pay employment taxes and workers' compensation; union contractors must also pay for sick time, vacation time, health insurance, pension benefits, and training. These additional costs are referred to as the *labor burden* and generally run 25 to 40 percent of actual wages. The labor burden for workers in trades considered to be extremely dangerous such as roofing and steel erection may be greater than their actual wages, however.

On a cost-plus contract, the contractor must ensure that its employee billing rates represent its actual costs. There are three common ways of billing for labor. The most accurate method is for the contractor to provide a certified payroll accounting that shows the cost of the labor burden, broken down by each of its components. Certified payroll is often required on government projects or projects where there is union labor. An alternative method is to specify the labor burden as a percentage of the actual payroll. This is less precise than calculating actual costs but is considerably easier to administer. A third method is have the contractor submit a schedule of labor rates for different classes of workers. Since labor costs are relatively fixed and easy to determine, contractors can usually calculate their labor rates fairly accurately.

8.2.2 Subcontracted Work

On a fixed-price contract, the contractor has an incentive to use the subcontractors that will perform the required work at the lowest price. On a cost-plus contract, there is no such incentive and the contractor may want to use a more expensive subcontractor for reasons that benefit the contractor rather than the owner. For example, the contractor may select a particular subcontractor as an incentive to encourage the subcontractor to bid on another project.

The owner can protect against this to a certain degree by requiring that all subcontracts be put out for bid, as if the contract were fixed price. The owner may also hire the A/E or a construction manager to review the subcontracts.

8.2.3 Heavy Equipment

The reimbursable cost of work generally includes the cost of heavy equipment. When the equipment is rented, the reimbursable cost is simply the invoice from the rental company. When the contractor plans to use its own equipment, a schedule of values specifying the rate for each piece of equipment is usually appended to the contract. Typically, these rates must be approved by the owner.

The contractor may calculate its equipment rates based on its actual costs or use rates equivalent to those of local rental companies. When a rental company calculates its equipment rates, it considers the cost of purchasing, licensing, maintaining, and insuring the equipment. These costs, together with some allowance for profit and overhead, are divided into an estimate of the total time that the equipment will be rented, generating a rental rate. A contractor would do a similar calculation to determine rental rates for its equipment.

8.2.4 Small Tool Allowance

Small tools such as chipping hammers and drills often last for several years, but contractors must still account for their replacement cost. Cost-plus contracts may include small tools in the reimbursable cost of the work as "partially consumable" items. The AIA cost-plus contracts set the reimbursable cost of a tool as the value of the tool when first used on the project less its value when it is no longer used on the project. However, most cost-plus contracts simply state that the cost of work includes a small tool allowance. The allowance is often a percentage of the total project cost (typically 3 to 6 percent).

8.2.5 Reasonableness or Necessity of Costs Incurred

Because the contractor has no financial risk on a cost-plus contract, it may have little motivation to perform the work efficiently. In an effort to guard against unscrupulous contractors, the AIA cost-plus contract documents state:

> *The Contractor accepts the relationship of trust and confidence established by this Agreement and covenants with the Owner to cooperate with the Architect and exercise the Contractor's skill and judgment in furthering the interests of the Owner.*

Some courts have held that such language makes the contractor a fiduciary of the owner, thereby increasing the contractor's duty to the owner and providing the basis for a constructive fraud claim if there are unreasonable cost overruns. *Constructive fraud* is essentially a legal fiction that courts adopt in the interest of fairness. Actual fraud requires a misrepresentation made with the intent of deceiving the other party and inducing it to act. A court may find that there has been constructive fraud if a party relies on the representation of a fiduciary and suffers a loss as a result of this reliance, even though there was no deceptive intent.

The AIA cost-plus documents also state that "costs shall not be at rates higher than the standard paid at the place of the project except with prior consent of the Owner" and require the contractor to perform the work in an "expeditious and economical manner consistent with the Owner's interests." Other industry standard form contracts state that the cost of work will include only the "reasonable and necessary" costs incurred in performing the work.

Even without such clauses, the contractor has a common-law duty of good faith and fair dealing. Failure to perform contractual obligations with good faith may be considered a breach of contract. In addition, because contracts typically give the owner the right to challenge the reasonableness of the costs, the contractor risks not being able to recover costs that are deemed excessive.

8.2.6   Contractor's Overhead and Profit

The "plus" portion of a cost-plus contract, also referred to as the *contractor's fee*, covers the contractor's profit and overhead. The contractor's fee is usually a percentage of the construction cost. Typical contract language when the fee is a percentage of the cost is:

> *The contract sum shall be the Cost of Work plus __%, which __% shall constitute the Contractor's exclusive compensation for overhead and profit.*

The fee can also be a fixed amount, or it can be time based, for example, a fixed amount per month. When the fee is a fixed amount, there is usually a provision to adjust the fee if there are significant changes to the project, such that the work is significantly more or less than what the parties anticipated when the contract was signed.

8.2.7   Estimates and Cost-Plus Contracts

An owner contemplating a cost-plus contract will typically want some idea of the cost of construction. The usual source of projected cost information is the A/E, who may do a formal cost estimate as an additional service. The owner may also ask the contractor for an estimate prior to awarding the contract. Because the contractor is generally not paid for the estimate, the owner may not be able to place too much reliance on it; in addition, the owner should be wary of a contractor that provides an artificially low estimate simply to obtain the work.

Many government contracts include clauses that cap the allowable costs at those set out in the estimate unless additional costs are approved in advance by the government. The government can choose whether to incur the additional costs, alter the scope of work, or terminate the contract. Such clauses do not guarantee that the project will be completed at the estimated cost, but they remove some of the incentive the contractor might have for providing an understated estimate. The ability to obtain approval of additional costs in advance also protects the contractor from incurring costs that the government will not pay.

8.2.8 Timely Payment Discounts

Contractors often have purchase agreements with vendors such that the contractor receives a discount for timely payment of invoices. Alternatively, timely payment may entitle the contractor to a credit against future purchases. When specifying the terms of a cost-plus contract, the parties should agree on how these discounts and credits will be handled. The contractor may be required to pass the discount or credit along to the owner if the owner pays the contractor's invoice by a certain date. The contract may also limit the contractor's reimbursement to the discounted price, even if the contractor did not pay the invoice by the date required to obtain the discount.

8.2.9 Audit Rights

On a fixed-price contract, the contractor has no obligation to disclose its costs to the owner. The owner has neither the legal right to know, nor any way to find out, how much profit the contractor included in its price. On a cost-plus contract, however, the owner may insist on the right to audit the contractor's records so that it can verify the accuracy of the contractor's representations concerning costs.

The owner may also require the right to audit the contractor's records for time and materials change orders, even if the contract itself is priced as a fixed fee. In such a case, the owner's audit rights would be limited to records related to the change order.

8.3   COST-PLUS WITH GUARANTEED MAXIMUM PRICE

By assuming the cost risks of a cost-plus contract, the owner can obtain considerable savings. However, the owner may also be at risk for massive cost overruns. To guard against this possibility, the owner can use a cost-plus contract with a guaranteed maximum price (GMP). Such contracts include a cost-plus term that sets out which costs are reimbursable and which are considered overhead. In addition, there is a separate cost limitation that establishes the maximum price. Typical wording to establish the GMP is:

The Contract Sum is guaranteed by the Contractor not to exceed $_____, subject to additions and deductions by Change Order as provided in the Contract Documents. Such maximum price is referred to in the Contract as the Guaranteed Maximum Price. Costs which would cause the Guaranteed Maximum Price to be exceeded shall be paid by the Contractor without reimbursement by the Owner.

A cost-plus with GMP pricing contract is thus a cost-plus contract up to the point that the GMP is reached, and a fixed-price contract thereafter. The owner bears the risk that the cost of work will be as much as the GMP; the contractor bears the risk of any costs over the GMP.

8.4 UNIT-PRICE CONTRACTS

Under a unit-price contract, the owner pays a fixed price for each unit of work performed or material supplied; the total price is the unit price times the number of units. The owner has some cost control in the form of a fixed price for each unit but assumes the risk of variations in estimated quantity.

Although it is rare for the contract between an owner and a contractor to be unit price, fixed-price contracts often contain items that are bid as unit prices. These items are usually for work whose quantities cannot be determined before the start of construction. The bid form will contain the A/E's estimate of the quantity required; the bid price will be the estimated quantity times the unit price.

As an example, in excavating for a foundation, it may not be clear how much blasting will be necessary. If the contractor is required to submit a fixed fee for the excavation work, it would probably include a fairly large contingency to cover the risk that much of the area will need to be blasted. To eliminate the need for a contingency, the bid can be structured so that there are two work items for excavation: one for soil that can be removed without blasting and one for rock that has to be blasted. The contractor would include a unit price for each work item, and the final price would be the unit prices times the respective quantities of work. When work items are to be paid as unit prices, the contract should specify who is responsible for measuring quantities for payment and how disputes in measurements will be resolved.

8.4.1 Variation in Estimated Quantities (VEQ) Clauses

Contracts for projects that include unit price work often have a Variation in Estimated Quantities (VEQ) clause that provides for an adjustment to the contractor's unit price if the actual quantities are significantly different from the estimated quantities. The provision for an adjustment acknowledges that the contractor's cost per unit for the work depends on the quantity of work done.

In some cases, this is because the contractor gets a volume discount for buying large quantities, and this discount is factored into its bid. In most cases, however, it is because the contractor has a relatively fixed cost for mobilization and demobilization. The contractor's unit price for the work will include the amount it needs to cover these fixed costs, based on the estimated quantity. If the actual quantity is significantly less than the estimated quantity, the contractor may not cover even its fixed costs unless the unit price is increased. Likewise, providing for a decrease in the unit prices when the quantities are much greater than anticipated prevents the contractor from receiving an unwarranted windfall.

Although the wording of VEQ clauses varies, the adjustment, whether upward or downward, is typically based on the change in the contractor's costs as a result of the change in quantity, not the actual change in quantity. Most VEQ clauses require the change in costs to be on the order of 15 or 20 percent before an adjustment is required.

8.5   UNBALANCED BIDDING

Any time a bid includes unit-priced work items, there is a potential for unbalanced bidding. Bids can be either mathematically or materially unbalanced. A mathematically unbalanced bid is one where the unit prices do not reflect the reasonable cost of doing the work. Mathematically unbalanced bidding is typically not a problem; bids always contain some variation in unit prices. In some cases, the variations may simply be the contractor's attempt to simplify the bidding by combining two or more bid items into one. However, when a bid is mathematically unbalanced, the owner will usually look at whether the bid is also materially unbalanced.

A bid with unit-priced items is materially unbalanced if there is a reasonable doubt that an award to the bidder will result in the lowest ultimate cost to the owner. In some cases, the contractor may have deliberately submitted unreasonable unit prices because it thinks the estimated quantities in the bid are incorrect. If the contractor thinks the actual quantity for a particular item will be considerably higher than estimated, it will increase the unit price for that item and lower the price on another work item to ensure that it still has the low bid. Likewise, if the contractor thinks the actual quantity of a particular item will be considerably lower than estimated, it will submit a low unit price but will increase the price of another work item.

In public contracting, a materially unbalanced bid will typically be rejected as nonresponsive. If all of the bids contain unbalanced unit prices, the estimated quantities may not be an accurate representation of the work. In such cases, the government may choose to cancel the bid advertisement and re-advertise the project with corrected quantities.

On a fixed-price project, a contractor may submit an unbalanced schedule of values to ensure that it receives a substantial amount of the contract price at the beginning of the project. This practice is referred to as *front-loading*. A bid that is front-loaded may be considered materially unbalanced, even if it is the low bid, because it essentially results in advance payments. Advance payments put the owner at risk if the contractor defaults, since the owner has paid for work that has not been done.

8.6   BIDDING WHEN THE DESIGN IS INCOMPLETE

A fixed-price contract is rarely appropriate for a project if the design is not complete at the time the project is put out for bid. Because the plans and specifications define the contractor's obligations, requiring a contractor to quote a fixed price on the basis of incomplete drawings virtually guarantees that there will be disputes over the scope of the work.

A cost-plus contract is more appropriate in such cases; the contractor will be compensated based on the work that is done, so the scope of work at the time of bidding is not an issue. The owner must be cautious when comparing estimates that are based on incomplete plans, however, as different contractors are likely to have made different assumptions about the final work. Likewise, the owner must be cautious about relying on the estimate of the contractor it selects, as the final design may be quite different from the project that the contractor was providing an estimate for.

9

SUBCONTRACTORS AND SUPPLIERS

Federal government procurement regulations define the word *subcontractor* to mean any supplier, distributor, vendor, or firm that furnishes supplies or services to a prime contractor or another subcontractor. Although the wording "subcontractors and suppliers" is sometimes used on federal projects, from a legal standpoint there is usually little difference between the two. In private contracting, as well as state and local contracting, however, a subcontractor is typically considered to be an entity that performs work, such as excavation or painting, at the project site. An entity that simply delivers materials or equipment is considered to be a supplier. There can be significant legal implications to the distinction.

9.1 SUBCONTRACTORS VERSUS SUPPLIERS

One of the key differences between subcontractors and suppliers in private contracting is that the Uniform Commercial Code (UCC) applies to the furnishing of goods by suppliers but not to the furnishing of services by subcontractors. The UCC is a model code that has been adopted as law, at least in part, in all states. The UCC may affect the parties' rights with respect to warranties, remedies for the other party's default, notice requirements, and the right to assurance of the other party's ability to perform. In addition, subcontractors and suppliers may be treated differently under mechanic's lien statutes and payment bonds.

Many transactions are mixed, in that the same firm furnishes both services and goods as part of its contract. Subcontractors may design and manufacture their own products, and firms that are primarily suppliers may sometimes install their products. To determine whether a contract is for services or supplies, many courts use the so-called *predominant factor test,* which looks at the relative value of the services versus the value of the goods. Courts may also look at whether the terms of the parties' contract more closely resemble the standard provisions of a contract for services or a contract for the sale of goods.

9.2   OWNER'S CONTROL OVER SUBCONTRACTOR SELECTION

Unless there are specific restrictions in the construction contract, the contractor has the right to subcontract portions of the work to others. Contracts often allow the owner to have input into which subcontractors and suppliers the contractor selects, however. AIA A201, for example, requires the contractor to furnish the names of prospective subcontractors and suppliers to the owner. The contractor cannot contract with an entity that the owner or A/E has a reasonable objection to.

An owner will sometimes ask its contractor to use certain subcontractors or suppliers after the contract has been awarded. On a fixed-price contract, or a cost-plus contract with a GMP, the contractor's basis for selecting a subcontractor or supplier is often cost. If the owner's preference results in a higher-priced subcontractor or supplier, the contractor may be entitled to an adjustment in the contract price. In addition, the contractor is not required to contract with anyone it has a reasonable objection to.

Alternatively, the bid documents may state that certain subcontractors or product brands must be used on the project. In this case, the owner's requirements must be factored into the contractor's bid; the contractor would not be entitled to a price adjustment. Nor would the contractor be allowed to object to using the specified subcontractors or products.

It is possible, although unusual, for the owner to negotiate a contract with a subcontractor or supplier and then indicate in the bid documents that the contractor will be required to accept an assignment of the contract. Typically, this is done only if the owner is in a position to negotiate a very favorable contract.

9.3   SUBCONTRACTOR BIDS

On most fixed-price projects, the contractor prepares its bid based on the bids of its subcontractors. Contractors typically receive bids from a number of competing subcontractors; the subcontractors, in turn, may submit bids to several contractors competing for the project. The subcontractors' bids are often received just before the contractor's bid is due, because subcontractors do not want the contractor using their bids to negotiate lower bids from their competitors.

Comparing subcontractor bids is not always easy, as each subcontractor may be bidding on a different scope of work; some subcontractors have very limited specialties, while others may work in several trades. In putting together its bids, the contractor must ensure that it has included all of the work required for the project, plus its overhead and profit, plus some amount of contingency for unforeseen events.

9.3.1 Enforcing a Subcontractor's Bid

A subcontractor's bid is an offer; a binding agreement (a contract) is not formed until the contractor accepts the offer. Despite the fact that the contractor uses the subcontractors' bids to calculate its own bid, the parties typically do not create a binding agreement before the prime contract is awarded.

Once the contractor is awarded the prime contract, it must formalize its agreements with its subcontractors. If a subcontractor refuses to honor its bid and execute the subcontract, it may cost the contractor considerably more to hire another subcontractor. In many states, the fact that the contractor has relied on the subcontractor's bid for its own bid is held to create a legally enforceable agreement, even without a formal contract. The basis for this holding is the legal theory of *promissory estoppel*. Under the theory of promissory estoppel, a party that has made a promise is prevented from going back on its promise if the other party reasonably relied on the promise and would be harmed if the promise were not enforced. The law requires the promissor to carry out its promise, in exchange for the other party's return promise, exactly as if a contract had been formed between the parties.

However, even if a court holds that the subcontractor's bid is subject to promissory estoppel, it will look to the specific circumstances before enforcing the bid. Courts typically will not enforce a bid if the subcontractor reserved the

---

CASE STUDY—PROMISSORY ESTOPPEL

In soliciting bids from subcontractors, a contractor stipulated that bids must be held open for at least 60 days and that subcontractors would be accountable for the prices submitted. A subcontractor bidding on the concrete work submitted a bid that clearly stated the price quote was for informational purposes only, did not constitute a "firm offer," and should not be relied on. The contractor nevertheless used the subcontractor's bid amount. The contractor was awarded the project, but the subcontractor refused to honor its bid. The contractor ended up using another subcontractor, which increased its costs by more than $200,000.

The contractor sued the subcontractor under the theory of promissory estoppel to recover its extra costs, but the court dismissed the claim. A key element of a promissory estoppel claim is that reliance on the other party's promise must be reasonable. The contractor's reliance on the subcontractor's bid amount was not reasonable, since the bid clearly stated that it should not be relied on.

Fletcher–Harlee Corp. v. Pote Concrete Contractors, Inc.,
482 F.3d 247 (3rd Cir. 2007)

right to withdraw its bid or the contractor's reliance on the bid was unreasonable because of an obvious mistake in the bid. In addition, courts generally will not enforce a subcontractor's bid if the contractor unreasonably delayed accepting the bid, the contractor engaged in bid shopping, or the contractor's acceptance varied the terms of the bid in such a way as to constitute a counteroffer.

9.3.2 The Subcontractor's Right to Enforce Its Bid

Although a subcontractor's bid is a promise to the contractor, the contractor's request for the bid is not a promise to the subcontractor. After having been awarded the contract, the contractor may decide to "shop" a subcontractor's bid to its competitors to see if it can get more favorable terms. Absent a binding agreement between the parties, the subcontractor cannot force the contractor to award it the work, even if the contractor has used the bid as the basis for its own bid. Thus, while the contractor may force the subcontractor to honor its bid, the subcontractor cannot force the contractor to award it the work.

Subcontractor trade associations have condemned the practice of bid shopping as unethical. In addition, they have alleged that the practice may affect the quality of the work. In response to concerns over the effects of bid shopping, a number of states have passed laws aimed at limiting the practice on public projects. These laws require contractors bidding on public projects to submit a list of their proposed subcontractors with their bids; a contractor must use its listed subcontractors if it is awarded the contract. Even in these states, however, bid shopping is typically legal on private projects. Some states do not allow contractors to enforce their subcontractors' bids because they consider it unfair to provide contractors this right without also providing it to subcontractors.

9.4 INCORPORATION BY REFERENCE

On many projects, the general contractor subcontracts out almost all of the work. This arrangement can create problems because the quality of the project depends on the work of subcontractors that the owner has no direct control over; while the GC is legally responsible for the project, it is the subcontractors that carry out this responsibility. To ensure that the project will be constructed in accordance with both the design and the requirements of the general conditions, the contractor normally wants to pass its obligations under its contract with the owner (the prime contract) on to each subcontractor. This can be done by incorporating the provisions of the prime contract into the contract between the contractor and its subcontractors by reference.

Incorporation by reference provisions are found in many of the industry standard form subcontracts. For example, the list of subcontract documents in §1.1 of AIA A401, *Standard Form of Agreement Between Contractor and Subcontractor*, includes the owner-contractor agreement and the other contract documents enumerated in the owner-contractor agreement. It then states: "These [documents] form the Subcontract, and are as fully a part of the Subcontract as if attached to this Agreement or repeated herein." It should be emphasized, however, that incorporating the prime contract by reference into a subcontract does not make the subcontractor either a party to, or a beneficiary, of the prime contract; it only binds the subcontractor to the terms of the prime contract.

9.5 FLOW-DOWN AND FLOW-UP PROVISIONS

The subcontract can also include a provision whereby the parties explicitly agree that the contractor's responsibilities under the prime contract "flow down" to the subcontractor. Most of the industry standard form subcontracts include flow-down provisions. Article 2 of AIA A401 states:

> *The Contractor and Subcontractor shall be mutually bound by the terms of this Agreement and, to the extent that the provisions of AIA Document A201 2007 apply to this Agreement . . . the Contractor shall assume toward the Subcontractor all obligations and responsibilities that the Owner, under such documents, assumes toward the Contractor, and the Subcontractor shall assume toward the Contractor all obligations and responsibilities which the Contractor, under such documents, assumes toward the Owner and the Architect.*

Under this type of provision, sometimes called a flow-up/flow-down provision, the contractor's rights and remedies against the subcontractor are the same as the owner's rights and remedies against the contractor. Likewise, the subcontractor's rights and remedies against the contractor are same as the contractor's rights and remedies against the owner. When the contract between the owner and the contractor requires that subcontracts contain flow-down provisions, the contractor typically requires its subcontractors to include similar provisions in their contracts with second-tier subcontractors.

9.5.1 Rights and Liabilities of the Parties under Flow-down Provisions

A flow-down provision in a subcontract nominally puts the contractor in a legally neutral position between its subcontractors and the owner. If the owner claims that work performed by a subcontractor does not conform to the contract requirements, the contractor can look to the subcontractor for a resolution. Likewise, if a subcontractor claims that the drawings or specifications are defective, the subcontractor can assert a claim against the owner through the contractor. Flow-down provisions are typically general provisions applying to unspecified rights and liabilities, however. When specific issues arise, it is not always clear whether these general provisions apply.

Generally the flow-down clause will state that if there is a conflict between the subcontract and the prime contract, the subcontract governs. If the flow-down provision is ambiguous as to which rights and remedies flow down, extrinsic evidence such as conversations between the parties may be considered. Courts have held that flow-down provisions do not limit the subcontractor's rights with respect to mechanic's liens, unless the limitation is specifically set forth in the subcontracts. In addition, some courts have held that flow-down provisions do not apply to specific insurance obligations or dispute resolution methods.

9.6 DUTY TO COOPERATE AND COORDINATE SUBCONTRACT WORK

The contractor has an implied duty to cooperate with its subcontractors and coordinate their work. The contractor also implicitly promises to provide the working conditions that its subcontractors need to carry out their contractual obligations. The contractor's implied duty includes a promise not to hinder, delay, or interfere with the work of the subcontractors. A contractor that interferes with the work of its subcontractor has breached this obligation, and the subcontractor may be entitled to recover its damages for any delays that occur.

Contractors tend to be wary of the implications of these obligations, however. Because they are responsible for the entire project, contractors must be able to direct the schedule and sequence of their subcontractors. Even the industry standard form subcontracts are relatively vague about the contractor's coordination obligation and give the contractor significant flexibility over scheduling subcontractor work. As an example, §3.1.1 of AIA A401 simply states:

The Contractor shall cooperate with the subcontractor in scheduling and performing the Contractor's Work to avoid conflicts or interference in the subcontractors' work.

In addition, subcontracts generally create a mutual obligation to cooperate. Section 4.1.2 of A401 requires the subcontractor to cooperate with the contractor in scheduling and performing its work to avoid delaying or interfering with the work of the contractor, other subcontractors, the owner, or separate contractors. Likewise, §4.1.8 requires the subcontractor to cooperate with the contractor, other subcontractors, the owner, and separate contractors whose work might interfere with the subcontractor's work.

9.6.1 Limiting the Liability for Coordination

The fact that the subcontract places some of the coordination burden on the subcontractor does not relieve the contractor of its duty not to interfere with the subcontractor's work. Concern over potential liability for the coordination of subcontracted work has resulted in contracts with provisions that are stronger than those found in AIA A401. These include provisions that give the contractor absolute authority to direct the subcontractor's schedule and obligate the subcontractor to follow those directions. The subcontract may also include a no-damages-for-delay clause, such that if the contractor's scheduling unreasonably interferes with the subcontractor's work, the subcontractor would be entitled to an extension of time but would not be entitled to damages. However, courts typically do not enforce no-damages-for-delay clauses if the contractor unreasonably hindered or delayed the subcontractor's work.

9.6.2   Coordination of Multiple Primes

Problems with coordination of the work of various construction trades arise most often on projects where the owner has contracted with multiple prime contractors. When multiple prime contractors are working on a project, there may be conflicts over who can work in a particular area at a particular time. Even when there are no conflicts with respect to where the trades are working, there may be conflicts over where they are storing materials or when a particular contractor's work must be done so that another trade can begin its work.

When an owner awards multiple prime contracts, it is responsible for coordinating the work of the prime contractors. Even on projects where there is only one prime contract, the owner is responsible for coordinating the work of the prime contractor with the work of any other contractors or personnel that it has on site. For example, §6.1.3 of AIA A201 states:

The Owner shall provide for coordination of the activities of the Owner's own forces and of each separate contractor with the Work of the Contractor, who shall cooperate with them.

Even without such a clause, if a prime contractor encounters delays or cannot work efficiently because of interference from another contractor working for the owner, the prime contractor may be entitled to compensation for any increase in its costs. The owner has a common-law duty of coordination unless the contract specifically provides otherwise.

9.7   SUBCONTRACTOR PAYMENT

Generally, the contractor pays its subcontractors after it receives payment from the owner. AIA A401 illustrates how such payments are typically handled when the subcontract is for a fixed fee. Article 11 of A401 provides that the subcontractor will receive progress payments pursuant to a schedule of values that allocates the contract sum among the various items of the subcontractor's work. Each month, the subcontractor submits a pay application indicating the percentage of each item of work completed during the month. The contractor then includes the amount of the subcontractor's pay application in its application to the owner. Within seven working days of receiving payment from the owner, the contractor must pay the subcontractor the amount of its application, less any amounts the owner has withheld for retainage or work needing correction.

Under AIA A401, if the contractor does not pay the subcontractor within seven days of receiving payment from the owner, the subcontractor must give the contractor an additional written notice. If the subcontractor does not receive payment within another seven days, it can stop work until it is paid. The subcontract amount will be increased by the subcontractor's cost for the delay, including demobilization and remobilization. The subcontractor can terminate the subcontract for the same reasons that the contractor can terminate the prime contract, including nonpayment for 60 days or longer.

Courts will uphold the subcontractor's decision to stop work or terminate the contract, as long as doing so was reasonable under the circumstances. However, if the subcontractor's work was defective, the contractor is justified in withholding payment. Under these circumstances, if the subcontractor decides to stop work or terminate the subcontract, it may be liable for any damages the contractor incurs as a result of its action.

9.7.1   "Pay-If-Paid" versus "Pay-When-Paid"

Subcontracts often contain pay-if-paid clauses. A pay-if-paid clause, also known as a *contingent payment* clause, states that the contractor does not have to pay the subcontractor until, and unless, the owner pays the contractor. Typical wording for a pay-if-paid clause is:

> *Payment of Owner to Contractor for Subcontractor's work is a condition precedent to Contractor's duty to pay Subcontractor under this Subcontract agreement.*

Such clauses essentially shift the risk of nonpayment to the subcontractor. Courts tend to view these clauses with disfavor, as the owner's reasons for withholding payment may have nothing to do with the subcontractor's work. In some states, pay-if-paid clauses are prohibited by statute, even in private construction. In other states, they are not prohibited, but the courts have held them to be unenforceable. They are unenforceable in California, for example, because they are held to violate the anti-waiver provisions of California's mechanic's lien laws. Even in states where pay-if-paid provisions are enforceable, courts have created exceptions. In particular, courts do not enforce a pay-if-paid clause unless the contractor has made a diligent, good-faith effort to obtain payment from the owner.

If the owner is withholding payment because of something the contractor itself did or failed to do, a court generally finds a pay-if-paid clause to be unenforceable under the prevention doctrine. The prevention doctrine is a principle of contract law which holds that if a promissor (the party making the promise) prevents a condition to his or her performance from being fulfilled, the condition may be waived. Thus, if it is the contractor's fault that the condition required for payment to the subcontractor (payment by the owner) is not fulfilled, the condition may be waived. The prevention doctrine does not require proof that the condition would have been fulfilled "but for" the wrongful conduct of the promissor; it requires only that the promissor's conduct materially contribute to the situation.

The wording of a pay-if-paid clause must be clear and unambiguous. If the wording is ambiguous, the clause is usually interpreted as a "pay-when-paid" clause. Under a pay-when-paid clause, the contractor must pay the subcontractor within a reasonable time, even if it has not received payment from the owner. Both AIA A401 and ConsensusDOCS CD 750, *Standard Form Agreement between Contractor and Subcontractor*, include pay-when-paid provisions that entitle the subcontractor to payment within a reasonable time if the owner, through no fault of the subcontractor, fails to pay the contractor.

It should be noted, however, that a court may interpret a clause titled "Pay-when-paid" as "Pay-if-paid" if the clause includes language stating that payment from the owner is a condition precedent for payment to the subcontractor. It is the language of the clause that controls, not the title or heading.

A surety cannot rely on a pay-if-paid clause in its principal's contract with the owner as a defense to a payment bond claim by a subcontractor. Allowing a surety to avoid its obligation under the payment bond because the owner did not pay the general contractor would defeat the purpose of a payment bond, which is to ensure that subcontractors are paid.

9.8   SUBCONTRACTOR CLAIMS AGAINST THE OWNER

On a design-bid-build project, the owner's contract is with the general contractor; it does not contract with the subcontractors that actually perform the work. The GC selects its subcontractors and determines the conditions of their employment. Direct dealings between the owner and the subcontractors are inconsistent with this arrangement and can prejudice the legal position of both the owner and the subcontractors.

Subcontractors often incur additional costs due to acts or events attributable to the owner, however. Like the GC, subcontractors base their bids on the conditions of the project represented to them at the time they priced their work. Design problems or differing site conditions may adversely affect the subcontractor's work; delays to the contractor's work will typically delay the subcontractor's work as well.

Because the subcontractor does not have a contract with the owner, it cannot bring a contract claim against the owner. In addition, the lack of contractual privity may prevent the subcontractor from bringing a tort claim against the owner; the court may hold that the owner does not owe a duty to the subcontractor. Even though the contractor is not the cause of the subcontractor's extra costs, the contractor is the party the subcontractor has an agreement with and may be the only party the subcontractor can bring a claim against. The contractor must then bring a claim against the owner.

9.8.1 The Pass-through System

The contractor may try to bring an action against the owner "on behalf of" the subcontractor; the legal basis for the claim would be that the contractor is liable to the subcontractor for the subcontractor's claim and is passing this liability on to the owner. However, contractors generally try to protect themselves from liability to their subcontractors, both through the provisions of the subcontract and through the terms of documents prepared during the project. If these efforts result in a legally binding release of the contractor's liability to the subcontractor, the contractor has no liability for a claim and, thus, cannot pass the claim through to the owner.

This issue was raised in the case *Severin v. United States*,[1] and the holding in that case has given rise to the so-called Severin doctrine. In *Severin*, the contractor sued the federal government on behalf of a subcontractor that had incurred damages as a result of the government's breach of contract. However, the subcontractor had released the contractor from liability for any damages caused by the government.

The court's holding was that in order to bring an action against the government, the contractor must have suffered damages, either by having reimbursed the subcontractor for its losses or by being liable for the subcontractor's losses. Because the subcontractor in *Severin* had released the contractor from liability, the contractor had not suffered any damages. In the court's view, the contractor was simply accommodating the subcontractor by letting the subcontractor use its name for the litigation; this is not allowed under federal law. If the contractor had settled with the subcontractor prior to bringing the action against the government, the contractor would be entitled to its damages, but the damages would be limited to the amount of the settlement, irrespective of the subcontractor's actual damages.

9.8.2 Liquidating Agreements

To avoid the problem encountered in *Severin*, it is common for the contractor and subcontractor to enter into a liquidating agreement before the contractor asserts

---

[1]*Severin v. United States*, 99 Ct. Cl. 435 (1943).

a claim against the government on behalf of the subcontractor. The name *liqui-dating agreement* comes from the fact that, although the subcontractor does not release the contractor from liability, it liquidates (determines) the amount of the contractor's liability to be the amount that the contractor recovers from the owner on behalf of the subcontractor.

Such agreements usually provide that once the contractor pays the subcontractor whatever money it receives from the owner for the subcontractor claims, the contractor is fully released from the claims. If the contractor does not receive anything from the owner, the contractor has no liability to the subcontractor for its claims. Typical wording for a typical liquidating agreement is:

> *Subcontractor hereby agrees to release Prime Contractor from any claims relating in any way to the Subcontractor Claims, except that Subcontractor does not release Prime Contractor from the payment of any money received on behalf of the Subcontractor Claims. It is agreed that Prime Contractor's liability with regard to the Subcontractor Claims is limited to the final award and payment on Subcontractor Claims by Owner.*

Although the *Severin* holding only applies to those cases involving federal government contracts brought in federal courts, the Severin doctrine has been adopted by a number of state courts. State court claims are less common, though, because in state and local contracting as well as private contracting, the prime contractor can generally assign its rights under the prime contract to the subcontractor. The subcontractor can then bring a claim against the owner. In federal contracting, the prime contractor is prohibited from assigning its rights against the government to anyone else.

9.9 CONDITIONAL ASSIGNMENT OF THE SUBCONTRACTS TO THE OWNER

If a contractor is terminated for default, the owner may want to preserve the subcontractors' obligation to continue work. To this end, the owner typically requires that the construction contract and all subcontracts contain a conditional assignment clause under which the owner has the right to assume the subcontracts in the event of the contractor's default, but is not required to do so.

Alternatively, the owner may require that it be made a third-party beneficiary of the contractor's subcontracts, with the right to assume the subcontracts if the contractor defaults. Generally, the owner also has the right to further assign the subcontracts to another entity (for example, the contractor hired to complete the project). Even if the owner assigns the subcontracts, it remains ultimately responsible for ensuring that the subcontractors are paid for any work performed after the subcontracts were assumed.

9.10   MINORITY AND DISADVANTAGED BUSINESS PROGRAMS

Many federal procurement contracts include preferences for small and disadvantaged businesses and require prime contractors to give such businesses the "maximum practical opportunity" to participate in federal contracts. This practice dates from 1961, when President John F. Kennedy issued an executive order instructing federal contractors to take "affirmative action to ensure that applicants are treated equally without regard to race, color, religion, sex, or national origin." In 1977, Congress furthered the effort to eliminate discrimination by requiring contractors to hire Minority Business Enterprises (MBEs) for at least 10 percent of all federal projects. This requirement was upheld three years later by the U.S. Supreme Court in the case *Fullilove v. Klutznick*.[2]

State and local governments then began implementing "set-aside" programs requiring that a certain percentage of all public construction projects be allocated to minority-owned businesses. The Supreme Court rejected this use of affirmative action in the 1989 case *City of Richmond v. J. A. Croson Co.*,[3] however. The case involved Richmond's set-aside program, which required prime contractors to award at least 30 percent of the dollar amount of the contract to MBEs. On the project at issue, the only MBE subcontractor that expressed interest submitted a bid that was higher than market rates. The contractor, J.A. Croson, which had already been awarded the prime contract, challenged the MBE requirement under the Equal Protection clause of the Fourteenth Amendment.

The case went to the U.S. Supreme Court. In striking down Richmond's MBE requirement, the Court held that affirmative action programs must be evaluated with a "strict scrutiny" test that looks at whether they are narrowly tailored to serve a compelling government interest. There must also be strong evidence that such remedial action is necessary. The Court declared Richmond's set-aside program unconstitutional because the city did not present any direct support of the need for any remedial action. The Court affirmed the *Croson* ruling in the 1995 case *Adarand Constructors, Inc., v. Pena*[4] and held that federal affirmative action programs must also undergo strict scrutiny.

MBE and Minority and Women Business Enterprises (MWBE) programs that work to remedy past or present discrimination are generally considered to serve a compelling government interest. Nevertheless, they may be challenged on the basis that they are overly broad, that the requirements are set arbitrarily, or that race-neutral alternatives would achieve the same goals. Challenges to construction industry programs often focus on the adequacy of the evidence of past discrimination. Under a strict scrutiny standard, a general claim of societal discrimination is not enough; patterns of discrimination must be persistent in the local construction industry. There must also be proof that the program at

---

[2] *Fullilove v. Klutznick*, 448 U.S. 448, 100 S.Ct. 2758, 65 L.Ed.2d 902 (1980).

[3] *City of Richmond v. J.A. Croson Co.*, 488 U.S. 469, 492, 109 S.Ct. 706, 102 L.Ed.2d 854 (1989).

[4] *Adarand Constructors, Inc., v. Pena*, 515 U.S. 200, 227, 115 S.Ct. 2097, 2113, 132 L.Ed.2d 158 (1995).

issue will counteract the effects of such discrimination. Testimony from both minority and nonminority contractors regarding their experiences with the local industry may be used to supplement evidence from census data, statistical disparity studies, local hearings, and phone surveys.

Programs that allow contractors to base their MBE/MWBE participation goals on the availability of such firms in the local market have withstood strict scrutiny. Likewise, programs that provide price evaluation preferences for MBE/MWBE businesses have survived challenges. Under a price evaluation program, contractors using MBE/MWBE subcontractors have their bids discounted by some percentage of the MBE/MWBE subcontracts.

Price evaluation programs (preferences) can also be used on prime contracts to encourage participation by specific groups. For example, tribal authorities contracting for construction on tribal land typically give a 5 percent preference to Native American–owned businesses. Under such a preference, if a bid from a responsive/responsible Native American–owned business is within 5 percent of the bid of the lowest responsive/responsible bidder, the contract is awarded to the Native American–owned business.

9.10.1 Federal Minority and Disadvantaged Business Programs

The Small Business Administration (SBA) administers a number of federal programs designed to encourage the development of small, minority, and disadvantaged businesses. The SBA negotiates business procurement goals with federal agencies and conducts an annual review of each agency's results. Procurement goals are typically a percentage of the agency's annual expenditure and may include separate goals for small businesses, small disadvantaged businesses, woman-owned businesses, and HUBZone businesses.

Implementation of the SBA programs is covered in Part 19 of the Federal Acquisition Regulation (FAR). The SBA defines a small business as a business that is independently owned and operated, organized for profit, and not dominant in its field. Depending on the industry, eligibility is based on either the average number of employees for the preceding 12 months or the average sales volume for three years. For general and heavy construction firms, annual receipts cannot exceed $13.5 to $17 million, depending on the type of construction; for specialty contractors, annual receipts cannot exceed $7 million. These standards apply for any federal government program where eligibility as a small business is a factor. Under the Small Business Act, federal agencies may set aside procurements for small businesses if enough qualified small businesses are expected to bid or offer services to ensure adequate competition.

A Small Disadvantaged Business (SDB) is a small business that is at least 51 percent owned, controlled, and operated by socially and economically disadvantaged individuals. Socially disadvantaged individuals are those who have been subjected to racial or ethnic prejudice or cultural bias because of their identity as members of a group. Social disadvantage must stem from circumstances beyond the individual's control. Economically disadvantaged individuals are individuals whose ability to compete in the free enterprise system has been impaired due to diminished capital and credit opportunities.

Under the SBA system, Black Americans, Hispanic Americans, Native Americans, Asian Pacific Americans, and South Asian Americans are presumed to be socially disadvantaged. An individual who is not a member of a group presumed to be socially disadvantaged must establish disadvantage on the basis of clear and convincing evidence. Women are not presumed to be socially disadvantaged for SBA programs.

Businesses receiving SDB certification from the SBA are eligible for special federal contract bidding benefits and set-asides. Federal agencies are authorized to set aside competitions solely for SDBs, and agencies are authorized to give up to a 10 percent price evaluation preference to SDBs. In addition, SDBs may qualify for SBA-guaranteed surety bonds on construction contracts.

9.10.1.1 The Section 8(a) Program

Small disadvantaged businesses can also apply to participate in the SBA 8(a) program. The 8(a) program, named for Section 8(a) of the Small Business Act, is a business development program designed to help SDBs access the federal procurement market. The program provides SDBs with technical and management assistance as well as access to the federal procurement market through sole-source contracts and set-asides.

To qualify for the 8(a) program, a firm must be owned and controlled by socially and economically disadvantaged individuals who are U.S. citizens of good moral character. To be considered economically disadvantaged, an individual's net worth, excluding its primary residence and its equity in the firm, cannot exceed $250,000. The firm must also be able to demonstrate its potential for success. In assessing a firm's potential for success, the SBA considers such factors as the technical experience of its managers, its operating history, its financial capacity, and its record of performance. Normally, a firm must have been in business for two years in order to be eligible for the 8(a) program.

Under the 8(a) program, the SBA acts as a prime contractor and enters into contracts with other federal government agencies. The SBA then awards a subcontract for the work to an 8(a)-certified company. An agency that wants a contract to be performed by an 8(a) firm will offer the contract to the SBA; the agency may also identify the 8(a) firm that will perform the work. Upon the SBA's acceptance of the contract, the agency awards the prime contract to the SBA, and the SBA awards the subcontract. In an effort to expedite this process, the SBA has signed Memorandums of Understanding (MOUs) with a number of federal agencies; these MOUs allow the agencies to contract directly with 8(a)-certified firms. The SBA is still the prime contractor on the contract, but the agencies are authorized to enter into the contract on behalf of the SBA.

Participants in the 8(a) program can be awarded sole-source federal contracts of up to $3 million for goods and services and $5 million for manufacturing. Each participant may receive up to $100 million in sole-source contracts during its program participation. The SBA does not guarantee contract awards, however; the firms in the 8(a) program are responsible for marketing themselves to the agencies. Participants may also compete for procurements that are set aside for 8(a)-certified firms. In addition, as certified SDBs, 8(a) participants can receive a price evaluation preference of 10 percent on full and open competitive procurements.

Firms remain in the 8(a) program for nine years. During the first four years, firms are provided business development assistance to help them overcome their economic disadvantage. There is then a five-year transitional stage to prepare them for leaving the 8(a) program.

9.10.1.2 HUBZone Program

The HUBZone Empowerment Contracting Program is designed to stimulate economic development and create jobs in areas designated as HUBZones (Historically Underutilized Business Zones). The HUBZone program provides federal contracting preferences to businesses that are HUBZone certified. To be HUBZone certified, a business must be considered a small business by SBA criteria, must employ staff who live in a HUBZone, and must maintain a principal office in a HUBZone.

All subcontracting plans for large business federal contractors must include a HUBZone subcontracting goal, and contracts can be awarded with a price preference for a HUBzone business. Contracts can also be set aside for HUBZone competition and, in certain circumstances, can be awarded on a sole-source basis to a HUBZone business.

9.10.1.3 Woman-Owned Businesses

Although there are no procurement set asides for woman-owned businesses, federal agencies are required to establish contracting goals that ensure full participation by women in the federal contracting process. In addition, federal acquisition regulations require agencies to actively encourage prime contractors to use woman-owned small businesses as subcontractors.

A business is defined as woman-owned if it is at least 51 percent owned and controlled by women who are U.S. citizens. There is no federal process for certifying woman-owned business; firms self-certify.

9.10.2 Agency DBE Programs

Agencies that provide federal funding for state and local projects have their own Disadvantaged Business Enterprise (DBE) programs for these projects. The two federal agencies that provide most of the federal funding for construction are the Department of Transportation (DOT) and the Environmental Protection Agency (EPA). In 1983, Congress enacted a statutory provision requiring the DOT to ensure that at least 10 percent of the funds authorized for highway and transit financial assistance programs went to DBEs. Congress reauthorized the DBE program in 1987 and amended it to include woman-owned businesses as well as businesses presumed to be disadvantaged by SBA criteria. The provision applies to projects with funding assistance from the Federal Highway Administration (FHWA), the Federal Aviation Administration (FAA), and the Federal Transit Administration (FTA).

The main objectives of the DOT program are to ensure that DBEs can compete fairly for federally funded transportation-related projects and that only eligible firms participate as DBEs. State and local transportation agencies that receive DOT funding are required to establish annual goals for DBE participation; they must also review the scope of large prime contracts and establish contract-specific DBE subcontracting goals. The DOT relies on the state and local agencies that are receiving funding to certify the eligibility of DBE firms to participate in DOT-assisted projects. Typically, certification is done by the state department of transportation.

Agencies must meet the maximum feasible portion of their DBE goal by using race-neutral means. Race-neutral DBE participation means the firm's DBE status are not actually considered in making the award. Race-neutral solicitation includes arranging solicitations to facilitate DBE participation, for example, by unbundling large contracts to make them more accessible to small businesses and encouraging prime contractors to subcontract work that they might otherwise perform with their own workforce.

The EPA does not have a minimum DBE participation requirement. Instead, it requires state and local agencies receiving EPA funding to make a documented good-faith effort to seek out qualified DBEs. They must include qualified DBE businesses on solicitation lists and must ensure that such businesses are solicited whenever they are potential sources of products or services. When economically feasible, the agencies are required to divide contract requirements into small tasks or quantities to permit maximum participation by DBEs and establish delivery schedules that encourage participation by DBEs. Contractors are required to make the same good-faith efforts to solicit DBE subcontractors. The DBEs must be certified through either the SBA or the state department of transportation.

10

TIME FOR PERFORMANCE

Delays, and the adjustments required to make up for them, are the primary contributor to cost overruns on most construction projects. As a result, disputes over which party is responsible for a delay are common in the construction industry. Although some delays are beyond the control of either the contractor or the owner, many delays can be attributed to the actions of one of the parties. Depending on the terms of the contract, the party responsible for a delay may be held liable for the resulting costs.

10.1 TIME IS OF THE ESSENCE

Historically, the inherent uncertainties of construction were so great that timely completion of a construction project was not a material element of the contract. Since time for completion was not a material element of the contract, the contractor only had to complete the project within a reasonable time after the date specified in the contract. A contractor's failure to complete the work by the promised completion date might allow the owner to recover damages, but it did not allow the owner to terminate the contract.

In an effort to make it clear that the completion date is important, owners began adding time-is-of-the-essence clauses to construction contracts. The wording for such a clause might be: "Time limits stated in the Contract Documents are of the essence of the Contract."

Under contract law, if a contract states that time is of the essence, the provision in the contract that sets the time of performance is an essential term of the contract, such that the breach of the provision allows the nonbreaching party to terminate the contract. Time-is-of-the-essence clauses are regularly used in contracts for real estate and the sale of goods, where courts typically follow a strict interpretation, even when the results are harsh. For example, courts may uphold a vendor's right to cancel a sale for late payment, even if the payment is only a few minutes late.

10.1.1 Time-Is-of-the-Essence Clauses in Construction Contracts

In contrast, time-is-of-the-essence clauses generally carry far less weight in construction contracts, and the parties usually cannot terminate the contract for a slight breach of a time condition. There are a number of reasons for this. First, construction contracts often contain specific provisions, such as liquidated damages clauses, that address delays in completion. Specific clauses almost always override general clauses such as time-is-of-the-essence clauses. When the contract stipulates liquidated damages, the owner has presumably indicated that the stipulated damages are an adequate remedy for a breach of the time obligation.

A second reason that time-is-of-the-essence clauses are given less weight in construction contracts is that there are time references for various duties, including such duties as giving notice of a delay claim or a differing site condition. There may also be deadlines or milestones for various segments of the project. Unless the contract specifically states that missing a milestone or failing to comply with a duty by the specified time allows the owner to terminate the contract, a court is unlikely to find that this was the parties' intent.

Third, as opposed to a sales transaction, where the parties often have little invested in the transaction, contractors may have invested very heavily in a construction project before a possibly minor delay in completion. A court is likely to consider it unreasonable for the owner to terminate the contractor under such circumstances. The owner also has a significant investment in a partially completed project, and a court typically would not consider it reasonable for the contractor to terminate the contract because a progress payment was a few days late.

Nevertheless, courts are likely to hold that the time for completion is a material element of the contract and will allow the owner to terminate the contract if there is a significant delay in completion. In commercial construction, it is well understood that the owner needs to be able to make financial commitments based on the expected completion date of the project. Even in residential construction, failure to complete the project by the agreed-upon date can result in considerable expense for the owner.

10.2 DATE OF COMMENCEMENT/TIME FOR COMPLETION

Most construction contracts specify both a date for commencement of the work and a time for completion. The date of commencement is often specified as the date that the owner issues a *notice to proceed* to the contractor but can also be the date the contract is executed, or the date of a third party's action, such as the date the building department issues the permit.

The time for completion is usually specified as a number of days (either calendar or working days) from the date of commencement. For example, AIA A101, *Standard Form of Agreement Between Owner and Contractor*, §3.3 states:

The Contractor shall achieve Substantial Completion of the entire Work not later than ___ days from the date of commencement, subject to adjustments of this Contract Time as provided in the Contract Documents.

Contracts typically state that by signing the contract, the contractor accepts the time for completion allowed by the contract as reasonable. The owner's specification of the time for completion does not necessarily provide an implied warranty that the work can reasonably be completed within that time period, however.

10.2.1   Delays in Commencement of the Work

By specifying the time for completion as a set number of days from the date of commencement, the required completion date is automatically adjusted if the start of the project is delayed. This is typically not a problem for relatively short delays, but long delays in the project start date can penalize the contractor unfairly, particularly on a fixed-price contract. The contractor's costs for labor and materials tend to increase with time. In addition, if a delay in commencement changes the season in which particular work must be done, there can be significant cost effects. For example, the contractor may have planned to have the exterior walls and roof completed before winter to minimize heating costs; a delay in the start of the project may mean that a temporary enclosure must be erected and heated. Delays may also cause problems with subcontractor scheduling and coordination.

To avoid such problems, the contract may limit the delay that will be allowed, with an adjustment to the contract price if this limit is exceeded. If there is no such restriction in the contract, a court may hold that the law implies the owner must issue a notice to proceed within a reasonable time of the contract's execution. This is not a well-established doctrine, however, and courts have allowed owners considerable latitude on project start dates.

10.2.2   Waiver of Time for Completion

Even if the contract states that "time is of the essence," the requirement for timely completion can be waived by the parties' conduct. For example, a court may find the owner has waived the substantial completion date if the owner continues to accept the contractor's performance after that date, without setting a new completion date. This is most likely to occur if there have been significant changes to the project, such that the original completion date is no longer applicable. In the absence of any established time for completion, the contractor is only responsible for completing the work within a "reasonable time" based on the circumstances of the contract. Unless a new completion date is set, the owner cannot terminate the contractor for default due to the delay. In addition, the owner generally cannot recover damages for late completion.

If the owner has waived the original substantial completion date, the parties can agree on a new date, which will become as material and enforceable a term of the contract as the original completion date. The owner can also establish a new completion date unilaterally. Provided the new date is reasonable and takes the contractor's performance capabilities into account, the new date will be enforceable.

10.3 SUBSTANTIAL COMPLETION

Under most contracts, the owner is not entitled to 100 percent completion and full compliance with the plans and specifications by the contract completion date. Instead, the project only needs to be "substantially complete" by that date. Substantial completion is generally defined as the point where the work is sufficiently completed in accordance with the contract documents that the owner can use the project for its intended purpose. Substantial completion is considered to be so close to what was bargained for that it would be unreasonable to deny the contractor the full contract price, subject to the owner's right to withhold an amount necessary to ensure full performance.

When the contractor believes the project is substantially complete, it will usually provide the A/E with a list of the items that need to be done before final completion. The A/E then inspects the project and adds any additional items that need to be completed or corrected. If the A/E agrees that the project can be used for its intended purpose, it will issue a *certificate of substantial completion*.

The list of what must be done between substantial completion and final completion is known as the *punchlist*. Although the punchlist for even a small project can be quite long, most of the work is likely to be minor items such as cleaning or touch-up painting. The punchlist may also include paperwork that cannot be completed until after substantial completion, such as manufacturers' warranties for equipment and "as-built" drawings that show variations between the construction drawings and what was actually built.

10.3.1 The Significance of Substantial Completion

Substantial completion is significant for several reasons. Once substantial completion is reached, the contractor cannot be terminated for default—any deficiencies in performance must be remedied by an award of damages representing the cost to correct or complete those deficiencies. In addition, the contractor has no further liability for delayed completion. If there are liquidated damages as a result of delayed completion, the liquidated damages will stop accruing upon substantial completion, unless the parties agreed otherwise in the contract.

Substantial completion also triggers the owner's obligation to release retainage, less an amount sufficient to cover the incomplete or incorrect work on the punchlist. Because the contractor is no longer subject to termination for default or the threat of delay damages for completion of the remaining work, many owners hold a multiple of the estimated value of the remaining work as an incentive to complete the remaining items promptly.

Since substantial completion means the project can be used for its intended purpose, control of the project is typically transferred to the owner. The owner thus becomes responsible for security, maintenance, utilities, and insurance. The callback period (the period during which the contractor must correct any work that does not comply with the contract requirements) generally begins at substantial completion.

10.3.2 Establishing Substantial Completion

Given the significance of substantial completion, there can be disputes as to whether it has been achieved. Although it is common to have the A/E certify substantial completion, the A/E's decision is to some extent subjective. If the A/E refuses to issue a certificate of substantial completion, the contractor may allege that the A/E is being unreasonable. Owners may therefore prefer to use some other means of establishing that substantial completion has been achieved.

As an example, the contract may specify that substantial completion is achieved when the *certificate of occupancy* is issued. Most localities require a certificate of occupancy to be obtained before a building can be occupied; the certificate of occupancy indicates that the building substantially complies with the plans and specifications that have been approved by the appropriate licensing authority.

By definition, once a certificate of occupancy is issued, the owner can occupy the premises. A certificate of occupancy does not necessarily mean that the owner can use the project for its intended purpose, however. Unless the contract specifically states that substantial completion is based on the certificate of occupancy, courts generally hold that a certificate of occupancy is relevant evidence of substantial completion but does not automatically prove it has been achieved. If the owner has taken control of the premises, there is a presumption that substantial completion has been achieved, whether or not a certificate of occupancy has been issued.

10.4 FINAL COMPLETION/FINAL PAYMENT

Final completion refers to the point when construction is 100 percent complete and all nonconstruction requirements, other than any warranty responsibilities, have been performed. Once the contractor believes it has achieved final completion, it submits its final application for payment. By certifying the final payment, the A/E represents that the contractor has submitted all required documents, including final lien waivers, operating manuals, warranty documentation, and project start-up procedures, and that any tests required to establish that the project meets performance standards have been run. Many contracts also require the

contractor to provide the owner with an "owner's manual" that includes maintenance instructions for the equipment, as well as a list of materials such as paint
that shows the brand and colors of paint used.

Final payment is significant with respect to both the owner's and the contractor's legal rights. The contractor's acceptance of final payment is generally considered to be a waiver of any claims not previously identified. For example, AIA
A201 §9.10.5 states the following:

> *Acceptance of final payment by the Contractor, a Subcontractor or material
> supplier shall constitute a waiver of claims by that payee except those previ-
> ously made in writing and identified by that payee as unsettled at the time of
> final Application for Payment.*

Under such language, the contractor cannot simply reserve the right to file a
claim for additional costs; claims must be specifically identified when the contractor submits its final application for payment. If the contract is silent with
respect to the contractor's waiver of claims but the owner made it clear that final
payment was being tendered as settlement of all claims not yet filed, acceptance
of payment generally bars any claims for additional costs.

10.4.1 Acceptance of Defective Work

Construction contracts typically state that the owner's acceptance of the work
does not occur until final completion, and that progress payments do not constitute acceptance of work that does not conform to the contract. In addition,
contracts often state that inspections and tests of the work by the owner during
the project are for the owner's convenience and do not constitute acceptance of
nonconforming work.

Specifying final completion as the point of formal acceptance allows the
owner to wait until the work is fully completed to reject any nonconforming
work. However, courts recognize that it is usually more efficient to correct defective work before it is covered or blocked by subsequent work. Thus, courts may
hold that the owner cannot reject work at the end of the contract when the
defects were actually discovered, or should have been discovered, much earlier.

Most industry standard form contracts state that, by making final payment,
the owner waives any unasserted claims with respect to defective work. However,
these contracts typically also state that the owner's final payment does not
constitute acceptance of defective work. If the defects are latent (hidden) and
unknown to the owner after conducting a reasonably diligent inspection, final
payment is not considered a waiver. Likewise, if the owner and contractor have
discussed the defective work, and the contractor has agreed to repair it, making
final payment does not constitute a waiver by the owner.

In contrast, when the work is patently (openly and obviously) defective and
the owner has not requested correction, final payment typically is considered
a waiver. Courts have held that a defect that is discoverable through testing

and inspection procedures called for by the contract may be considered patent, regardless of the owner's actual knowledge of the defect. If the owner discovered, or should have discovered, a defect and did not require the contractor to correct it, the owner may be deemed to have accepted the work.

CASE STUDY—WAIVER OF DEFECTS

The contract for construction of a winery stated that final payment would waive all claims for defective work except claims for defects that appeared after substantial completion. The contract contained provisions for arbitration of disputes but specifically excepted claims that had been waived by final payment.

Upon completion of construction, the owner made final payment for the work. Several years later, defects were found in the roof. The court dismissed the owner's petition for an order compelling the contractor to participate in an arbitration to determine liability. During construction, the owner had a representative with considerable expertise in roofing on-site full-time to oversee and inspect the contractor's work. The owner's representative observed the methods by which the roofing materials were applied on a daily basis and often made comments and suggestions. The court found that the defects were apparent to the owner through its representative upon reasonable inspection and were thus known to the owner at the time it made final payment. Therefore, final payment constituted a waiver of those defects.

Renown, Inc., v. Hensel Phelps Construction Co.,
201 Cal.Rptr. 242 (Cal. App. 1984)

10.5 DELAYS

Even though the contract usually establishes a time for completion of the project, almost all projects encounter delays; very few projects are completed by the specified date. Delays can be characterized as either inexcusable, compensable, or excusable. A delay that is caused by, or within the control of, the contractor is considered an inexcusable delay. In such cases, the required completion date is not extended and the contractor is not entitled to additional compensation. Depending on the contract, the contractor may be charged either liquidated damages or actual damages if the project completion date is not met. In contrast, if the delay is caused by the owner or within the owner's control, the delay is generally compensable—the contractor is entitled to both a time extension and compensation for any costs it incurs as a result of the delay.

Delays caused by events that are beyond the control of either the owner or the contractor are considered excusable delays. These include so-called Acts of God such as fires, floods, hurricanes, and earthquakes. The expense caused by such delays is not allocated to either party, so neither party may recover damages from the other. However, because the contractor is not liable for damages for late completion due to such a delay, the net effect is that the contractor receives an extension of the time for completion.

AIA A201 addresses the circumstances under which the contractor is entitled to a time extension for either a compensable or an excusable delay in §8.31. Per §8.31:

> *If the Contractor is delayed by the Owner or Architect or a separate contractor employed by the Owner, or by changes ordered in the Work, or by labor disputes, fire, unusual delay in deliveries, unavoidable casualties or other causes beyond the Contractor's control, or by delay authorized by the Owner pending mediation or arbitration, or by other causes that the Architect determines may justify delay, then the Contract Time shall be extended by Change Order for such reasonable time as the Architect may determine.*

The listed events are not excusable per se, however. A delay caused by an event such as a fire due to the contractor's negligence is not considered excusable. Similarly, a delay is not excusable if the event causing the delay was foreseeable at the time the contract was signed. Thus, a strike that started before the contract was signed would typically not give rise to an excusable delay. Likewise, flooding that occurs regularly cannot be claimed as an unforeseeable event. Contractors must make allowances for such events in their time and cost estimates.

The contractor is typically required to give the owner written notice that it will be making a delay claim within a certain number of days of the event or condition that gave rise to the claim. If the owner is aware that its actions are causing a delay, it may be able to take steps to mitigate the delay. The owner may also require the contractor to keep a record of the effects of the delay.

10.5.1 Determining Whether a Delay Was within a Party's Control

Delays caused by an employee or agent of either party, or by an entity with whom a party has contracted, are considered to be within the control of that party. Thus, delays caused by subcontractors and suppliers are considered to be within the control of the contractor and are inexcusable; delays caused by the A/E are considered to be within the owner's control and are compensable. The underlying rationale is that a party can choose whom to employ and contract with, and should therefore be responsible for problems created by its employees and agents. In addition, the contractor's duty to complete the project by the specified completion date cannot be delegated. As a result, the contractor is responsible to the owner, even if the delay was caused by a subcontractor or supplier.

Financial inability to perform, by either the contractor or a subcontractor or supplier, is generally considered to be within the contractor's control and thus an inexcusable cause of delay. This holds true even when the financial problems are caused by events beyond the contractor's control, for example, the unexpected bankruptcy of a major client with a large outstanding balance. Even in these cases, the inability to perform is far more under the control of the contractor than the owner and thus is attributed to the contractor. The exception is where the contractor's financial difficulties are directly caused by the owner's actions, such as the owner's failure to make timely payments.

FAR §52.249-10 includes examples of delays that are considered to be beyond either party's control in federal government contracts. These include delays caused by:

- Acts of God
- Acts of the government in either its sovereign or its contractual capacity
- Acts of another contractor in the performance of a contract with the government
- Fires, floods, epidemics, quarantine restrictions, strikes, and freight embargoes
- Unusually severe weather

In addition, delays of subcontractors or suppliers that arise from unforeseeable causes beyond the control of either the contractor or its subcontractors and suppliers may qualify as excusable. The contractor must notify the contracting officer within ten days of the beginning of any delay; the contracting officer will determine whether the circumstances warrant an extension of time.

10.5.2 Delays Due to Weather

In planning and pricing its work, the contractor is expected to take normal weather variations at the site into account. Although unusually adverse or "abnormal" weather can be grounds for an excusable delay, snowstorms, heat waves, and extended periods of rain could all be considered normal, depending on the location. To avoid disputes over whether a particular event or series of events is normal, contracts may specify a means for determining if weather conditions are abnormal, or state the number of days of precipitation each month that are considered normal. The most common means of evaluating weather conditions was developed by the Army Corps of Engineers and compares the conditions experienced on the project to a ten-year average, using the weather records from the nearest National Oceanic and Atmospheric Administration (NOAA) monitoring location.

Even when weather has been abnormal, there can be a dispute over whether there was a delay to any activities that were critical to the project completion date. Abnormally heavy rains typically do not delay activities such as interior painting, for instance. In addition, the contractor is responsible for mitigating the effects of abnormal weather where practicable and reasonable. As an example, heavy rains can prevent the contractor from performing site work; wet soil after the rain ends may extend the delay period. The portion of the delay due to soil conditions after the rain may not be excusable if the contractor did not take reasonable steps to provide adequate site drainage.

10.5.3 Concurrent Delays

Disputes concerning delays often involve so-called concurrent delays. A concurrent delay is one caused by both the owner and the contractor. In other words, both parties contributed to a delay or delays that ultimately caused the project completion date to be delayed. Most courts hold that neither party should benefit from a concurrent delay. Thus, the contractor is entitled to an extension of time but is not entitled to any delay damages. Because delays caused by subcontractors and suppliers are considered to be within the control of the contractor, the contractor cannot recover damages from the owner for a delay that was caused by both the owner and a subcontractor. However, depending on the terms of its subcontracts, the contractor may be liable for damages to other subcontractors that incurred costs because of the delay.

Courts sometimes attempt to apportion the delays and expenses attributable to each party but they will only do so when the evidence presented by the parties establishes a reasonable basis for such apportionment. Apportionment has been made easier by the use of CPM schedules that show what caused a particular delay and how the delay impacted the project schedule.

10.5.3.1 Pacing

In some cases, the contractor will disclaim any responsibility for what appears to be a concurrent delay. Instead, the contractor alleges that once the owner's actions had caused a delay, it simply paced its work so that activities were not completed any earlier than necessary. Such pacing is sometimes advisable; completing an activity before subsequent activities can be performed might create a safety hazard or require the work to be protected from the elements. Even in such cases, however, courts usually hold that the contractor was required to notify the owner that it was intentionally altering its schedule because of the owner-caused delay.

10.6 LIQUIDATED DAMAGES

In lieu of requiring the owner to calculate and prove actual damages from a contractor-caused delay, the contract may contain a liquidated damages clause, which provides that the contractor will be charged a specified amount per day of delay. Courts generally enforce liquidated damages, as long as they are a reasonable approximation of actual damages, as of the date the contract was executed.

If actual damages can be calculated easily, or the liquidated damages amount is considerably greater than the owner's probable loss, a court may hold the liquidated damages clause unenforceable as a penalty. A contractual penalty—an amount intended to punish the contractor for late completion—is unenforceable as a matter of public policy. To increase the chance that liquidated damages will be enforceable, liquidated damages clauses often explicitly state that actual damages for delayed completion would be difficult to determine and the specified amount is intended as an estimate of actual damages rather than a penalty. However, even without such a statement, courts seldom challenge the amount of liquidated damages.

If the contract provides for liquidated damages, such damages are usually the owner's only remedy for late completion; the owner cannot recover its actual delay damages even if they exceed the liquidated amount. Some states allow an exception if the contractor has abandoned the project, on the theory that the liquidated damages provision was not intended to cover abandonment. In such cases, the owner can typically choose between liquidated damages and actual damages.

Liquidated damages are usually assessed at the end of the project, but AIA A201 allows the owner to withhold liquidated damages from the contractor's progress payments. Per A201 §9.5.1, the architect can withhold a certification of

CASE STUDY—LIQUIDATED DAMAGES

The transportation department hired a contractor to raise a section of highway to protect it from flooding. The contract stated that liquidated damages of $600 per day would be assessed for every day after the specified completion date that any work remained uncompleted. The highway was open to traffic by the completion date, but work such as signage and landscaping was not complete. The project was not fully complete until 156 days after the contractual completion date, and the contractor was assessed $93,600 in liquidated damages.

The contractor filled suit to protest the charge, stating that liquidated damages should not have accrued, since the project was substantially complete by the specified date. The court held that the doctrine of substantial completion did not apply in this case. It was appropriate to charge liquidated damages until the work was fully complete, to compensate the department for overhead expenses such as equipment rental, salaries, and utility bills that continued to accrue.

Reliance Ins. Co. v. Utah Dept. of Transp.,
858 P.2d 1363 (Utah 1993)

payment because of "reasonable evidence that the Work will not be completed within the Contract Time, and that the unpaid balance would not be adequate to cover actual or liquidated damages for the anticipated delay."

Liquidated damages clauses sometimes include an early completion bonus. These so-called bonus/penalty provisions typically state that the contractor will be paid a daily bonus amount for completing the project sooner than the required completion date and will be charged a penalty for each day the project is late. Although the use of such clauses has increased in recent years, courts have sometimes refused to enforce a penalty, holding that it is against public policy.

10.7 CONSTRUCTIVE ACCELERATION

If the owner requires a fixed-price project to be completed earlier than the date specified in the contract, the contractor may incur additional costs for overtime work, rescheduling subcontractors, and expediting material deliveries. There is typically no dispute that the contractor is entitled to reimbursement for reasonable expenses in such cases.

Disputes may arise, however, if the contractor alleges that there has been constructive acceleration. Constructive acceleration occurs when the owner refuses to grant a time extension for an excusable or compensable delay and requires the contractor to complete the project according to the original schedule. To prove a claim of constructive acceleration, the contractor must show that:

1. The owner was given notice and appropriate proof that a time extension was warranted;
2. The owner required the contractor to work on the unadjusted schedule; and
3. The contractor was forced to accelerate the work and, in doing so, incurred extra costs.

10.8 RIGHT TO FINISH EARLY

Most courts hold that the contractor is entitled to finish before the specified contract date and may claim damages for owner-caused delays, even if the project is completed ahead of schedule. To sustain a claim for damages in such a case, the contractor must show that it intended to finish ahead of schedule, had the capacity to finish ahead of schedule, and would have finished earlier "but for" the owner's actions. Typically, the damages claimed would be the extended general conditions costs for field office expenses, supervision, utilities, and insurance.

10.9   MILESTONES

In addition to specifying a substantial completion date, the contract may specify dates for the completion of certain activities. Although these milestones may simply be intended to track job progress, the contract can specify damages if these dates are not met. Damages can either be actual damages or liquidated damages. If liquidated damages are specified, they must be an approximation of actual damages; they cannot be assessed as a penalty.

11

CONSTRUCTION SCHEDULING

On many projects, the project specifications require the contractor to provide the owner with a schedule that shows how the work will be executed. Even when the contractor is not explicitly required to create a schedule, the contractor must coordinate its manpower and equipment, as well as its subcontractors and materials deliveries. Thus every construction project involves some amount of scheduling.

The project schedule can be a valuable management tool that allows the contractor to use resources efficiently and provides advance notice of situations that may cause the project to be delayed. It can also be an important tool for evaluating and proving delay claims.

11.1 BAR CHARTS

There are two different scheduling methods used on construction projects: bar charts and CPM (critical path method) networks. Bar charts, sometimes referred to as *Gantt charts*, were developed in the early 1900s by Henry L. Gantt. They consist of a vertical list of work items accompanied by a horizontal scale that is broken down into time increments such as days or weeks. Horizontal bars are drawn to represent the time required to complete each work item; cost and manpower curves can be superimposed on the bars to calculate cumulative cost and labor requirements.

Bar charts are easy to understand and help provide less sophisticated project participants with a general understanding of the schedule. They can also be useful for short-term planning and are often distributed at subcontractor coordination meetings as "two-week look-ahead schedules." They are not appropriate for planning and scheduling complex construction projects, however, because they do not show the relationships among work items. Consequently, they do not show which work items must be completed before others or how a delay in one work item will impact others.

11.2 CRITICAL PATH SCHEDULING

Critical path scheduling uses a graphic network model to show the activities that must be carried out, the relationships among these activities, and their estimated durations. The network model tells the contractor the range of dates within which specific activities must be performed in order to ensure timely completion of the project. The chain of activities that takes the longest time to complete is referred to as the *critical path*. Because the critical path is the key feature of a network analysis, these types of analyses are typically referred to as *critical path modeling* or the *critical path method* (CPM).

The current version of CPM evolved from programs developed independently in the 1950s for the U.S. Navy and the DuPont Company. Both the Navy's Project Evaluation and Review Technique (PERT) and DuPont's Critical Path Planning and Scheduling used network analysis to schedule and manage projects. CPM was widely introduced into the construction field in the 1960s; by the 1990s, CPM programs had evolved to the point that they ran on personal computers and could be used by people with limited computer skills. CPM is now the standard for scheduling in almost all industries, including construction.

CPM is used to schedule and manage virtually every large project that involves work by different trades, particularly when some or all of the work is subcontracted. It is also used forensically to analyze and prove delay claims. Many project specifications require a CPM analysis to establish entitlement to a time extension. Likewise, courts often require that parties to a construction project use CPM to identify the cause and responsibilities for project delays.

11.2.1 Activity Logic

CPM networks are constructed from discrete items of work referred to as *activities*. An activity is a specific task that has a recognizable beginning and end, and a required time for accomplishment. The sequence in which the activities are carried out is called the *activity logic*. To establish the activity logic, the scheduler must determine which activities have to be completed before a particular activity can start, which activities can be performed concurrently, and which activities cannot start before that particular activity is completed. The logic should also consider resource availability and physical requirements such as access and safety, as well as preferential relationships among the activities. Preferential relationships mean that it is more efficient, but not necessary, to perform the activities in a certain sequence.

11.2.2 Arrow Diagramming

There are two types of CPM networks: arrow diagramming networks and precedence diagramming networks. In an *arrow diagramming method* (ADM) network, arrows and circles (nodes) indicate the planned sequence and relationships of the work activities. The arrows represent activities, while the nodes are points in time that represent the start or finish of an activity, or the junction of two or more activities. The node at the activity's start (the tail of the arrow) is referred to as its "i" node; the activity's end (the head of the arrow) is its "j" node. Because activities are identified by their i-j numbers, each activity must have a unique i-j node sequence.

All of the activity relationships in an ADM network are finish-to-start, which means that an activity cannot start until all of its predecessor activities have finished. Dummy activities, also called *restraints*, are used to enforce proper logic sequencing and ensure that all activities have unique i-j sequences.

11.2.3 Precedence Diagramming

In a *precedence diagramming method* (PDM) network, the activities are represented by boxes connected by lines that indicate the work flow. Whereas ADM only allows finish-to-start activity relationships, PDM also allows start-to-start and finish-to-finish relationships. In addition, PDM relationships can include lead time and lag time. Lead time creates a relationship where an activity cannot finish until a specific amount of time after another activity finishes. Lag time creates a relationship where one activity cannot start until a specific amount of time after another activity has started. These additional relationships eliminate the need for dummy activities and thus reduce the number of activities required to model a project.

Although ADM was the dominant scheduling method for many years, it has now been almost completely replaced by PDM, and most commercial software programs no longer support ADM models. ADM principles are still relevant, however, because scheduling specifications sometimes limit the PDM model such that only finish-to-start relationships are allowed.

11.2.4 As-Planned (Baseline) Schedule

The contractor's intended approach to executing the project is referred to as the *as-planned (baseline) schedule*. The first step in preparing the baseline schedule is to identify the activities that are required to perform the work. To be useful as a management tool, the schedule must include an appropriate number of activities. If too few activities are used, there will be little flexibility with respect to scheduling; if too many activities are used, the relationships between activities may be difficult to follow. The appropriate number of activities depends on the nature, size, and complexity of the project. The specifications may try to ensure appropriate detail by requiring a minimum number of activities or limiting activity duration to a certain number of days.

Once the activities have been identified, the next step is to determine the activity logic and estimate the amount of time required to perform the work represented by each activity. When estimating activity durations, factors such as anticipated weather conditions; available labor, equipment, and materials; and other constraints are considered.

The final step is to enter the information into the CPM software and calculate the schedule. The first calculation, known as the *forward pass*, calculates the project completion date and the critical path. It also calculates the early start and finish date for each activity. The early start date of an activity is the earliest that it can start, based on the date that all of its preceding activities will be completed. The early finish date is the earliest the activity can be completed; it is determined by adding the activity's duration to its early start date.

The software then does a *backward pass* to determine late start and finish dates. The late finish of an activity is the latest that it can finish and still allow the project to be finished by the calculated completion date. The late start of an activity is the latest that it can start if the project completion date is to be met. The late start is calculated by subtracting the activity's duration from its late finish date.

11.2.5   Float

The backward pass also calculates float for each activity. There are two types of float: total float and free float. *Total float* is the amount of time an activity can be delayed without delaying the project's completion date. An activity's total float is calculated by subtracting either its early start date from its late start date or its early finish date from its late finish date. Any activity with zero total float is a critical activity because a delay in its finish date will delay project completion.

Free float is the amount of time an activity can be delayed without delaying the early start of any succeeding activity. Free float will always be less than or equal to total float. An activity on the critical path will have zero free float as well as zero total float.

Float values can change throughout the project due to progress (or lack thereof), changes in activity duration, or changes to the project completion date. Float values are important because a contractor may be able to prevent a delay in project completion by shifting resources from an activity that has float to a critical activity that is behind schedule.

Issues often arise if the owner does something that reduces the float in the schedule, thus depriving the contractor of scheduling flexibility. Unless float is specifically addressed in the contract, however, most courts hold that it is a resource that belongs to the project, and that it can be used by any party on a first-come, first-served basis, as long as the party acts in good faith. When float is considered a project resource, a party acting in good faith will not be held liable for a project delay, even if the party delayed an activity until its float was exhausted. Although disputes over how changes affect float are typically over total float, free float values can also be important, particularly when there are resource constraints.

11.2.6   Critical Path

The critical path establishes the project duration. By definition, none of the activities on the critical path have any float. If an activity on the critical path is delayed, there will be a delay in the project's completion.

An activity that was not originally on the project's critical path can become part of the critical path as a result of a delay or schedule change that uses all of the activity's float. If more than the original float is used, the activity's early start date will be later than its original late start date, and the activity's float will become negative. Unless the activities are resequenced or an activity on the critical path is compressed (accelerated), there will be a delay in the project's completion. Activities can be accelerated in a number of ways, but the most common way is to assign additional resources so the work can be completed in less time than originally planned.

11.2.7 Multiple Calendars

Many of the software programs used for scheduling include multiple calendars that allow work to be done according to different schedules—for example, some activities may have a seven-day workweek, while others are restricted to a five-day workweek. Multiple calendars can also be used to specify restrictions that apply only to certain activities, such as date restrictions that prevent certain activities from being done during the winter. When such restrictions exist, a short delay in the start of an activity might cause it to fall within the restricted period, which could significantly increase the delay. By incorporating these restrictions into the schedule, potential problems can be identified early and can often be prevented.

11.3 SCHEDULING SPECIFICATIONS

Most contracts require the contractor to provide the owner with a baseline schedule for review and approval. The owner should review the time allowed for shop drawing approval to ensure that it is not being required to act in an unreasonably short time. In addition, the owner's approval should explicitly state that the contractor remains responsible for the means, method, and timing of performance.

Increasingly, construction specifications are dictating the format of the project schedule and including requirements for updating the schedule. The specifications may require the contractor to submit fully operational electronic versions of all schedules, including updates. The owner can use these files to evaluate the effect of a proposed schedule change before negotiating a change order. It can also use the files to monitor progress and verify that the contractor's scheduled completion date is reasonable.

Because the major trade subcontractors carry much of the risk of labor productivity on many projects, they may be required to provide input on activity sequences and durations. They may also be required to participate in updates related to their work. The specifications may also require that the schedule show resource usage (*resource loading*). This helps the owner determine whether projected activity durations are reasonable and allows the owner to compare proposed resource usage to actual resource usage when evaluating delays or requests for time extensions.

Scheduling software that masks the logic and allows calculated dates to be overridden has led to serious scheduling abuses. As a result, specifications often specifically prohibit schedule alterations that override the activity logic. The specifications may also prohibit use of default updating mechanisms such as automatic entries for actual start and finish dates.

11.4 SCHEDULE UPDATES

Most project specifications require the schedule to be periodically updated to reflect the progress to date, the delays encountered, and the sequence actually followed. The specifications typically indicate how often the schedule must be updated and how the updates should address planned changes to the schedule for the remaining work. Many contracts require the owner and contractor to conduct joint monthly updating meetings, where they agree on the progress of the various activities during the preceding month and review the contractor's plans for going forward. The contract may also require the owner to approve any major logic changes.

Even if updating is not required by the specifications, the schedule must be updated regularly if it is to be useful as a management tool. The updates should reflect the work completed and the contractor's plans for completing the remaining work, including any significant changes in logic or duration. Each time updating information is entered, the schedule must be recalculated to determine the effect of the changes.

11.5 RESOURCE LEVELING

Maintaining fairly constant resource usage throughout the period of time that a resource (equipment or labor) is needed is usually more efficient than intermittent periods of high resource usage. Many scheduling software programs provide an option for resource leveling that allows activity durations to be determined by resource availability. The activity durations are entered as work-days or equipment-days; the actual durations are then calculated based on the resources allocated to the activity. This allows the program to create the schedule based on a preset resource level.

Different programs use different algorithms, but the amount of the resource available is typically allocated over all activities going on at a particular time, with priority given to the activities with the least float. Usually, a minimum and maximum duration can be set for each activity. Some programs also allow the resource usage to vary within preset limits if increasing the amount of the resource will shorten the critical path.

This type of automatic resource leveling is not used very often, however. Changing project conditions would require the schedule to be updated frequently, and in most cases the extra effort is not considered worthwhile. In addition, it may be difficult to understand the program's logic with respect to how activities are sequenced. When there is a critical resource, it is often simpler to manually control resource usage through activity sequencing.

11.6   CPM-BASED METHODS FOR PROOF OF DELAY CLAIMS

There are a number of CPM-based methods for proving delay claims, as well as several variations to each method. This proliferation of options, combined with the fact that the terminology used to discuss their relative merits is not always consistent, has created considerable confusion. In general, however, these methods all compare the as-planned project schedule to the actual schedule. The comparison looks at the variations in activity sequences, start dates, and durations; the party that was responsible for these variations; and how these variations impacted the project completion date.

The different methods incorporate delays differently, however, and as a result the method selected can affect the outcome of the analysis. In addition, each method requires various assumptions to be made. The results of a particular analysis can be very different, depending on what assumptions are made.

The most common methods of proving delay claims are:

- Total time analysis
- Impacted as-planned
- Collapsed as-built
- As-planned versus as-built
- Windows analysis

Of these five, only the as-planned versus as-built and windows analysis methods are generally accepted by courts.

11.6.1   Total Time Analysis

A total time analysis compares the contractor's baseline schedule with the actual as-built schedule and holds the owner responsible for the variances. Courts almost always reject this approach because it assumes that the baseline schedule was reasonable and the contractor performed as efficiently as planned, without making any mistakes. It should be noted, however, that a scheduling expert seldom says that it is using a total time approach. Typically, the approach is labeled as such by a court that has been presented with an analysis which fails to account for any of the delays caused by the contractor.

11.6.2   Impacted As-Planned ("What-If")

The impacted as-planned approach (also referred to as the "what-if" approach) was one of the first CPM-based delay analysis techniques. In this approach, the claimed delays are inserted into the contractor's baseline (as-planned) schedule and the critical path is recalculated. The impacted version is compared with the as-planned schedule, and any delay in the project completion is attributed to the claimed delays.

Although the simplicity of the approach is attractive, it is generally rejected by the courts because it assumes that the project was built in accordance with the as-planned schedule logic. Thus, it ignores the actual project history and does not reflect schedule adjustments and logic changes made during the project. As a result, it is extremely susceptible to manipulation.

11.6.3   Collapsed As-Built ("But For")

In contrast to the impacted as-planned approach, the collapsed as-built approach (also referred to as the "but-for" approach) is based on the as-built CPM schedule. To use this approach, an as-built schedule must be developed from either a contemporaneously updated CPM schedule or project records such as daily logs and time sheets. The claimed delaying events are then removed from the as-built schedule, thereby collapsing the schedule and theoretically showing what would have occurred "but for" the delays.

The collapsed as-built approach has the advantage of using actual activity durations and sequences, and it has occasionally been accepted by courts, but it is generally disfavored. The analysis is highly subjective, particularly if the analyst must create the as-built schedule from project records. Even if the as-built schedule was regularly updated throughout the project, the analyst must still assign preferential logic, choose which delays to address, determine which activities were impacted by these delays, and then choose how to eliminate the delays. The analyst's choices often determine the results of the analysis. The collapsed as-built approach also fails to take the as-planned schedule into account and relies on after-the-fact assumptions that may not reflect the contractor's actual decision-making process.

11.6.4   As-Planned versus As-Built

The as-planned versus as-built approach uses a retrospective analysis of the project to determine the cause and effect of delays. The analysis requires a sufficiently detailed as-planned schedule to use as a baseline. In addition, an accurate as-built schedule must be developed from contemporaneous schedule updates or detailed project records. The as-built schedule is compared with the baseline schedule to identify the differences between the planned and the actual progress. These differences are then analyzed to determine both their causes and their effect on the progress of the work.

Comparing the baseline schedule to a reconstructed as-built schedule allows the project's as-built critical path to be determined and delaying events to be identified. Nevertheless, the approach is somewhat imprecise. The comparison process involves subjective determinations about the as-built critical path and the extent to which the contractor's as-planned performance was impacted by various delays.

If contemporaneous records are incomplete, it can be difficult to reconstruct an accurate as-built schedule. Even with good records, the as-built CPM can never be a completely accurate document, since it is difficult to determine which restraints actually prevailed during construction. The logic of the as-built schedule and the dates it produces are thus somewhat speculative. Nevertheless, most courts accept the as-planned versus as-built approach as a valid means of proving delay claims.

11.6.5 Windows Analysis

The windows analysis is the favored method of proving delay claims. In a windows analysis, the as-built project is divided into periods of time, referred to as *windows*. The windows are analyzed in chronological order, and the schedule for each window is updated with either contemporaneous updates or project records. This results in a step-by-step determination of the events that impacted the schedule and a quantification of the loss or gain in time during each window.

Typically, the critical path and project completion date are calculated immediately before the start of the first claimed delay in the window. The actual events and delays encountered during the window are then introduced into the schedule, and the schedule is recalculated. Thus, the contractor's contemporaneous schedule changes and the as-built history of the project are factored into the analysis.

The main criticism of the windows approach is that the choice of windows is subjective, and the outcome of the analysis can be controlled by how the windows are chosen. There are also concerns when a windows approach is used only to quantify a specific delay in a specific time period, as opposed to analyzing the entire project. Selective use of a windows analysis may not correctly address the effect of delays occurring in a different time period. Despite these concerns, the windows analysis is a widely accepted method of proving delay claims.

11.7 EXPERT WITNESS TESTIMONY

Although the use of CPM to prove delay claims is now common, as courts have become more knowledgeable about CPM techniques they have also become more skeptical about expert witness testimony by scheduling experts. Under Rule 702 of the Federal Rules of Evidence, the trial court is required to determine whether an expert's testimony should be admitted. Rule 702 states that if scientific or technical knowledge will help the judge or jury understand the evidence or determine a fact at issue, a witness who is qualified as an expert by "knowledge, skill, experience, training, or education" may provide testimony. However, Rule 702 requires the testimony to be based upon sufficient facts or data and to be the product of reliable principles and methods.

The Supreme Court provided guidance on the interpretation of these requirements in *Daubert v. Merrell Dow Pharm., Inc.*[1] and subsequent cases such as *Kumho Tire Co. v. Carmichael.*[2] The court stated that in the context of expert testimony, "scientific knowledge" must be known facts, or ideas inferred from such facts, or accepted as truths on good grounds; it cannot be subjective belief or unsupported speculation.

The *Daubert* court also found that the trial court has the duty to act as a gatekeeper to determine the reliability of proposed expert scientific testimony before admitting it into evidence. Under *Daubert*, courts have the power to exclude so-called junk science, as well as testimony that is unreliable for other reasons, such as failure to establish a proper foundation. Rule 702 was subsequently amended to include the requirement that the trial court must ensure the reliability of expert testimony. Although the *Daubert* holding and the Federal Rules of Evidence apply only to federal courts, most of the states have adopted similar rules.

Even when expert scheduling testimony has passed the Daubert test and is admitted, unless it is based on a fair and impartial review of the project record, it is likely to be found unpersuasive. In claiming damages for a delay or entitlement to a time extension, the contractor's expert witness cannot rely solely on the contractor's estimates of the time required for various tasks. In addition, the contractor usually cannot obtain delay damages for owner-caused delays if the schedules submitted during the project did not show that the activities in question were on the critical path.

11.8 USING CPM TO ESTIMATE EXTENSIONS OF TIME

In addition to being used to evaluate delay claims, CPM is often used to determine how delays resulting from a proposed change order will affect the schedule. The most widely accepted approach for evaluating such delays is a chronological and cumulative method that uses the critical path at the time of the delay. This method is often referred to as the time-impact-analysis (TIA) method and is a windows approach, similar to the windows analysis used in evaluating delay claims.

---

[1] *Daubert v. Merrell Dow Pharm., Inc.*, 509 U.S. 579, 113 S.Ct. 2786, 125 L.Ed. 2d 469 (1993).

[2] *Kumho Tire Co. v. Carmichael*, 526 U.S. 137 (1999).

In using this method, the as-planned schedule is updated to record the progress to date. The proposed change is then introduced into the schedule, and the effect on the critical path is evaluated. If the proposed change extends the critical path, the contractor is entitled to an equivalent extension of time to complete the project. When the delay is significant, the contractor may also look at whether any weather-sensitive activities will be impacted. An activity initially scheduled for warm weather might take considerably longer and cost considerably more if the schedule has slipped to the extent that the work must be done during the winter. In such cases, the contractor might be entitled to both an extension of time and an increase in the contract price.

Some contracts require that time extensions be evaluated using a fragnet (network fragment) of the activities impacted by the proposed change. To create a fragnet, the impacted activities are extracted as a partial schedule, the change is introduced, and the partial schedule is recalculated. The recalculated fragnet is then put back into the schedule and the impact on the overall schedule is determined. The fragnet approach may overestimate the impact of the proposed change, however, because activities unrelated to the proposed change can often be rescheduled to mitigate the effect of the change.

11.9   USING BAR CHARTS TO PROVE DELAY CLAIMS

Developing a baseline CPM schedule and performing regular updates can require a considerable investment of time and money. As a result, bar charts continue to be used to schedule projects where there are only a small number of activities and the relationship between the activities is linear. Courts have allowed contractors to prove delay claims with bar charts when CPM was not used to schedule the project, the cost of doing a CPM analysis was unreasonable compared to the amount of the claim, and there were obvious owner-caused delays. Nevertheless, bar charts are of limited help in proving the impact of construction delays on construction projects with a large number of activities and varying logic relationships.

12

CONTRACT ADMINISTRATION

In the context of a construction project, *contract administration* refers to a wide range of activities designed to ensure that the project is constructed in accordance with the contract documents. Although licensing regulations for design professionals may require certain activities to be performed either by, or under the supervision of, a licensed professional, the owner is not required to engage the A/E that prepared the plans and specifications as a contract administrator.

Experienced owners such as developers often have their own staff to provide contract administration. Public owners may use their own staff or hire a second A/E firm to provide independent contract administration. Nevertheless, most owners retain the A/E that prepared the plans and specifications to provide contract administration services.

12.1 THE A/E'S ROLE IN CONTRACT ADMINISTRATION

The nature and scope of the A/E's role in contract administration is established by the terms of its contract with the owner and the principles of agency law. During contract administration, the A/E is a limited agent for the owner. The contract documents give the A/E express authority to act for the owner on certain matters. For example, the A/E generally does not need the owner's approval for minor changes that are consistent with the intent of the contract documents and do not involve any adjustment in the contract sum or contract time. However, most contracts state that the owner must approve all change orders that affect the contract price or schedule. Thus, the A/E would not have authority to approve additional work on behalf of the owner.

In addition to express authority, the A/E will have implied authority for certain acts. Authority may be implied from provisions of the contract documents or from the circumstances. For example, the A/E's contract may require

139

it to measure floor flatness. Unless the contract stated otherwise, the A/E would have the implied authority to reject any floors whose profile exceeded allowable tolerances.

12.2 A/E'S LIABILITY FOR CONTRACT ADMINISTRATION

The industry standard design agreements differ somewhat in how they define the A/E's role during contract administration, but most design agreements antic-ipate that the A/E will be responsible for answering requests for information (RFIs), making site visits, and preparing change orders. In addition, the A/E is typically expected to review shop drawings, approve pay applications, and cer-tify substantial completion. An A/E that acts outside the scope of its authority has breached its contract with the owner and may be liable to the owner for any damages incurred as a result of the breach. The A/E may also be liable for breach of contract if its actions were within its scope of authority but vio-lated the professional standard of care.

The A/E may be liable to the contractor, subcontractors, or third parties such as adjacent landowners in tort if there is injury or property damage as a result of its actions. To limit such liability, most A/Es insist that their contract with the owner contain a number of disclaimers about their responsibilities.

12.2.1 Approval of Shop Drawings and Other Submittals

One particular area of concern to A/Es is approval of the contractor's submit-tals. The contract documents typically require the A/E to approve submittals, including drawings and documents for various construction details. Drawings showing construction details are commonly referred to as *shop drawings* and are often provided by subcontractors and suppliers. For example, the precast con-crete supplier will provide drawings showing how the precast façade panels will be attached to the steel framing members. Likewise, the structural steel supplier will provide connection details. Other required submittals may include product samples and technical information from manufacturers and suppliers.

Reviewing this information allows the A/E to verify that construction will conform to the design concept set forth in the plans and specifications. However, A/Es have become increasingly careful to avoid contractual responsibility for approving shop drawings and other required submittals, except for the limited purpose of confirming that the submittals conform to the applicable design con-cepts. In approving a submittal, the A/E usually makes it clear that any such approval does not give the A/E control over construction means, methods, tech-niques, or procedures.

The contract documents sometimes allow the contractor to propose substitu-tions for equipment and materials required by the specifications. Typically, pro-posed substitutions need to be submitted to the A/E for approval. As with shop drawings, the A/E generally stamps these submittals to indicate that they have only been reviewed for conformance with the information given in the contract documents. If a substitution is approved before the contract is awarded, the A/E will distribute an addendum to the other bidders, informing them of the allowable substitution.

12.2.2 Site Visits and Inspections

Usually, one of the A/E's duties during contract administration is to visit the site to observe the progress of the work. The A/E's liability for failure to discover and reject defective work depends, in part, on the terms of its contract; in particular, whether the A/E has contracted to provide "general supervision" through periodic visits or is providing continuous on-site inspection through a full-time project representative.

When the A/E has a full-time representative (*clerk of the works*) on-site, it is more likely to be found liable for defective construction. Courts have not been consistent in their interpretations of the A/E's obligations under general supervision, however. Many design agreements contain provisions similar to the following:

> *The Architect shall make periodic visits to the site to familiarize himself generally with the progress and quality of the Work and to determine in general if the Work is proceeding in accordance with the Contract Documents. On the basis of his on-site observations as an Architect, he shall endeavor to guard the Owner against defects and deficiencies in the Work of the Contractor.*
>
> *The Architect shall not be responsible for the acts or omissions of the Contractor, or any Subcontractors, or any of the Contractor's or Subcontractors' agents or employees, or any other persons performing any of the Work. The Architect shall not be responsible for construction means, methods, techniques, sequences or procedures, or for safety precautions and programs in connection with the Work, and he shall not be responsible for the Contractor's failure to carry out the Work in accordance with the Contract Documents.*

Despite the qualifying language in these provisions, courts have sometimes held the A/E liable for failing to discover defective work, based on the A/E's obligation to familiarize itself with the progress of the work and to "endeavor to guard the Owner against defects and deficiencies in the Work of the Contractor." These courts have interpreted the wording "shall not be responsible for the Contractor's failure to carry out the Work in accordance with the Contract Documents" and "shall not be responsible for the acts or omissions of the Contractor" to mean only that the A/E does not guarantee or insure the contractor's work. Other courts have held that the qualifying language relieves the A/E of liability except in cases where the A/E knew, or should have known, of the defect and failed to bring it to the owner's attention.

Even when the A/E has authority to reject work that does not conform to the contract requirements, it does not have the authority to accept such work. Only the owner has the right to change the contract requirements by accepting non-conforming work. The owner will typically seek the A/E's advice on the matter, but it is ultimately the owner's decision.

12.2.3 AIA B101 Provisions

In an effort to clarify the A/E's obligations with respect to defective work, the relevant provisions were revised in the 2007 AIA documents. The wording in the 2007 version of AIA B101 is:

> *§3.6.2.1 The Architect shall visit the site at intervals appropriate to the stage of construction . . . to become generally familiar with the progress and quality of the portion of the Work completed, and to determine, in general, if the Work observed is being performed in a manner indicating that the Work, when fully completed, will be in accordance with the Contract Documents. . . . On the basis of the site visits, the Architect shall keep the Owner reasonably informed about the progress and quality of the portion of the Work completed, and report to the Owner (1) known deviations from the Contract Documents and from the most recent construction schedule submitted by the Contractor, and (2) defects and deficiencies observed in the Work.*

The design agreement thus specifically limits the A/E's obligation to reporting known deviations and observed defects to the owner; the commentary for B101 notes that the A/E may not detect every deviation from the contract documents, regardless of how often it visits the site. The 2007 AIA documents also include the provisions contained in previous versions, which state that the A/E is responsible for its own negligent acts or omissions but is not responsible for the acts or omissions of the contractor or any other entities performing work.

AIA B101 specifically states that the A/E's authority to reject work does not give rise to any duty or responsibility to the contractor, subcontractors, or suppliers. As long as the A/E acted in good faith, the contractor typically cannot hold the A/E liable for failing to discover defective work before subsequent events have increased the cost of correction.

12.2.4 The Right to Stop Work

In addition to giving the A/E the authority to reject defective work, the contract documents may authorize the A/E to stop work. Having the authority to stop work may create a significant liability for the A/E, however. In particular, the A/E's authority to stop work has been used as a basis to impose liability on the A/E when work was not stopped despite an obvious safety hazard.

In the often-cited 1967 case *Miller v. DeWitt*,[1] the court found that because the A/E had the duty to evaluate the work and the right to stop the work, it had a duty to prevent the contractor from carrying out the work in a faulty manner. It was thus found liable for workers who were injured when the roof collapsed during construction. The *Miller* decision was actually contrary to the prevailing view at the time, which was that the A/E's duty is to provide a completed structure in accordance with the owner's requirements, but not to dictate the methods by which the contractor performs the work. The court in *Miller* focused on a clause in the A/E's contract that required the A/E to "supervise" the contractor. Following this decision, many of the industry standard form documents were revised such that the A/E no longer supervises the work but instead "observes" the work.

In addition, A/Es routinely disclaim any responsibility for safety precautions and programs in connection with the work and are careful to limit other obligations where such obligations might expose them to liability for injuries. Most A/Es now insist that the design agreement explicitly state that the A/E does not have control over, and is not responsible for, the construction means, methods, techniques, sequences, or procedures.

If the A/E does have the right to stop work, it may be held liable for both the owner's and the contractor's extra costs if it fails to stop work during adverse weather conditions. At the same time, the A/E may be held liable for stopping work unnecessarily. The A/E generally is not held liable for making a poor decision, though, as long as it acted in good faith. The A/E incurs liability only for decisions that were negligent, such that the A/E failed to exercise reasonable care, or acts that were done in bad faith. Nevertheless, the A/E may insist that the contract documents explicitly state that the A/E has no authority to stop the work.

12.2.5 Approval of Progress Payments

As part of its contract administration service, the A/E is often responsible for approving payment applications, where such approval is a representation to the owner that the work was properly performed. The A/E may be liable to the owner for approving payment applications when the work was defective or incomplete. However, unless the design agreement requires the A/E to obtain lien waivers, the A/E is not responsible for ensuring that the contractor is paying its subcontractors and suppliers.

Because the A/E does not have a contract with either the owner's lender or the contractor's surety, the lender and surety may not be able to recover against an A/E that approves payment for defective work or approves payment in excess of the value of the work. If the lender is concerned about the payments or worried that the contractor will default, it may engage an independent A/E to review

[1] *Miller v. DeWitt*, 37 Ill.2d 273, 226 N.E.2d 630 (1967).

the contractor's applications and verify that the stated percentage of completion is accurate. An independent A/E may also be required on projects that receive government funding.

12.2.6 Responding to Change Order Requests

An A/E providing contract administration usually has a significant role in the change order process. The A/E typically reviews all proposals or requests for changes in the work and prepares the change order, including any plans and specifications required by the change. Preparing the change order is usually part of the A/E's basic services during contract administration. Likewise, preparing a construction change directive is usually part of the basic services. However, creating and assembling supporting documentation such as new or revised plans and specifications generally constitutes an additional service, for which the A/E is entitled to receive additional compensation.

12.2.7 Requests for Information, Interpretations, and Clarifications

During the construction phase, questions about the plans and specifications may be referred to the A/E through requests for information (RFIs), also known as requests for interpretation or clarification. Because the A/E is working as the owner's agent, the owner may be liable if the A/E's failure to respond to RFIs promptly causes a delay.

In some cases, the contractor may claim that defects in the drawings have required an unusually large number of RFIs and that this has led to expenses not covered by the construction contract. However, an unusually large number of RFIs may also be a sign that the contractor does not have the proper qualifications for the project. In such cases, the A/E may claim additional compensation for providing contract administration services beyond those contemplated by its contract with owner.

12.3 A/E'S ROLE IN CONTRACTOR TERMINATION

Contract documents often require the A/E to advise the owner as to whether the contractor should be terminated for default. Although this advice nominally constitutes the tort of interference with a contract, the A/E has an obligation to guard the interests of the owner. The A/E is thus granted the privilege to intervene in the contractual relationship between the owner and the contractor so that it can advise the owner honestly, without risk that it will be liable for its actions. Some contracts even state that unless the A/E certifies that there is adequate cause for termination, the owner does not have the right to terminate the contractor for default.

An A/E that acted within the scope of its contractual obligations to the owner is not liable for wrongly advising the owner to terminate a contractor's performance unless it acted with malice or in bad faith. Mere negligence or poor judgment is not sufficient for the contractor to recover damages from the A/E, even if the termination was unjustified.

12.4 INITIAL DECISION MAKER (IDM)

The design agreement may require the A/E to serve as the initial decision maker (IDM) when disputes arise between the owner and the contractor during construction. In this role, the A/E is expected to serve as a neutral mediator or referee. The owner is paying the A/E for this service, however, and the contractor may dispute any decisions it believes are unfavorable. The 2007 version of the AIA documents allows the parties to select someone other than the A/E as the IDM, but specifies that the A/E will act as the IDM unless the parties specify someone else.

13

THE PAYMENT PROCESS

Large construction projects can last for several years and even relatively small projects can last for several months. Because few contractors or suppliers are able to wait until final completion to receive payment for their work, regular progress payments are necessary. Progress payments are particularly important to subcontractors, which tend to be smaller and less well capitalized than general contractors. In addition, subcontractors must usually pay their suppliers monthly and often pay their employees weekly. A subcontractor that is struggling financially because of cash flow problems can put the entire project at risk.

13.1   PROGRESS PAYMENTS

Most contracts provide that progress payments will be made monthly, with the amount of the payment based on the work that has been done. The way the payment is calculated depends on the type of the contract. If the contract, or a part of the contract, was bid on a unit-price basis, the payment is the unit price times the number of units done during the billing period. On a cost-plus contract, the payment is the costs incurred during the billing period plus the agreed-upon fee for overhead and profit. On a fixed-price (stipulated sum) project, payment is typically made according to a schedule of values prepared by the contractor.

13.1.1   Schedule of Values

A schedule of values breaks down the bid according to the various items of the work. Each billing reflects the percentage done on each item of work during that billing period. For example, if the scheduled value for excavation is $100,000, and the contractor performed 40 percent of this work during the first month, it would be entitled to bill for $40,000 on its first payment application.

On a fixed-price project, bidders are typically required to submit a schedule of values as part of their bid. This allows the owner to identify any obvious discrepancies between the bids. It also allows the owner to identify possible problems with *front-loaded* bids. A front-loaded bid skews the schedule of values by assigning items such as excavation and foundation work that are performed at the beginning of the project a value much higher than their actual cost, while later work such as painting is undervalued. In some cases, the contractor may have front-loaded the bid because of financial problems. Once the work reaches the point where items have been undervalued in the schedule, the contractor may be financially unable to complete the project. If the contractor defaults, the owner will have trouble finishing the project for the contract price as a result of overpaying for the work that has been completed.

13.1.2   The Application for Payment

On most projects, the contractor must submit an application for payment, also known as a *draw request*, to be paid for its work. The contractor's application for payment is a representation as to the status and quality of the work. The application for payment is typically submitted to the A/E, who reviews it, compares it to the work in place, and advises the owner as to whether the contractor is entitled to the requested payment.

The A/E may refuse to recommend payment for a number of reasons, including defective work and third-party claims, such as a claim that the contractor caused damage to an adjacent property. Under the AIA contract documents, the A/E may also refuse to recommend payment if there is reasonable evidence that the work cannot be completed for the contract balance or within the contract time. If work that the contractor has been paid for is subsequently found to be defective, the owner can withhold an appropriate amount from a subsequent payment until the defective work is corrected.

The application for payment that a subcontractor submits to the contractor is likewise a representation as to the status of the subcontract. The contractor may withhold payment from a subcontractor for defective construction, disputed work, or third-party claims.

13.1.3   Certification of Payment

The AIA contract documents refer to the A/E's approval of the application for payment as a *certificate of payment*. Per AIA A201 §9.4.2, a certificate of payment is a representation that the A/E believes the work has progressed to the point indicated and the quality of the work is in accordance with the contract documents. However, §9.4.2 qualifies the certification by stating that it is not "a representation that the Architect has made exhaustive or continuous on-site inspections to check the quality or quantity of the Work." Section 9.4.2 further qualifies the A/E's representation by saying that it is:

> . . . *subject to an evaluation of the Work for conformance with the Contract Documents upon Substantial Completion, to results of subsequent tests and inspections, to correction of minor deviations from the Contract Documents*

prior to completion, and to any specific qualifications expressed by the Architect.

Even though the representation made by the A/E in a certification is not a warranty concerning the quality of the work, the A/E must exercise reasonable care and diligence. Because the A/E should reasonably foresee that the owner will rely on the accuracy of the A/E's certification, the owner may have a claim for negligent misrepresentation against an A/E that overcertifies the amount of work completed.

Section 9.4.2 of A201 also states that the certificate is not a representation that the A/E has reviewed the subcontractors' and material suppliers' requisitions to substantiate the contractor's right to payment or determine how the contractor has used money previously received. In other words, the A/E does not verify that the contractor is paying its subcontractors and materials suppliers. If the owner wants to ensure that payments are being made, it must require the contractor to obtain lien waivers from its subcontractors and suppliers.

13.2 RETAINAGE

Construction contracts typically state that a certain percentage of each payment will be retained until substantial completion of the project. The purpose of this retainage is both to ensure that the contractor has an incentive to complete the project and to create a fund to cover correction of defective work. Retainage also gives the owner, the lender, and the surety protection against liens from unpaid suppliers and subcontractors, as well as against tort claims from third parties.

The bulk of the retainage is typically released once substantial completion is achieved. If the contractor is liable for damages because of a delay in achieving substantial completion, the owner usually takes the accrued amount out of retainage. The owner is also entitled to hold back an amount that will cover the incomplete or defective items on the punchlist. Once final completion is achieved, the owner must release the remaining retainage. The owner is not allowed to continue withholding retainage to ensure that the contractor performs warranty work.

Retainage is typically either 5 or 10 percent of the draw request. On some projects, retainage is 10 percent until the project is 50 percent complete. Subsequent payment applications are then paid in full, effectively reducing the retainage to 5 percent by the end of the job. The rationale for this approach is that as the contractor completes more of the work, both the risk that the project will not be completed and the costs to correct defects decrease. Owners usually reserve the right to reinstate the full retainage if they deem it necessary to do so, however.

Although retainage protects owners, it can create cash flow problems for contractors. Some states have tried to strike a balance between protecting owners and protecting contractors by setting a limit on the allowable retainage. Other states require that the retainage decrease as construction progresses or allow contractors to provide a bond in lieu of retainage.

13.2.1 Payment of Subcontractor's Retainage

When a subcontractor's payment is contingent on the contractor's receiving payment from the owner (i.e., the subcontract has a "pay-when-paid" clause), there can be a significant delay before the subcontractor receives the retainage held on its work. Because the contractor's retainage is typically not released until the project reaches substantial completion, subcontractors that complete their work early in the project may have to wait months or even years to receive their retainage. Despite the unfairness of this arrangement, courts typically uphold the terms of the subcontract with respect to payment of retainage.

13.2.2 Claims on Retainage

Retainage held by the owner can become the subject of claims by third parties. If the contractor has defaulted and its performance bond surety is required to complete the project, the surety is entitled to collect the contractor's retainage under the doctrine of equitable subrogation. The surety's right of *subrogation* (right to step into the owner's shoes) continues even if the contractor declares bankruptcy—the contract balance and any retainage is the property of the surety rather than the bankruptcy estate. The surety is responsible for paying subcontractor retainage claims out of the funds received, however.

In cases where the contractor has not defaulted on the contract, third-party claims to retainage are governed by state law. In some states, a subcontractor's lien has priority over all other interests, including court judgments.

13.3 ACCORD AND SATISFACTION

An accord and satisfaction is essentially a substitute contract between a debtor and a creditor that settles a debt for an amount that is different from what is allegedly owed. The *accord* is the agreement between the parties to settle the debt. The *satisfaction* is the acceptance of the amount agreed to. In the context of a construction project, an accord and satisfaction typically involves payment for less than what is owed, in exchange for work that is in some way less than what was contracted for.

An accord must have the three essential elements of a contract: offer, acceptance, and mutual consideration. As an example, a contractor agreed to rebuild a homeowner's porch for $10,000. The contract called for a $5,000 payment before the start of construction and a $5,000 payment at completion of the work. At completion, the owner complained about the quality of the work and refused to make the final payment. After a settlement conference, the contractor agreed to accept $4,000 as its final payment if the owner released it from all claims.

The owner's consideration for the accord was that it gave up the right to a well-constructed porch; the contractor's consideration was that it gave up its right to the full contract amount.

Before an accord and satisfaction can be established, there must be a bona fide, good-faith dispute between the parties as to the amount that is owed. Mere refusal to pay the full claim does not make it a disputed claim; the party owing the money must demonstrate a valid basis for refusing to pay. The accord does not discharge the original contract; it merely suspends the right to enforce it. If there is a breach of the accord, the nonbreaching party has the right to sue under either the original contract or the accord agreement. Satisfaction of the accord (payment) discharges both the original contract and the accord agreement.

13.3.1 Payment of an Accord by Check

When payment of an accord is by check, the debtor must make it clear—by appropriate and conspicuous wording—that the check is intended to settle the outstanding claim between the parties and that by cashing the check, the creditor accepts the settlement. Typically, the debtor writes this on the check or the accompanying voucher, using language such as "Payment in full settlement of the stated accounts" or "Endorsement of the check constitutes a complete settlement of your claim."

The amount of the accord does not need to be negotiated in advance—the debtor can simply send the creditor a check for an amount that is less than what is owed, with the notation that it is settlement of the debt. If a creditor receives a check for less than the full amount owed and the check contains a conspicuous notation that it was tendered as satisfaction of the entire debt, the creditor can either reject the offer by returning or destroying the check, or cash the check and accept the accord.

Although the concept of accord and satisfaction developed through case law (common law), the requirements for an accord and satisfaction for the sale of goods paid for with a check were codified in the Uniform Commercial Code at UCC §3-311. Many of the states have extended the language of this code section such that it applies to services as well. Under the common law, a creditor could not prevent a satisfaction by crossing out the settlement language or writing a disclaimer on the check before cashing it. However, the UCC allows a creditor to accept a partial payment without giving up its claim to the balance by writing "under protest" on the check. Many states have held that this right now applies to both goods and services.

Even in states that do not let creditors cash a partial payment under protest, courts typically make an exception when the payment was not made in good faith. A payment would not be in good faith if the debtor knew it had no basis for refusing to pay the full amount owed, or the debtor knowingly took advantage of the creditor's financial need. In addition, state statutes typically allow a creditor who has cashed a check written for less than the full amount owed to return the money within a certain amount of time, thereby undoing the satisfaction. A creditor may also require that any payment be sent to a particular office or particular person. This prevents a settlement from being accepted by someone without the proper authority.

13.4   JOINT CHECKS

If an owner is concerned that the contractor may not be paying its subcontractors or suppliers, the owner can issue checks that are jointly payable to the contractor and the subcontractor or supplier. Joint checks are not negotiable unless they are endorsed by both of the payees.

Contractors generally do not want joint checks, as they restrict the contractor's ability to pay whatever bills it considers most pressing. The contract may specifically state that the owner is allowed to issue joint checks, however. For example, AIA A201 §9.5.1 allows the owner to issue joint checks if the A/E withholds a certificate of payment because of a reasonable belief that the contractor is not paying its subcontractors or suppliers. There is no standard wording for a joint check agreement, and the language of such agreements can vary considerably.

A subcontractor's supplier will sometimes require the contractor to issue joint checks to the subcontractor and the supplier. These joint check agreements can work in the subcontractor's favor, particularly if the subcontractor does not have good credit and would not otherwise be able to purchase the required materials. The joint check agreement may require the contractor to write two checks, one that is a joint check for the materials and a second made out to the subcontractor for the balance of the subcontract. Although the joint check agreement creates a contractual relationship between the contractor and the supplier, the contractor is generally protected from claims as long its payments are in accordance with the agreement. For example, the contractor would generally not be liable if the subcontractor forged the supplier's signature.

13.4.1   Joint Payee versus Alternative Payee

It should be noted that a joint payee is not the same as an alternative payee. When there are two or more payees and the payee names are separated by the word *and*, they are joint payees; when the names are separated by the word *or*, they are alternative payees. Only one of the alternative payees needs to endorse the check for it to be negotiable.

13.5   TITLE INSURANCE

Title insurance protects against liens and other encumbrances on the title to the property; separate policies are issued to the owner and the lender. When title insurance is provided during construction, a *date-down endorsement* is typically issued with each progress payment. The endorsement increases the amount of insurance by the amount of the payment.

Title insurers may also serve as escrow agents for disbursements to the contractor, even if they are not providing title insurance during construction. Prior to disbursing funds, the title insurer will do a title search to confirm that the title is free and clear of claims. If the title search discloses a lien or other encumbrance for which the contractor is responsible, an appropriate amount is withheld from the disbursement.

13.6   OBLIGATIONS OF THE LENDER

Construction loan agreements often state that disbursements on the loan will be made on the basis of the owner's draw requests and property inspections by the lender's inspector. Courts have held that while such language gives the lender the right to make inspections, it does not create a duty to do so. The owner is responsible for ensuring that its draw requests are proper. If the lender fails to make an inspection and pays a draw request for more than the work done, the owner cannot hold the lender liable for any problems due to the excess payment.

13.7   EVIDENCE OF FINANCING

The owner's ability to finance the project is of considerable importance to the contractor; contractors do not want to advance their own money or assume liabilities to third parties without some assurance that they will be paid. Although a contractor can file a mechanic's lien against a project if it is not paid, the lien may be of little value if the owner goes bankrupt and the contractor's lien rights are subordinate to those of the lender.

Contracts often state that the contractor is entitled to proof of adequate financing before starting work, and owners generally do not dispute the need to provide reasonable assurance of their ability to pay before the start of construction. Acceptable evidence of financing can include a construction loan commitment, a credit report, or documentation of the government appropriation for the project.

Most disputes occur when the contractor requests evidence of financing after the start of construction. The AIA contract documents provide that the contractor may demand evidence of financing if the owner has failed to make payments in accordance with the contract documents or a change in the work has materially changed the contract sum. However, the parties may disagree over what evidence the owner must provide, over and above what it has already provided. Such disagreements can be problematic if the contract allows the contractor to terminate for cause unless it receives adequate assurance.

13.8 PROMPT PAYMENT ACTS

Because late payments can impair a contractor's or supplier's ability to meet its cash flow needs, timely progress payments are a major concern to both contractors and suppliers. In an effort to lessen the burden of late payment from federal agencies, Congress enacted the federal Prompt Payment Act (PPA) in 1982. The PPA requires federal agencies to pay for construction work on a timely basis, pay interest penalties when payments are late, and take discounts only when payments are made by an agreed-upon discount date.

The PPA applies to all contracts involving a federal agency acquiring property or services from a business concern. It requires the agency to pay the prime contractor within 14 days of receiving a proper payment request unless the contract provides for an extension if the agency requires more time to inspect the work. It also allows the contractor to negotiate for an earlier payment by offering the agency a discount.

13.8.1 The Progress Payment Request

To be deemed "proper," a progress payment request must include substantiation of the requested amounts. Under Office of Management and Budget (OMB) guidelines, the contractor can substantiate progress payment requests by itemizing the work done, the amounts requested, and the amount tendered to each subcontractor. The prime contractor must also certify that to the best of its knowledge and belief, the requested amounts are for the performance defined by the contract and that debts to subcontractors and suppliers have been, or will be, satisfied from prior payments or the payment requested. If the contractor is holding retainage on a subcontract, it may not request payment for those amounts; the funds are retained by the agency rather than the contractor.

If an agency receives a proper progress payment request and fails to make timely payment, the PPA requires the agency to pay an interest penalty. Absent a material breach of the contract, a contractor's only remedy for late payment is the interest penalty. The interest rate is the rate determined by the secretary of the treasury. If an agency refuses to pay interest on a late payment, the contractor can file a claim under the Contract Disputes Act of 1978.

13.8.2 Payment on Subcontracts

In 1988, Congress added provisions to govern the manner in which prime contractors pay subcontractors and suppliers on federal projects. Under the 1988 PPA amendments, subcontracts must include payment provisions that are substantially similar to those required in prime contracts. Subcontracts must include a payment clause requiring the prime contractor to pay the subcontractor within seven days of receiving payment from the agency. The interest penalty for late payments is the same as the penalty for late payments to the contractor. A flowdown clause must be included in each subcontract, and the subcontractor must include a payment clause and interest penalty in any contracts with second-tier subcontractors.

13.9 THE OWNER'S PAYMENT OBLIGATION ON PRIVATE CONSTRUCTION

A number of states have enacted prompt payment acts for work done under contracts with state agencies. However, neither federal nor state prompt payment acts apply to private construction; on private construction the owner's payment obligation must be stated in the contract. Most contracts indicate when payment must be made and the interest rate to be applied to late payments. If the contract does not specify an interest rate for late payments, courts will use the legal rate of interest. Almost every state sets a legal rate of interest by statute. The rate is typically the same rate that applies to late payments by state agencies; it changes periodically to match other prevailing interest rates.

Contracts often stipulate that if the owner fails to make payment of undisputed amounts within the time allowed by the contract, the owner has materially breached the contract, and the contractor is allowed to stop work. For example, §9.7.1 of AIA A201 states:

> *[I]f the Owner does not pay the Contractor within seven days after the date established in the Contract Documents . . . the Contractor may, upon seven additional days' written notice to the Owner and Architect, stop the Work until payment of the amount owing has been received.*

However, unless the contractor's decision to stop work is reasonable and made in good faith, a court may find that the contractor has defaulted on its contract. In determining whether the decision to stop work was reasonable, courts generally consider the owner's reasons for withholding payment, the amount that is being withheld, and the duration of the withholding in light of the circumstances and the contractual language.

The contractor must also ensure that it has not waived its right to stop work by continuing to work on previous occasions when the Owner has withheld payment. A contractor that has waived its right to stop work, but stops working nonetheless, may be liable for any expenses the owner incurs as a result of the stoppage.

13.10 THE FALSE CLAIMS ACT

The goal of the federal False Claims Act (FCA) is to prevent fraud in government contracting. Enacted in 1863 in response to privateering during the Civil War, it has been revised several times to accommodate changes in government contracting practices. In recent years, it has primarily been used to combat fraud in the health-care industry, but a number of cases have arisen in the construction industry.

False claim liability arises under the FCA when an individual knowingly presents or causes to be presented a "false or fraudulent claim for payment or approval" to the United States or conspires to get a false claim paid. Liability also attaches to any person who knowingly makes or uses a false statement to get a false claim paid by the government or knowingly makes or uses a false statement to avoid an obligation to pay the government.

The FCA defines *claim* to include all payment demands on both federal projects and projects receiving federal funding. This includes demands to the United States itself, to a government agency, to a contractor or agent of the government, and to an entity receiving federal funding. The FCA does not require the government to prove the individual's intent to deceive; it merely requires the government to prove that the individual knowingly submitted a false claim. The FCA defines *knowingly* to mean that the individual either had actual knowledge that the claim was false, acted in deliberate ignorance of the claim's truth or falsity, or acted in reckless disregard of the claim's truth or falsity.

13.10.1 Liability for False Claims

Under the FCA, a contractor can be liable for submitting overstated progress payment requests, overpriced change orders, inflated equipment rental rates, or unjustified claims of delay impacts. A contractor can also be liable for passing through a false claim from a subcontractor. Likewise, design professionals and construction managers can be liable for the claims of subconsultants, contractors, and subcontractors that they have passed through.

As an example, a CM who submits a contractor's invoice without reviewing it may be charged with knowledge that the invoice was false if the CM was reckless in not reviewing the invoice and finding that the amounts requested were too high. The CM need not actually know that the invoice amount was overstated; it is enough that the CM had no reasonable basis for believing that the amount was proper or had reason to believe that it might be false but took no steps to determine its accuracy.

Design professionals and CMs may also be liable if they bill for services not rendered, misrepresent the scope of additional services, overstate employee or firm qualifications in order to justify higher rates, or conspire with the contractor to approve deficient work. Innocent mistakes and mere negligence do not create liability under the FCA, however; liability attaches only if the action was reckless or intentional.

13.10.2 Prosecution of False Claims

Violators of the FCA may be sued by either the attorney general (AG) or a private individual. Private individuals sue as *qui tam* plaintiffs; *qui tam* is an abbreviation of the Latin phrase "*qui tam pro domino rege quam pro si ipso in hac parte sequitur*," which means "who sues on behalf of the King as well as for himself." A *qui tam* plaintiff must notify the AG upon filing a complaint. If the AG declines to prosecute the claim, the *qui tam* plaintiff is allowed to prosecute it. When the AG prosecutes an action commenced by a *qui tam* plaintiff, the *qui tam* plaintiff will receive at least 15 percent, but no more than 25 percent, of any recovery. If the *qui tam* plaintiff prosecutes the claim, it will receive at least 25 percent, but no more than 30 percent, of any recovery, as well as its costs.

Violators of the FCA are liable for both treble damages (three times the damages sustained by the government) and punitive damages of up to $10,000 per claim. Violators are also liable to the government for the costs incurred in bringing the action; if the action is brought by a private individual, violators are liable for reasonable attorneys' fees. In addition to civil damages and penalties, violators may be subject to criminal liability. Violators can mitigate their damages somewhat by providing the government with information related to the violation prior to the commencement of prosecution and fully cooperating with the investigation.

13.10.3 State False Claims Act

A number of states, including California, Illinois, Florida, Montana, Massachusetts, Hawaii, and Virginia, have enacted their own false claims acts. Most of the state acts are based on the federal act and apply to any claims that are paid from state funds. However, with the exception of California, these acts have rarely been used to prosecute violations related to construction projects.

14

CHANGES TO THE WORK

It is rare for a construction project to be built exactly as originally designed. Changes may be necessary because of errors or omissions in the plans or specifications, unforeseen site conditions, or a change in the owner's needs. Changes may also be the result of cost savings proposed by the contractor or new government regulations. Alternatively, the budget for the project may need to be revised because the owner has suffered a financial setback. In some cases, the owner may simply have changed its mind about some aspect of the design, for either aesthetic or functional reasons.

Even if a change is not explicitly requested, the contractor may think it is being required to do work that is outside the scope of its contract. In such cases, the contractor may file a claim for a constructive change.

14.1 CONTRACT CHANGES

Many of the changes that occur over the course of a project, for example, changing a paint color, are minor. Most contracts allow the A/E to direct changes that are consistent with the intent of the contract documents and do not require adjustment to the contract price or time. Such changes do not have to be approved by the owner, and, when made by a written order signed by the A/E, are binding on both the owner and the contractor.

However, there may also be substantial changes that require considerable negotiation of both price and time adjustments. When a substantial change is contemplated, the owner may start by asking the contractor to provide a quote for the work. A request for a quote, sometimes referred to as a *contemplated change notice* (CCN), allows the owner to evaluate the cost and schedule impacts of a potential change before being making any commitment.

Almost all contracts include a *changes clause* that allows changes to the work to be negotiated under the terms of the contract rather than as a separate contract. The changes clause typically establishes the owner's right to make a change and defines the requirements for the documents memorializing the change. It may set the parameters for pricing work and adjusting the completion

159

date. It may also set the notice and documentation requirements for a constructive change claim and specify the dispute resolution process.

Under current versions of most of the industry standard contracts, the term *change order* refers to a written modification, signed by the contractor and the owner, that defines the scope of the work, its price, and its effect on the schedule. Many contracts also require that the change order be reviewed and signed by the A/E to ensure that the change does not negatively affect the design.

14.1.1 Construction Change Directives

If the parties are unable to agree on cost and schedule adjustments before the contractor must begin the work, most contracts allow the owner to issue a *construction change directive*. A construction change directive is a written order signed by the owner (and often the A/E) that directs a change in the work and states that adjustments to the contract price and time will be negotiated according to the terms of the contract. The owner can order additions, deletions, or other revisions to the work as long as the changes are within the general scope of the contract.

The fact that the changes clause allows the owner to direct the contractor to do the work, without having the contractor voluntarily agree, is somewhat unique in contract law. The common rule in contract law is that both parties to a contract must agree to the terms of a modification. However, if the changes clause gives the owner the right to make unilateral changes, this right will be upheld in court because, by signing the contract, the contractor has agreed the owner has this right. Absent a changes clause, such unilateral directives could be considered a breach of contract, particularly if the change involved deleting work.

14.2 PRICING CHANGE ORDERS

If the parties cannot agree on the price for a change order, the work is often done on a *time and materials* (T&M) basis. T&M pricing is much like a cost-plus contract. The contractor is reimbursed for the costs incurred and receives an agreed-upon amount for overhead and profit. The changes clause may identify which costs are reimbursable (chargeable to the owner) and which costs must be included in the contractor's overhead. Depending on the type of change, the costs to be allocated as reimbursable or overhead may include:

- Labor, including taxes and benefits
- Materials, supplies, and machinery
- Equipment rental or use
- Bond premiums, insurance, permit fees, or taxes related to the change
- Supervision and field office personnel directly attributable to the change

While a time and materials calculation is nominally fair to both sides, there can be disagreements over how certain costs are calculated. One common point of disagreement is the rate that the contractor is entitled to charge for the use of its own equipment. To avoid such disputes, the contractor may be required to submit a list of equipment rates as part of its bid.

14.2.1 Determination of Price by a Third Party

Instead of using time and materials pricing, the contract may state that if the parties cannot agree on a lump-sum price for a change order, the price will be determined by a third party, such as the A/E. While having the price determined by a third party involves the risk of favoritism or ignorance, the parties usually do not challenge the price, unless the change order is for a substantial amount. On small change orders, the transaction costs (attorney's fees and arbitration or litigation costs) to dispute the price are likely to far outweigh any potential price change.

14.2.2 Schedule Adjustments

Under most of the industry standard form documents, schedule adjustments for changed work are handled in the same way as price adjustments. If the parties agree on the schedule adjustment, the change order will typically include an adjustment to the completion date. Otherwise, a third party such as the A/E will determine the adjustment. Determining an appropriate schedule adjustment is sometimes difficult, however. Even if the contract time is increased to allow for the change itself, the adjustment may not account for all of the impacts resulting from the change.

14.3 CONSTRUCTIVE CHANGES

While there may be disagreements over the pricing of change orders, most disputes over changes involve constructive changes. A constructive change occurs when the contractor believes it is being required to perform work that is outside the scope of its contract, but the owner refuses to acknowledge the work is a change. The most common source of constructive changes is errors or ambiguities in the plans and specifications.

Contracts typically require bidders to bring any ambiguities in the plans and specifications to the owner's attention before submitting their bids. This prevents the contractor from asserting a claim for a constructive change arising out of a patent (obvious) ambiguity. However, it does not bar a claim based on a latent ambiguity that could be reasonably discovered only once construction had begun.

Under the legal principle of *contra proferentum*, if the plans contain latent ambiguities such that there is more than one reasonable interpretation of the work required, the ambiguities will be construed against the party that provided the plans (typically the owner). As long as the contractor's interpretation is reasonable and consistent with industry custom, an owner's directive to perform work that was not clearly required by the plans constitutes a constructive change.

14.3.1 Owner's Direction or Improper Rejection of Work

Another situation in which a constructive change may arise is when the owner requires the contractor to perform the work in a way that increases the contractor's costs. Normally, owners contractually disclaim all responsibilities for the contractor's means and methods. However, in some cases, the owner needs to impose certain restrictions on the contractor. Such restrictions may be necessary because of an environmental regulation, or to allow the A/E to verify that the work is being done in accordance with the specifications. Nevertheless, if the restrictions were not included in the contract, the contractor may have a claim for a constructive change.

A constructive change can also arise when work is required to meet a standard that is higher than what is required by the specifications. The contractor is only obligated to perform the work in accordance with the plans and specifications. If the standards specified in the contract are not sufficient to ensure a successful project, or do not produce the result the owner desires, the owner must issue a change order. If the owner requires a higher standard without issuing a change order, the contractor is entitled to recover its additional costs as a constructive change. Likewise, improper rejection of work constitutes a constructive change, even when done by mistake. If work that complies with the specifications is rejected as defective, the contractor is entitled to recover the costs of implementing the unnecessary corrective work.

Constructive changes arise most often on fixed-priced contracts and cost-plus contracts with a guaranteed maximum price. However, even on a cost-plus contract without a GMP, the contractor may allege there has been a constructive change if work is rejected and must be redone at the contractor's expense. On unit-priced work, a constructive change may result from a dispute over how the work is being performed or how it is being measured or tested.

14.3.2 Notice Requirements for a Constructive Change

Under many contracts, the contractor must give the owner written notice before doing work that it claims is a constructive change. Timely notification of a potential claim allows the owner to explore less costly options for performing the work, request documentation of the costs, and adjust its budget to cover the claim. Whether failure to provide the required notice bars a claim depends on both the contract language and the state in which the claim is litigated. Some states strictly uphold notice requirements as a condition precedent to the right to recover on the claim. In these states, the requirement is waived only if the owner's actions prevented or hindered compliance with the notice requirement, or the work resulted from an emergency endangering life or property.

When the claim is due to work that was improperly rejected or work that was held to an improper standard, the contractor must typically provide written notice within a certain number of days after the event that gave rise to the claim.

14.3.3 Waiver of Notice Requirement

Much of the litigation over whether a claim is barred by failure to comply with a notice provision involves public contracts. Courts tend to be very protective of public funds and may require strict compliance with notice requirements on public projects but waive similar requirements on private projects. Even on public projects, however, strict compliance with the notice provisions is not always required. Courts look at whether the government was prejudiced by the contractor's failure to provide the required notice and may not require strict compliance if the government was aware the contractor considered the change to be extra work.

On private construction, courts are more likely to allow the contractor to recover costs without providing the required notice when the work was ordered by the owner as opposed to the A/E, or the owner verbally agreed to additional compensation for the work. In addition, if the owner repeatedly allowed the contractor to bill for change orders without providing the required notice, the owner may be held to have waived strict compliance with the notice requirements.

14.3.4 Extra Work versus Additional Work

Although the terms *extra work* and *additional work* are often used interchangeably on construction projects, contractors sometimes make a distinction to avoid the notice requirements for a constructive change. If the contract requires written notice for extra work, the contractor may characterize the work as additional work so that it would be entitled to a contract adjustment, despite not having given the required notice.

Under this argument, *extra work* is defined as work that is not required at all by the contract, whereas *additional work* is work that is not precisely required but is a necessary extension of work that is required. Some courts have allowed the contractor to recover for additional work even though it did not comply with the notice requirements. The justification is that because the additional work was necessary, the owner was not prejudiced by the lack of notice.

14.4 FEDERAL GOVERNMENT CONTRACTS

Contracts for private construction typically define a change order as a document that memorializes the parties' agreement as to the scope of the changed work and the corresponding adjustments to the contract price and the schedule. In contrast, on federal government projects, a change order is a unilateral directive from the government that requires the contractor to do work that is different from what is required by the contract. Change orders are authorized by §52.243-49 of the Federal Acquisition Regulation (FAR). Per FAR §52.243-49(a):

The Contracting Officer may, at any time, without notice to the sureties, if any, by written order designated or indicated to be a change order, make changes in the work within the general scope of the contract, including changes—
  1. In the specifications (including drawings and designs);
  2. In the method or manner of performance of the work;
  3. In the Government-furnished facilities, equipment, materials, services, or site;
  4. Directing acceleration in the performance of the work.

14.4.1 Equitable Adjustments

Under §52.243-49(b) of the FAR, the contractor may assert a constructive change by stating that an order from the contracting officer should be treated as a change order even though it was not designated as such. The contractor must give the contracting officer written notice that the order is regarded as a constructive change within 20 days of performing the work.

When a change order causes an increase or decrease in the cost or the time required for the work, the contracting officer must make an equitable adjustment and modify the contract in writing. If the contractor intends to request an adjustment to the contract price or time because of a change order, it must submit a written statement with a proposed amount for the adjustment. The statement must be submitted within 30 days of receiving a change order or furnishing notice of a constructive change. Although the amount of the adjustment can be determined after the work is done, the preferred method is to determine the adjustment before the work begins. The adjustment will be based on the amount proposed by the contractor, along with any backup documentation, such as subcontractor or supplier pricing.

When the adjustment is determined after the work is performed, the contractor is sometimes required to submit a record of its actual costs. The measure for determining the amount of an equitable adjustment is the reasonable cost of the work, however; there is no presumption that the contractor's actual costs are reasonable.

14.4.2 Escrow of Bid Documents

On some projects, the contractor is required to provide the owner with a set of its bid documents to be held in escrow. When determining an equitable adjustment for a change order, the owner can then refer to the takeoffs, quotes, and other information that the contractor used to calculate its bid price. Escrowing bid documents tends to be unpopular with contractors, who fear it may give competitors access to their cost and bidding data. Nevertheless, it is required by a number of government agencies, particularly on transportation projects. Usually, contractors are not required to provide their bid documents until after the bid opening. Often only the apparent low bidder is required to provide its bid documents. Some agencies make escrowing bid documents optional; others require it only on projects that exceed a certain cost threshold.

14.5   AUTHORITY TO ISSUE CHANGES

The dispute over an alleged constructive change often centers on whether the individual issuing the change directive had the authority to do so. On federal government contracts, only the contracting officer or the officer's authorized representative has the right to order changes in the work. Most state and local government contracts are similarly structured.

In most cases, the contractor on a government project is not receiving its direction from the contracting officer but is dealing with a project representative, such as the contracting officer's technical representative (COTR) or a project engineer. The contracting officer necessarily delegates certain responsibilities and authority to the project representative, who acts as an agent for the owner. In addition to the authority that is explicitly delegated, the representative has implied authority. For example, if the representative has been delegated the authority for materials testing, it would have the implied authority to reject defective materials. The contractor can rely on the project representative's express and implied authority to make decisions.

14.5.1   Apparent Authority and Ratification

Contracts for private construction typically require the owner to designate a representative. On private construction, the contractor can rely on the representative's apparent authority as well as its express and implied authority. Apparent authority exists when the owner has acted in such a way that a third party reasonably believes that the owner has authorized the representative to take the action in question.

The federal government does not allow contractors to rely on apparent authority, however. On a federal project, the agent must have actual (express or implied) authority for its actions. This principle was articulated in *Federal Crop Ins. Corp. v. Merrill*,[1] where the Supreme Court held that the contractor must verify that the government agent issuing an order has the authority to do so. The contractor cannot rely on an agent's claim of authority, even when the agent

---

[1] *Federal Crop Ins. Corp v. Merrill*, 332 U.S. 380 (1947).

honestly believes it has such authority. The underlying principle for this requirement is that public funds must be protected against unauthorized expenditures.
Most states have a similar requirement for state and local government projects.
A contractor that relies on an agent's apparent authority to request extra work
on a government project is generally not entitled to an adjustment for the work.

However, the contractor may be entitled to compensation if the government
ratifies an unauthorized directive to perform extra work. As long as the government received the benefit of the directive's performance, the government will be
deemed to have ratified the directive if the contracting officer knew of the directive and did not stop the work. Ratification is valid even when the contractor
knew that the person who issued the directive had no authority to do so. In federal contracting, the principle of ratification is codified at §1.602-3 of the FAR.

14.6   DUTY TO PERFORM THE CHANGED WORK

Under both FAR §52.243-4 and the provisions in the industry standard contracts for a change directive, when the owner requests a change, the contractor
has a duty to perform the work without knowing how much, or even whether,
it will be compensated. Contract clauses that require the contractor to continue
work in the face of a pricing dispute are generally enforceable, and a contractor that suspends work pending resolution of the dispute could be terminated.
Because disputes over change orders can take years to resolve, most contracts
have an interim payment clause. An interim payment clause allows the contractor to request payment for the work before the final determination of the cost;
the A/E typically certifies payment for the amount that it determines to be reasonably justified.

An owner's right to require a contractor to perform extra or changed work is
not without limits. If a directive is so absurd or the consequences of compliance
so damaging as to cause an unconscionable result, the contractor may be justified in refusing to carry out the directive. Rather than risk termination by refusing to perform the work, the contractor may file suit for a declaratory judgment
stating that the work is not within the scope of its contract. If the court finds
that the work is not within the scope of the contract, the contractor cannot be
terminated for refusing to comply with the directive.

14.7   RESERVATION OF RIGHTS

Even if the owner and contractor agree to the terms of a change order, the
potential for a dispute remains, particularly when the scope of the change is not
well defined. As an example, when an addition to an existing structure includes
an ADA (Americans with Disabilities Act) ramp, a change to the dimensions

of the addition may require modifications to the ADA ramp to maintain the required slope. The owner may believe that the change order covered all required work, including the ADA ramp. The contractor, on the other hand, may believe that the agreed-upon price for the change order covered only the changes to the addition itself.

A change may also impact other aspects of the project, with a resulting increase in costs. At the time the change order is signed, it may be impossible for the contractor to determine the extent of these additional costs or even to know they will arise. Similarly, the change may impact the schedule in ways that were not foreseeable at the time the change order was signed. The contractor may believe that the change order only covered the cost of performing the extra work, not the indirect costs associated with subsequent delays.

To prevent claims for additional compensation, owners often include a provision in the change order agreement stating that the agreed-upon sum constitutes payment for all costs directly or indirectly attributable to the change. This is sometimes referred to as an *accord and satisfaction*, since it is intended to be a satisfaction of a potentially disputed amount. Typical wording is:

The change order sum constitutes an accord and satisfaction and represents payment in full for any and all costs, impact effects, and/or delays arising out of or incidental to the work.

CASE STUDY—ACCORD AND SATISFACTION FOR A CHANGE ORDER

The bid documents for construction of underground storage facilities at several air force bases contained errors and ambiguities that caused delays and cost overruns. After lengthy negotiations, the parties agreed to a change order that increased the contract sum by $535,000. The change order included a release of all claims related to the errors and ambiguities.

The contractor subsequently submitted a request for an equitable adjustment of $4,707,922 for extra costs due to the delays, saying the change order just addressed the additional construction costs. The court denied the request, holding that the change order contained all the elements of an accord and satisfaction between the parties. The language of the release clearly stated the parties' intent to discharge all claims through payment of the $535,000. The payment, although different from what the contractor subsequently claimed was due, thus constituted full satisfaction of the contractor's claims.

Bechtel National, Inc., v. Roche,
65 Fed.Appx. 277 (Fed. Cir. 2003)

Alternatively, a change order may bar further claims on the basis of a release that waives all claims, known or unknown.

Contractors that are concerned about waiving claims for delays caused by changes to the work typically require that change orders include a reservation of rights. The reservation of rights can simply state that the contractor reserves all rights against the owner for costs incurred due to any delays arising from the change order. Courts have upheld the contractor's right to assert an additional claim relating to a change order when the change order included a reservation of rights.

14.8   CHANGES CLAUSES IN SUBCONTRACTS

On most projects, much of the work is actually done by subcontractors. Thus, it is likely to be the subcontractors that are most impacted by changes to the work. Since the changes clause in a subcontract usually mirrors the changes clause in the prime contract, the subcontractor has a duty to perform the work required in a change directive.

In addition, the subcontractor has a duty to perform work it considers to be a constructive change. The subcontractor typically recovers its additional costs from the general contractor, which would be required bring a claim against the owner. The subcontractor's rights to recovery may be affected by the wording of a pay-if-paid or pay-when-paid clause in its subcontract.

14.9   DOCUMENTATION OF COSTS

Some contracts require the contractor to submit daily or weekly time and materials records when performing work it claims is a constructive change, or when performing acknowledged extra work if an agreement on price was not reached in advance. If the contractor fails to comply with this requirement, it may waive its right to compensation for the work.

Even if such records are not required, the contractor should keep a record of its costs. If there is a dispute over the pricing of the work, courts will look with disfavor on a contractor that relies on its estimates rather than the actual costs, particularly when it would have been easy to track the actual costs. On a government contract, the equitable adjustment for a change order is based on the contractor's reasonable costs. While there is no presumption that the contractor's actual costs are reasonable, they can serve as a basis for the claim. When the change order is being done as time and materials, but the contract itself is fixed price, the owner may require documentation showing that costs charged to the change order were actually attributable to the changed work rather than to the work of the original contract.

14.10   CARDINAL CHANGES

A *cardinal change* is a change to the work that goes so far beyond the scope of the original contract that the project has become a materially different undertaking. The owner's imposition of a cardinal change on the contractor amounts to a breach of contract. A cardinal change can result from one isolated but extremely significant change, or from a series of changes, related or unrelated. There is no formula for determining when a change or series of changes must be considered beyond the scope of the contract; it depends on the circumstances. While the number of changes may be grounds for invoking a cardinal change, the cumulative impact of the changes is more significant. The critical factor is whether the change or changes radically alter the nature of the contract, whether by the character or quantity of the work, the method of performance, or the cost.

The doctrine of cardinal change originated in federal government contracting; even now cardinal change claims arise most often on federal government projects. In most cases, the claim is not brought by the contractor doing the work, but by another contractor that wants an opportunity to bid on the new work. When the change requested by the government amounts to a cardinal change, the government is required to rebid the work, thus allowing other contractors to compete.

The doctrine is also recognized by a number of states, but the states vary as to whether it is recognized for public construction, private construction, or both. In private construction, only the contractor doing the work would have the right to assert that there had been a cardinal change to the project—procurement regulations meant to ensure that all bidders have an equal opportunity to compete for work do not apply to private construction. A contractor is most likely to bring a claim of cardinal change when it has underbid the work that is being increased and the change will cause it to incur a loss on the project. Some states do not use the term cardinal change, but instead refer to a significant change as an abandonment of the project.

14.10.1   The Contractor's Options

A contractor who believes that work requested under a change order constitutes a cardinal change can refuse to perform the work and treat the contract as terminated. However, contractors are unlikely to do so, except in very extreme cases. If a court ultimately rules that it was not a cardinal change and the termination was unjustified, the contractor will be held in default of its contract. The consequences of such a determination would likely be so severe that it is seldom worth the risk. Instead, the contractor may file suit for a declaratory judgment that absolves it of the requirement to proceed with the work.

Alternatively, the contractor can proceed with the work and sue under a theory of *quantum meruit*, on the basis that the work is not part of the contract. Under *quantum meruit*, the contractor is compensated according to what it deserves for the work, rather than the contract terms. If the contractor underbid the work, it may be able to recover more under *quantum meruit* than it would under the contract.

15

DIFFERING SITE CONDITIONS

Differing site conditions are unforeseen physical conditions at the project site that are not discovered until after the contract has been executed. The most common source of differing site conditions claims are subsurface soil conditions. Claims can be based on misclassification of the soils at the site, discrepancies in the reported depth to bedrock, or buried debris. Other common sources of claims are discrepancies in the reported depth to groundwater and the locations of utilities. Differing site conditions are not strictly limited to conditions at the project site; off-site borrow pits and access roads are usually covered as well.

Differing site conditions can also arise when existing buildings are being renovated or demolished. Conditions can include the unforeseen presence of hazardous materials and unexpected structural conditions that make it impossible for the work to be completed as planned.

15.1 THE PURPOSE OF THE DIFFERING SITE CONDITIONS CLAUSE

When a construction contract is for a fixed price, the contractor bears the risk that the cost of performing the work will be higher than anticipated. Historically, fixed-price contracts were rigidly adhered to, even when unanticipated site conditions materially changed the cost of the work. The Supreme Court stated this position in the 1918 case *Spearin v. United States*:

Where one agrees to do, for a fixed sum, a thing possible to be performed, he will not be excused or become entitled to additional compensation because unforeseen difficulties are encountered.

Although courts acknowledged that the contractor could suffer considerable losses with this approach, they generally held that if the contract did not allocate the risk of unanticipated conditions, the contractor should be the one to bear the expense. Contractors thus added contingencies to their bids to cover the risk that they were forced to assume. Because contractors were often bidding on a worst-case scenario, the owner would significantly overpay for the work if no unanticipated site conditions materialized.

To avoid this situation, the federal government began adding a Changed Conditions Clause to construction contracts in the 1920s. The clause is now called the Differing Site Conditions clause, but its purpose is still the same—to shift the risk of unknown physical conditions to the government so that the contractor does not have to inflate its bid. Federal procurement regulations require the government to include a Differing Site Conditions clause in any fixed-price contract that exceeds the simplified acquisition threshold.

In addition to eliminating the need for contingencies in the bid, a Differing Site Conditions clause reduces the risk that the owner will be held liable in breach of contract for describing the site conditions incorrectly. The damages that an owner would be liable for in breach of contract are likely to be much greater than the adjustment the contractor is entitled to under the Differing Site Conditions clause. All of the industry standard form contracts have Differing Site Conditions clauses.

15.2 DIFFERING SITE CONDITIONS CLAIMS

Most Differing Site Conditions clauses include two kinds of conditions that entitle the Contractor to an adjustment of the contract sum. These are referred to as *Type I conditions* and *Type II conditions*.

15.2.1 Type I—Conditions Materially Different Than Indicated

A Type I condition is a subsurface or concealed physical condition that differs materially from what is indicated in the contract documents. To establish entitlement to an adjustment, the contractor must prove that the conditions encountered during performance were materially different from those indicated in the contract documents. The contractor cannot claim a Type I differing site condition adjustment unless the contract documents make a specific representation as to the conditions that will be encountered. In addition, the contractor must have relied on the information in the documents, and its reliance must have been reasonable. If the contractor knew or should have known of the actual conditions prior to bidding, it is not entitled to a differing site conditions adjustment, regardless of what was in the contract documents.

Typically, the owner is not liable if the documents indicate that a condition may exist and require the contractor to investigate and determine the extent of the condition. However, the contractor may be entitled to an adjustment if the documents were ambiguous and the contractor's interpretation was reasonable. The representations in the contract documents do not have to be explicit, but they must provide sufficient grounds to justify the contractor's expectation of conditions materially different from those actually encountered. The contractor must consider all of the information provided to it; the owner will not be liable if the contractor decided to ignore certain information. Likewise, the owner will not be liable if the contractor made incorrect inferences from the information that was supplied.

CASE STUDY—DIFFERING SITE CONDITIONS

A subcontractor encountered wet soil while drilling caissons for the foundation of a new jail. The Differing Site Conditions clause in the subcontract allowed for a price adjustment if the subcontractor encountered conditions either at variance with those indicated in the subcontract or at variance with those ordinarily encountered. A soil report accompanying the bid documents indicated that the soil was dry, but the bidding instructions stated that this soil report was for information only and was not part of the contract documents. The subcontract further disclaimed all responsibility for the accuracy of the soils investigation.

The court held that the subcontractor was not entitled to a price adjustment. Although the conditions encountered were different from those identified in the soils report, the soils report was not part of the subcontract. Thus, the requirements for a differing site conditions adjustment were not met.

Millgard Corp. v. McKee/Mays,
49 F.3d 1070 (5th Cir. 1995)

15.2.2 Type II—Conditions of an Unusual Nature

A Type II condition is not based on the owner's representations; instead, it is a physical condition that differs materially from conditions normally encountered in the type of work being done. Under a claim for a Type II condition, the contractor must prove that the condition encountered was unknown, unanticipated, and unusual; that it varied from what would be expected in similar work in the area; and that neither a site visit nor the general knowledge of the contractor would have revealed it.

Claims for a Type II condition are rare, as it is difficult for the contractor to prove that a condition is so unusual that it could not have been anticipated. For example, even if drawings for a 1960s-era building did not show the presence of asbestos pipe insulation, it would probably not be considered an unusual condition, because asbestos was commonly used as insulation at that time. Similarly, a contractor dredging in a military zone would probably not be entitled to an adjustment for damage sustained after hitting unexploded ordnance, as it would not be considered unusual to encounter dangerous debris in a military zone. The contractor cannot rely on its own ignorance or inexperience to recover for a Type II differing site condition; it is presumed to possess the knowledge of an experienced, prudent contractor familiar with work of that type and in that geographic area.

Some Differing Site Condition clauses include only a Type I condition. Under these contracts, Type II conditions are the contractor's risk.

CASE STUDY—DIFFERING SITE CONDITIONS

A contractor contracted to perform excavation work for a highway authority. Elevations shown on the contract drawings were incorrect, causing the contractor to do more work than anticipated. The contractor filed a claim for this extra work, alleging that the incorrect elevations breached the owner's implied warranty of the accuracy of the plans. The court allowed the claim, holding that the elevations were positive assertions that purported to describe the land. Contractors may recover additional costs if unintentionally false statements in the contract drawings appear as positive assertions and not simply as estimates.

The contractor also filed a claim for the cost of removing wet materials not shown on the plans. The court dismissed this claim, however. The plans contained no statements as to whether such material would be encountered, and the specifications specifically disclaimed any information concerning subsurface conditions.

Golomore Associates v. New Jersey State Highway Authority,
413 A.2d 361 (N.J. App. 1980)

15.3 LIMITATIONS ON CLAIMS FOR DIFFERING SITE CONDITIONS

The Differing Site Conditions clause does not shift the risk to the owner anytime an unanticipated adverse site condition is encountered. The clause only applies to conditions that existed when the contract was executed; it does not apply to conditions that developed afterward. In addition, the unanticipated condition must be a physical condition. So-called Acts of God and impediments such as strikes or denial of access to the site by a third party are not covered.

Furthermore, it is not enough for the contractor to show that its costs were higher than expected; it must prove that the cost increase was a direct result of the unanticipated site conditions. It must also prove that the conditions encountered were reasonably unforeseeable based on all the information available to it at the time of bidding.

15.3.1 Duty to Make a Site Inspection/Duty to Investigate

Contracts typically require bidders to inspect the job site before submitting a bid and state that the contractor is responsible for any conditions observed in the field. For example, AIA A201 §3.2.1 states:

Execution of the Contract by the Contractor is a representation that the Contractor has visited the site, become generally familiar with local conditions under which the work is to be performed and correlated personal observations with the requirements of the Contract Documents.

On federal government projects, §52.236-3 of the Federal Acquisition Regulation requires the contractor to warrant that it has reviewed all subsurface exploratory work performed by the government, as well as all plans and specifications.

When a site visit is required, the contractor will be held responsible for knowing about any patent (obvious) site conditions, and is expected to possess the judgment of an experienced contractor when interpreting these conditions. Absent a specific requirement in the bid documents, however, the contractor is not expected to conduct an independent technical investigation or hire expert assistance to interpret the site conditions. In addition, while contractors have a duty to review information that is explicitly mentioned in the contract documents and made available for inspection, they have no duty to review documents that are not mentioned.

Even if the contractor is not explicitly required to perform a site inspection before submitting its bid, it has an implied duty to do so if conditions at the site will affect the cost of the work. Often, the bid advertisement will state that bidders should inspect the site and satisfy themselves as to all general and local conditions that may affect the cost of the work to the extent such information is reasonably obtainable. The advertisement may also state that failure to inspect the site, or failure to observe or appreciate the significance of an obvious condition, does not constitute either grounds for withdrawal of a bid after the bid opening or grounds for a claim after the contract is awarded.

On most projects, prospective bidders are required to attend a prebid conference. Even if the prebid conference is not mandatory, bidders are usually held responsible for any information conveyed at the conference, whether or not they attended.

15.3.2 Disclaimers

Because the owner typically does a site investigation while preparing the design documents, the owner's understanding of conditions at the site is generally better than the contractor's. Thus, it makes sense to allocate the risk of unforeseen conditions to the owner. However, even when there is a Differing Site Conditions clause, the owner may want to shift the risk of certain conditions to the contractor.

To shift specific risks to the contractor, the contract must disclaim the conditions at issue. Disclaimers will typically state that the information provided in the bid documents may not accurately reflect actual conditions and is provided as general guidance rather than as a representation of fact. It will disclaim the owner's responsibility for any conditions encountered and state that the contractor is solely responsible for determining the actual conditions. It may also explicitly state that the contractor is not entitled to any additional compensation as a result of the conditions encountered.

In public contracting, use of such disclaimers may be limited by procurement regulations. However, even in public contracting, disclaimers can be used to highlight a lack of information or indicate information that was intentionally not included in the bid documents because it could not be verified. Disclaimers can also be used to indicate that certain information was included even though it could not be verified. When information has been identified as unreliable, it would be unreasonable for the contractor to rely on it.

Private owners are free to include broad disclaimers stating that bidders cannot rely on the information in the bid documents and must do their own investigation before submitting their bids. Although such disclaimers are generally enforceable, courts have recognized exceptions. The most common exception

CASE STUDY—DISCLAIMER OF IMPLIED WARRANTY

An owner solicited bids for a project that included extensive excavation work. The owner provided bidders with plans and specifications for the project, as well as the soil borings and analyses that the plans were based on. It also provided bidders with the opportunity to conduct further tests. Soils at certain areas were different from those shown on the plans, requiring the contractor to use a more costly excavation method and excavate more material than it had anticipated. The contractor filed a claim alleging that the owner breached its implied warranty that the plans would be adequate to determine the quantities of material to be removed.

The court dismissed the claim, however. The contract stated that bidders had to determine the quantities of work that would be required and the conditions under which it would be performed and assumed all risks as to any variations in the quantities. It further stated that bidders would not be allowed to dispute the approximate quantities. Given these explicit disclaimers, the contractor's reliance on the plans was unreasonable.

Brant Const. v. Metro. Water Reclamation Dist.,
967 F.2d 244 (7th Cir. 1992)

is when the owner intentionally withheld relevant information. For example, if the owner knew that the site contained a significant amount of buried debris and failed to disclose that information, it would generally be liable for a differing site condition, despite a disclaimer. Likewise, the owner would generally be held liable if it did not indicate that a building contained asbestos and did not allow bidders access to areas it knew contained asbestos. The owner might also be liable for a differing site condition if it did not give bidders enough time to investigate the site conditions.

15.3.3 Notice

Differing Site Conditions clauses typically require the contractor to leave the condition undisturbed and inform the owner. AIA A201 requires the owner to be given notice within 21 days of the first observance of the condition; federal procurement regulations require "prompt" notice. Notice allows the owner to investigate the condition and evaluate how the contractor should proceed before any additional costs are incurred. Depending on the circumstances, the owner may decide to redesign or delete part of the project, or may ask the contractor to submit a proposal for dealing with the problem.

A contractor that fails to provide adequate notice will generally not be barred from recovering its costs unless the owner was prejudiced by the lack of notice. In addition, the notice requirement is typically waived if the owner knew or should have known of the condition. The requirement that the condition be left undisturbed will be waived if doing so would risk injury or property damage.

15.3.4 Waiver of Claims

Most Differing Site Conditions clauses state that the contractor cannot assert a claim for a differing site condition after it has accepted final payment. Even without such language, the contractor will typically be held to have waived its right to a claim unless it asserted the claim before final payment and expressly reserved the claim when accepting final payment.

If the contractor agrees to a change order for a differing site condition, the change order may state that the agreed-upon increase to the contract price is the total compensation for the changed work and that the contractor will not assert any other claims for the matter. If the contractor anticipates that the differing site condition will impact later work, it should expressly reserve the right to assert claims related to the differing site condition.

15.4 VARIATIONS IN ESTIMATED QUANTITIES CLAUSE

Contracts for projects that include unit-price work often have a Variation in Estimated Quantities (VEQ) clause that provides for an adjustment to the contractor's unit price if the actual quantities are significantly different from estimated quantities. A VEQ clause is thus similar to a Differing Site Conditions clause in that it allows a change in the price of the work due to unforeseen site conditions. A Differing Site Conditions clause only allows the contractor to claim for an increase in costs, however; a VEQ clause typically also allows for a reduction in the unit price. Most VEQ clauses require the change in costs to be on the order of 15 or 20 percent before an adjustment is required. A Differing Site Conditions clause typically does not require a minimum adjustment.

15.5 GEOTECHNICAL BASELINE SUMMARY REPORT

By their nature, subsurface conditions cannot be completely known at the time a project is planned, designed, and priced. To ensure that bidders are bidding on the same set of assumptions, the owner will sometime have the geotechnical engineer prepare a baseline summary report that summarizes the conditions that the foundation design was based on. The report is then included in the bid package; when differing site conditions are encountered during construction, the report can be used to help determine whether an adjustment to the contract price is necessary and, if so, how it should be priced.

15.6 HAZARDOUS MATERIALS

Although hazardous materials generally constitute a differing site condition, a contractor encountering unanticipated hazardous materials should first look to any contract provisions that specifically address such materials. AIA A201 deals with hazardous materials, including asbestos and polychlorinated biphenyl (PCB), in §10.3. Per §10.3, if hazardous materials are discovered, the contractor is required to stop work and report the discovery to the owner. The owner must then engage a licensed laboratory to identify the substance and render it harmless. The owner must also extend the contract performance time and allow the contractor reasonable costs for the shutdown and delay.

15.7 TORT AND BREACH-OF-CONTRACT ACTIONS

It should be noted that there is no implied right to an adjustment for a differing site condition. If a fixed-price contract does not have a Differing Site Conditions clause, the contractor must complete the work in accordance with the contract documents and at the contract price, regardless of the physical conditions encountered at the site. A contractor that enters into a fixed-price contract without a Differing Site Conditions clause thus assumes the risk that its cost of performance may be substantially higher than anticipated. However, the contractor may be entitled to an adjustment in the contract price if the owner misrepresented conditions at the site, the plans and specifications were defective in that they should have accounted for the conditions, or the owner failed to disclose its knowledge of hidden conditions. The contractor may also be entitled to an adjustment if there was a mutual mistake.

15.7.1 Misrepresentation (Intentional or Negligent)

If the owner makes either an intentional or an unintentional (negligent) misrepresentation as to the existing conditions at the site, a contractor that relies on the owner's misrepresentation may be entitled to sue for its damages under tort law. Claims of negligent misrepresentation may be barred by the state's interpretation of the economic loss doctrine, however. Under the economic loss doctrine, many states hold that if there is a contract between the parties, disputes cannot be brought as tort claims but must be settled under the terms of the contract.

The economic loss doctrine does not bar claims of intentional misrepresentation (fraud), but intentional misrepresentation is difficult to prove. The contractor must show that the owner made the representation with the knowledge that it was false or with reckless disregard for whether it was true or false. In addition, the contractor must show that the owner made the representation with the intention of misleading the contractor.

15.7.2 Owner's Breach of Implied Warranty of Plans and Specs

Under the Spearin doctrine, an owner that furnishes plans and specifications to the contractor provides the contractor with an implied warranty against the consequences of any defect in the plans and specifications. The owner does not need to have known the plans or specifications were defective; mere negligence in providing defective plans is enough to find a breach of this implied warranty. The implied warranty extends to maps or plans that show anticipated site conditions; thus, plans that fail to accurately depict site conditions may be considered defective. The implied warranty also extends to specifications that incorrectly indicate specific means or methods as being suitable or required for performing the work.

The implied warranty only applies to affirmative representations, however. There is no implied warranty that the information completely and accurately describes the existing conditions. For example, borings and soil tests are necessarily done at discrete locations throughout the project site. While the owner warrants that the information from these tests is accurate, it does not warrant that the tests identify all of the relevant soils on the site. Nor does it warrant that the soil conditions between borings are the same as those at the borings.

15.7.3 Failure to Disclose Superior Knowledge

Often, the information supplied to bidders is accurate but provides the bidders with an incomplete or inaccurate picture of the site. The contractor may have a claim against the owner if the owner failed to disclose its superior knowledge of a hidden condition that significantly affected the cost of the contractor's performance. Claims of superior knowledge are typically only recognized in public contracting, however, and are hard to prove. Often, a contractor claiming that the government failed to disclose superior knowledge cannot point to any specific representation as being responsible for its increased costs. Courts are generally reluctant to find an owner liable for the contractor's decisions unless the decisions were based on the owner's affirmative representations.

To recover under a superior knowledge claim, the contractor must show that the government possessed information that materially affected the contractor's costs, and that the contractor lacked that knowledge, had no reason to be on notice of it, and was not responsible for discovering it. In addition, the contractor must show that the government either knew or should have known that the contractor was ignorant of the relevant information. The contractor does not have to prove that the failure to disclose the information was intentional, however; even an inadvertent failure to disclose information can be sufficient for a claim if the required elements are met.

15.7.4 Mutual Mistake

When site conditions are other than what was anticipated, the contractor may be entitled to rescind (void) or reform (alter) the contract based on a theory of mutual mistake. Mutual mistake applies if both parties were under the same misunderstanding about an essential fact at the time of contracting, such that the contract does not represent the actual agreement between the parties.

A party's negligence in discovering the facts that resulted in the mutual mistake does not necessarily preclude the rescission or reformation of the contract. However, mutual mistake is generally not a successful claim. It is typically difficult for either party to prove that the mistake was not a unilateral mistake on its part, and courts do not allow a contract to be rescinded or reformed simply because one of the parties made a mistake.

16

TERMINATION OF
THE CONSTRUCTION
CONTRACT

Because a contract is a voluntary agreement between the parties, the parties can mutually agree to terminate it. In legal terms, this is referred to as a *rescission*. The requirements to rescind a contract are the same as the requirements to enter into a contract. The parties must mutually assent, there must be a meeting of the minds, and each party must provide consideration. However, a party's consideration is often just the release of the other party's obligations under the contract.

In many cases, the consideration provided is not equal. For example, the contractor may have started work but will agree to rescind the contract even though the owner has not yet paid for the work. Courts typically do not look to whether the consideration for an agreement is sufficient or reasonable. They will enforce a mutual agreement to rescind a contract unless one of the parties shows it acted under duress or was fraudulently induced to agree to the rescission.

16.1 UNILATERAL TERMINATION

Although contractual rescissions are possible, they are rare; in most cases, termination is a unilateral decision by one of the parties. Construction contracts typically allow either party to unilaterally terminate "for cause" if the other party has materially breached the contract. In addition, many contracts allow the owner to terminate for convenience (without cause). Nevertheless, a termination can be costly for both parties and, as a result, is likely to give rise to legal disputes. To minimize such disputes, both the grounds for termination and the procedure to follow in the event of a termination should be clearly stated in the contract.

16.2   CONTRACTUAL TERMINATION PROVISIONS

If a contract is unilaterally terminated for cause, the terminating party has the burden of proving that the termination was justified. Termination for cause requires a material breach of contract; a breach is material when it is reasonable for the nonbreaching party to infer that the party committing the breach is either unwilling or unable to meet its contractual obligations.

Once a party has materially breached a contract, the other party is excused from its duties under the contract and may terminate the contract. However, the terminating party must strictly follow the termination procedures stated in the contract, as failure to do so may amount to a wrongful termination.

16.3   TERMINATION BY THE CONTRACTOR FOR CAUSE

The requirements for termination by the contractor in AIA A201 are typical of those found in many construction contracts. Section 14.1 of A201 provides that the contractor may terminate the contract if the work is stopped for 30 consecutive days for one or more of the following reasons:

- A court order or act of government requires all work be stopped.
- The architect has not issued a certificate for payment and has not told the contractor why it is withholding the certificate.
- The owner has not made payment on a certificate for payment within the time stated in the contract documents.
- The owner has not furnished evidence of financing.

In addition, the contractor may terminate the contract if the owner suspends or delays the work for more than the total number of days scheduled for completion, or for more than 120 days in any 365-day period, or if the work is stopped for 60 consecutive days because the owner has failed to comply with its contractual obligations. In each case, the work must have been stopped through no fault of the contractor or any entity performing work for the contractor. The contractor must give seven days' written notice to the owner and the architect. After the seven-day notice period, the contractor may terminate the contract and recover payment for the work it has done, including reasonable overhead and profit, as well as the costs of the termination, and damages.

The AIA provision limits the contractor's right to terminate to the specific reasons provided, which, from an owner's perspective, can be beneficial. In addition, if the contractor is even partially at fault for the delays or the owner's failure to fulfill its obligations, the contractor does not have the right to terminate.

16.4 TERMINATION BY THE OWNER FOR CAUSE

The AIA provisions for termination by the owner for cause are broader than the provisions for termination by the contractor. Under §14.2 of AIA A201, the owner may terminate the contract for any of the following reasons:

- The contractor repeatedly fails to supply enough properly skilled workers or proper materials.
- The contractor fails to make payments to subcontractors for materials or labor in accordance with its agreements with the subcontractors.
- The contractor repeatedly disregards applicable laws, ordinances, codes, rules, and regulations.
- The contractor is otherwise guilty of a substantial breach of the contract documents.

However, the owner cannot terminate the contractor for cause until the initial decision maker certifies that the termination is justified. Once the contractor is terminated, the owner is allowed to take immediate action to mitigate its damages. Subject to the rights of the surety, the owner may exclude the contractor from the site and take possession of any construction equipment, tools, or materials that are still on-site. Section 5.4 of A201 grants the owner an assignment of the contractor's subcontracts; this means the owner can decide which, if any, of the subcontractors it wants to retain.

Unless the termination is deemed wrongful, the contractor loses its entitlement to payment until the work is finished. The owner may finish the work by whatever reasonable method it deems expedient, without regard to whether it is the cheapest or best method, and the owner can deduct all reasonable expenses from the balance of the contract funds. Although the contractor is entitled to any funds that remain once construction is complete, the cost to complete the project with another contractor will almost always be greater than the balance remaining on the contract, in which case the contractor is liable for the difference. The A/E must certify the amounts due to either the owner or the contractor at the end of construction. In addition, the owner must give the contractor a detailed accounting of the costs incurred to finish the work upon request.

Termination does not prejudice or waive the owner's other rights or remedies under the construction contract. Thus, the owner may also institute an action for damages caused by the contractor's default, if this is allowed by the contract.

16.4.1 Notice and Opportunity to Cure

AIA A201 requires the owner to provide seven days' written notice of the termination to the contractor and its surety. Often, this is enough time for the contractor to remedy the identified problems and thus avoid termination.

If the notice period specified in a contract is clearly too short to allow the contractor to cure the default, courts may interpret the notice of termination as simply giving the contractor an opportunity to mitigate its damages by laying off employees, removing equipment from the premises, and canceling orders. Nevertheless, courts generally disfavor any kind of forfeiture and tend to interpret a notice of termination as giving the contractor an opportunity to either remedy the problems or provide adequate assurances that they will be remedied within a reasonable time. If the parties negotiate a remedy to avoid termination, the owner may require reasonable assurances that the problems will not occur again.

If the contract does not specify a notice period, courts will generally find that one is required and that it gives the contractor the opportunity to cure its default. A court will generally find that notice is unnecessary only when the breach is truly incurable, such as when the contract completion date has passed or the contractor has abandoned the project. When the breach is potentially curable, the owner must give notice that adequately describes the circumstances of the default. In addition, the contractor must be made aware that its failure to comply with the contract is considered serious enough that the contract will be terminated for cause unless the default is corrected. Routine correspondence and deficiency reports typically are not considered adequate notice to alert the contractor that its performance may lead to termination.

If the notice period is not intended to provide the contractor an opportunity to cure, the termination provisions should make it clear that the termination will occur at the end of the notice period, regardless of the contractor's attempt to cure or change its conduct. Likewise, if the notice period is intended solely as an opportunity for the owner to evaluate its decision to terminate, this must be clear from the contract language.

16.5 WRONGFUL TERMINATION

Once the contract has been terminated, the terminated party is excused from any further performance of its contractual obligations. In addition, it may immediately sue for damages if it believes that the termination was wrongful. Termination may be wrongful because the allegations of inadequate performance were untrue, because the inadequate performance did not rise to the level of a material breach, or because the nonbreaching party had waived (excused) compliance with the requirements at issue.

A wrongful termination is itself a material breach of contract and entitles the terminated party to expectation damages. Expectation damages attempt to place the terminated party in the position that it would have been in if the contract had been performed. Punitive damages are not awarded for wrongful termination, however; as long as a party makes good on the other party's expectation interest, it is entitled to terminate a contract if it feels that doing so is in its economic interest.

Even without punitive damages, a wrongful termination can be quite costly for the terminating party. A contractor that is wrongfully terminated is generally entitled to its termination costs, the reasonable cost of labor and materials incurred in performance of the contract, and lost profits on the entire job. The contractor is typically entitled to its lost profits even if it has not started work, particularly if it has foregone bidding on other projects. If the contract was wrongfully terminated by the contractor, the owner is entitled to the extra costs incurred in completing the project. The owner's cost to complete a project after the contract has been terminated can be considerably higher than the original contract price.

CASE STUDY—DAMAGES FOR TERMINATION

In soliciting bids for a contract to build 100 miles of pipeline, the owner stressed that construction had to be completed by April 30, 1997. Although the contractor increased its bid by approximately 10 percent because of this deadline, it was still the low bidder and was awarded the contract. The parties agreed to a 14-week schedule, but after 8 weeks, the contractor had only completed 15 miles. The owner terminated the contractor for default and completed the work with another contractor. The owner then sued the contractor for breach of contract to recover the cost of completion. The contractor countersued for breach of contract, alleging that the termination was wrongful; the contractor sought its damages and lost profits.

The Texas Supreme Court held that there was virtually no way the contractor could complete construction on time. Because time was clearly of the essence on the project, failure to complete construction by the deadline was a material breach of contract. Therefore, the termination was not wrongful and the contractor was not entitled to damages and lost profits. However, the owner failed to show that its costs to complete construction were reasonable. The court thus reversed the court of appeals award of damages to the owner.

Mustang Pipeline Co., Inc., v. Driver Pipeline Co., Inc.,
134 S.W.3d 195 (Tex. 2004)

16.6 THE ROLE OF THE PERFORMANCE BOND SURETY

If the contractor materially breaches the contract, the owner is allowed to terminate the contractor and require the surety that provided the performance bond to complete the project. To trigger the surety's obligation under the bond, the owner must provide proper notice of the contractor's default and formally terminate the contractor. If the owner fails to provide the required notice to the surety or fails to terminate the contractor properly, its rights under the performance bond may be prejudiced.

16.7 TERMINATION FOR CONVENIENCE

Construction contracts often allow owners to terminate the contract for convenience. Under a termination-for-convenience provision, the owner can terminate the contract without having a specific reason, as long as it follows the requirements of the contract. Termination-for-convenience provisions are found in many of the industry standard forms and are generally upheld in court.

Under §14.4.3 of AIA A201, a contractor that is terminated for convenience is entitled to payment for work performed, costs incurred because of the termination, and reasonable overhead and profit on the work not performed. However, the allowance for overhead and profit on work not performed is not consistent with the common-law rule governing termination for convenience, which excludes damages for lost profits; courts generally do not award lost profits unless this is specifically included in the contract. The federal procurement regulations do not allow lost profits to be awarded when government contracts are terminated for convenience.

A termination for convenience is generally easier than a termination for cause because the owner does not have to prove that the contractor has materially breached the contract. In addition, the owner does not risk a claim of wrongful termination. However, if the contractor has defaulted, the owner will not be allowed to recover its costs due to the default unless the contractor is terminated for cause. These costs, which include the difference between the cost to complete the project and the remaining contract balance, can be significant.

17

MECHANIC'S LIENS

A *lien* is an encumbrance (legal hold) that is placed on the title to a particular property as security for a debt. The most common example of a lien is a mortgage, whereby a borrower grants the lender an interest in the property as security for the amount borrowed. A *mechanic's lien* is a lien that allows the lienor (the entity filing the lien) to obtain payment for services or materials furnished to the property. In contrast to a mortgage, which is a voluntary lien, a mechanic's lien is involuntary. However, both types of liens arise out of a contract with the owner and give the lienor rights in the property that are superior to the rights of the owner.

Mechanic's liens are one of the most effective means that those supplying labor, services, or materials to a construction project can use to protect themselves against the risk of nonpayment. A mechanic's lien is considered a "cloud on the title" to the property and makes it difficult for the owner to sell the property. A perfected mechanic's lien is effective against subsequent purchasers as well as third parties (parties other than the owner) that claim a legal right to the property.

17.1 PURPOSE OF A MECHANIC'S LIEN

The primary purpose of a mechanic's lien is to ensure that payment is made for labor, materials, or services furnished to increase the value or improve the conditions of a particular property, thereby providing a benefit to the property owner. The holder of a perfected mechanic's lien can file suit to foreclose the lien and have the property sold to pay the lien. Mechanic's liens also give subcontractors and suppliers a way to let the owner know that they have not been paid for their work or materials. All 50 states and the District of Columbia have laws creating the right to file a mechanic's lien. These laws vary widely, however, both in terms of who is entitled to file a lien and the procedures required to file and foreclose on a lien. Unless the specified procedures required by state law are strictly followed, the lien may be unenforceable.

Despite the differences in the statutes, the basis for the lien is the same in all states. If the lienor is a prime contractor, it must have a contract with either the owner or a person authorized by the owner to enter into a construction contract. The work that the contractor performs, or the materials it supplies, must fall within the state's lien statute. In addition, the contractor must either satisfy all of the contract requirements or establish that the owner has waived the requirements. If the lienor is a subcontractor or supplier, it must have a valid contract with a prime contractor or another subcontractor. The lienor must also establish a valid chain of contracts between the owner and itself, must furnish lienable materials or services to the property, and must perform as required under its contract.

17.2   PROCEDURES FOR FILING A LIEN

There are two steps to creating an enforceable lien: attachment and perfection. A lien attaches (arises) automatically when materials or services are provided to improve property. However, a lien claimant cannot file suit and foreclose on a lien unless the lien is perfected. The statutory requirements for perfecting a lien vary considerably from state to state, but all states require the claimant to file a *claim of lien* that provides public notice of the lien. The claim of lien, also called a *notice* or *affidavit of lien*, must be filed with the appropriate government office, often the city or county recorder of deeds.

In addition, potential claimants that do not have contractual privity with the owner (subcontractors and suppliers) are typically required to furnish a preliminary notice of lien, also called a *notice to owner* or *notice of intent to furnish services or materials*. The notice puts the potential claimant in statutory privity with the owner. It does not create a lien or encumbrance on the property; it simply tells the owner that the potential claimant is providing services and materials to the project and allows the owner to verify that they have been paid for their work.

Statutes vary with respect to who must be served with this preliminary notice of lien, and when. In California, for example, a subcontractor must serve a notice on the owner, contractor, and lender within 20 days of first performing work. In Illinois, a subcontractor must serve a notice on the owner within 90 days of completing work. A subcontractor that has not provided notice within the required time frame generally is not allowed to file a mechanic's lien. Many states require either the owner or the prime contractor to file a notice of commencement with the appropriate government office before starting work and to post a similar notice at the job site. The notice provides subcontractors and suppliers with the information they need to file a lien, such as who holds the title to the property.

17.3   LIEN ENTITLEMENT

A mechanic's lien only attaches when the work contracted for is an "improvement" to the property. Construction is typically considered to be an improvement if it enhances the value, beauty, or utility of the property or adapts it for a new purpose. Many states explicitly define the term *improvement* in their mechanic's lien law. If improvement is not defined by statute, some courts only allow a mechanic's lien if the work resulted in a visible change; others look at whether the change is permanent, or whether the work was necessary.

17.3.1 Liens for Services

Most statutes include specific language indicating who is entitled to assert a lien. All statutes allow prime contractors, first-tier subcontractors, and their suppliers to file liens. Some statutes extend lien entitlement to second-tier subcontractors and their suppliers, but the more remote the subcontractor or supplier, the more difficult it becomes to prove entitlement. Services such as maintenance, cleaning, and ordinary repairs are typically not lienable, as they are not considered improvements. In addition, liens usually cannot be filed to recover the cost of unpaid utilities or telephone service. Statutes vary as to whether services such as equipment rental, asbestos removal, and demolition are lienable.

Many statutes specifically include design professionals in the list of those entitled to file a mechanic's lien; when statutes do not specifically list design professionals, it is not always clear whether they are covered. Surveying work, such as setting stakes and establishing monuments, is generally considered to improve the property and is thus lienable if design professionals are covered by the statute. Services such as legal work related to the construction contract or title services are typically not covered, however. Some states allow A/Es to lien for services even if the project is not built, but most states do not allow a mechanic's lien to be filed until construction actually starts.

If the statute does not specifically indicate who is entitled to file a mechanic's liens, courts may look at the language of the statute. A statute that provides rights to all those engaged in the "scheme of improvement" is likely to be interpreted more broadly than one that is limited to work that is "directly connected" to the improvement.

17.3.2 Liens for Materials

In order to file a lien on the basis of materials, the supplier may need to show that the materials were actually incorporated into the project. In many states, however, it is enough to show that the materials were delivered to the job site. The owner then has the burden of showing that the materials were not incorporated into the project and that the failure to incorporate the materials was not the owner's fault. A supplier that supplies materials to a subcontractor is generally allowed to file a lien. A supplier that supplies the materials to another supplier is typically not allowed to file a lien, however, particularly for fungible (interchangeable) materials like sheetrock or lumber, as it is generally impossible to prove the materials in question were used on a particular job.

Many states allow a supplier that has not been paid to repossess materials that have not been incorporated into the project. However, this remedy is only allowed when the project has either been completed or abandoned before completion, and repossession can be done without a breach of the peace—in other words, only if there is no opposition. The supplier waives the right to enforce its lien for the value of the repossessed materials.

Mechanic's liens cannot attach to personal property (*chattels*) unless the personal property is connected to real property (land or a building) in such a way that it has lost its character as personal property and become part of the real property. Items that are permanently connected to the real property are typically considered fixtures and are lienable. Movable items such as furniture are typically considered chattels and are not lienable, unless specifically provided for by statute. In determining whether an item is a fixture, courts consider whether the item is attached to the real property, whether the item has been adapted to fit the purpose of the real property, and whether the parties intended to make the item a permanent attachment.

17.4 ENFORCEMENT OF THE LIEN

In most states, the proceedings for the enforcement of a mechanic's lien are similar to the proceedings used to foreclose on a mortgage. Once the lien has been perfected, the lienor can file suit with the court to foreclose on the property. The property will then be sold and the proceeds disbursed according to the priority of the liens on the property.

17.4.1 Priorities

A contractor with a perfected mechanic's lien has priority over the owner's interest in the property to the extent of its lien. However, there are often a number of other liens against the property. These may include other mechanic's liens, mortgage liens, tax liens, and court (judgment) liens. In many cases, the proceeds from a foreclosure sale are not sufficient to settle all of the liens. The question of priority for payment is determined by the state's mechanic's lien statute; the entity that filed the foreclosure suit does not have any special priority with respect to payment.

Some states base priority solely on the date of filing the lien. However, most mechanic's lien statutes have adopted the concept of "relation back." *Relation back* means that the priority for a mechanic's lien is determined not by the date that the lien was filed, but by an earlier date set by the statute. This is typically the date the contract between the owner and the contractor was signed, the date that the notice of commencement was filed, or the date the contractor started work. If all of the mechanic's liens relate back to the same date, they all have equal priority, regardless of when they were filed. Although mechanic's lien claimants typically share pro rata in the proceeds of the sale of the property, some statutes provide a preference for certain classes of lienholders. For example, some statutes provide that laborers with valid mechanic's liens will be paid before suppliers.

Even if the mechanic's liens relate back to the date the contract was signed, the mortgage lien typically predates the mechanic's liens and thus has priority. When the mortgage lien has priority over a mechanic's lien, the mechanic's lien will be of no value unless the foreclosed property is sold for more than the loan amount. To avoid rendering the mechanic's lien statute useless, some statutes provide that mechanic's liens have priority in the value of the actual improvement (the construction), regardless of when the liens were filed.

Under most statutes, liens are automatically discharged unless the lienor files a foreclosure action within a specified period of time after recording the claim of lien. In addition, many statutes allow an owner to file a notice of contest of lien, which requires the lienor to institute an action to enforce the lien within a shorter period. If the lien is preventing a sale, the owner may contest the lien to get it resolved.

17.4.2 Bonding Off

Most states allow a lien to be bonded off. *Bonding off* is a process whereby a lien can be discharged by filing a bond in the amount of the lien. It is typically done by an owner who would be unable to sell the property if it were encumbered by a lien. If the lien is determined to be valid, the amount owed to the lienor is satisfied from the bond. In addition, most states allow the contractor to provide a bond that protects the owner against potential liens if a subcontractor or supplier refuses to furnish a lien waiver. An owner may require the contractor to bond off any potential liens prior to receiving final payment.

17.5 INTERESTS SUBJECT TO A LIEN

Each state's mechanic's lien statute dictates the scope of the property that is subject to a lien in that state; typically, it is the improvement, together with such land as is required for the use and occupation of the improvement. For example, if a contractor filed a lien on a house being built in a subdivision, the lien would only attach to the house and that particular lot, even if the owner owned all of the other lots in the subdivision. When a condominium unit is liened, the fraction of the common elements belonging to the unit is also subject to the lien.

Property may be subject to a lien for work completed at the request of a tenant, but only if the tenant was acting as an agent of the property owner. If the tenant was acting on its own behalf and the improvement did not benefit the property owner, the work is generally not lienable. If the lease stipulates that the tenant may deduct the expense of any improvements from its rent, the tenant is typically regarded as the property owner's agent, and the work is lienable. Similarly, if the work was done as a condition of the lease, it is generally lienable. A mechanic's lien typically does not attach to property when the entity contracting for the work simply has an easement, such as a right-of-way over the property.

17.5.1 Subcontractor and Supplier Claims

When the lienor is a subcontractor or supplier that does not have a contract with the owner, mechanic's lien statutes generally follow one of two systems. The statute creates either a dependent (derivative) claim or an independent (original) claim. Under the derivative system, also called the New York system, the subcontractor or supplier does not have a direct lien on the property—its lien is dependent on the prime contractor's lien. Recovery under a derivative mechanic's lien is limited to the amount the owner owes the prime contractor. The amount of all liens, and thus the owner's liability, is limited to the amount of the owner's contract with the prime contractor.

Statutes that create a derivative lien protect owners from having to pay a subcontractor if they have already paid the prime contractor for the subcontractor's work. However, if the owner has not complied with all statutory requirements, such as posting a notice of commencement at the job site, it is typically not protected from paying a subcontractor's lien, despite having paid the contractor for the work.

In the direct system, also called the Pennsylvania system, a subcontractor or supplier's claim is independent of the amount owed to the prime contractor. Because subcontractors and suppliers have a direct lien on the property, the owner may be subject to double liability if it has already paid the prime contractor. Although this is potentially unfair to the owner, it protects subcontractors and suppliers from collusion between the owner and the prime contractor.

17.5.2 Amount of the Lien

The lienor's contract serves as evidence of the amount recoverable under a mechanic's lien; a contractor typically cannot enforce a lien for an amount greater than its contract price. In addition, the contractor must have substantially performed its contract in order to file a mechanic's lien. If a contractor has not substantially performed, through no fault of its own, it is typically entitled to a lien for the reasonable value of the work performed and the materials furnished, irrespective of the cost to complete the work.

Many states allow the prevailing party in a mechanic's lien action to recover reasonable attorney's fees from the other party. A claimant is usually considered to be the prevailing party if judgment is granted in its favor, even if the judgment is for less than the amount claimed in the lien. A lien filed by a party that knows the lien contains false information or a lien that fails to meet the statutory requirements may be considered fraudulent. In several states, it is a statutory violation to knowingly or willfully file a fraudulent lien, and courts may award monetary damages and attorney's fees to the owner. A minor mistake or filing error or a good-faith dispute over the amount does not constitute a fraudulent lien, however.

17.6   LIEN WAIVERS

To minimize the risk of mechanic's liens, owners often require the contractor to provide a list of the subcontractors and suppliers that will be working on the project. Prior to making progress payments, the owner will require the contractor to submit a lien waiver for its own work and obtain lien waivers from its subcontractors and suppliers.

A *lien waiver*, also called a *lien release*, is a sworn statement from the contractor, a subcontractor, or a supplier that acknowledges receipt of payment and waives (releases) the right to file a claim against the property.

Waivers may be for a progress payment (a partial waiver) or for final payment (a final waiver). Partial lien waivers typically waive claims for work performed through the invoice date or up to a stated amount, with the exception of any retainage that has been withheld. Final lien waivers waive all claims. The contractor may be required to submit final lien waivers to receive its final payment, even if it was not required to submit partial lien waivers.

Lien waivers may be conditional or unconditional. An unconditional waiver waives lien rights even if payment is not received or the check does not clear. In contrast, a conditional waiver only becomes effective once payment has actually been received and has cleared the bank. Requirements for lien waivers, like the requirements for mechanic's liens, are governed by state law. Some states allow unconditional waivers for final payment but only allow conditional waivers for progress payments. Other states require unconditional waivers to include a clear warning as to the rights that the claimant is waiving. For example, Arizona requires that unconditional waivers include the following language, in type at least as large as the remainder of the document:

Notice: This document waives rights unconditionally and states that you have been paid for giving up those rights. This document is enforceable against you if you sign it, even if you have not been paid. If you have not been paid, use a conditional release form.

When specific language is required for an unconditional lien waiver, the waiver is likely to be unenforceable unless the required language was included. In states where subcontractors only have a derivative suit (the New York system), a lien waiver agreement between the contractor and the owner may affect the subcontractor's right to enforce a lien.

17.6.1 No-Lien Contracts

Contracts will sometimes include a provision stating that the contractor promises it will not assert any liens against the owner's property and will keep the property free from the liens of subcontractors and suppliers. Known as *no-lien* contracts, these contracts essentially require the contractor to waive its right to file a lien as a condition of obtaining the contract. Some states consider these contracts to be against public policy and thus unenforceable. However, even in these states, lien waivers that are submitted after the contract has been signed are generally enforceable, as long as the party waiving its right to file a lien did so knowingly.

17.7 RIGHTS OF OWNERS AND THIRD PARTIES

Mechanic's lien laws protect the owner in that they require that claims against the property be filed within a certain amount of time after the work has been completed. An owner can defend against a mechanic's lien by proving that the lienor failed to comply with the statutory time requirements or that the lien is fraudulent or otherwise invalid. Mechanic's lien laws also protect lenders and subsequent purchasers from having their interests in the property encumbered by liens that they were unaware of. A valid mechanic's lien must be recorded against the title and can be found by anyone doing a title search.

17.8 THE EFFECT OF BANKRUPTCY ON A MECHANIC'S LIEN

When the owner of a project under construction declares bankruptcy, the rights conveyed by a mechanic's lien depend on whether the lien has been perfected. There are two types of creditors under the federal Bankruptcy Code:secured and unsecured. Secured creditors are those such as mortgage holders and contractors that hold perfected liens on the property of the debtor. Unsecured creditors are those that are owed money by the debtor but do not have perfected liens against any of the debtor's property. Until an unpaid contractor perfects its mechanic's lien, it is an unsecured creditor.

 If a lien has not been perfected when the property owner files for bankruptcy, the contractor can continue to take steps to perfect it. However, a petition for bankruptcy creates an automatic stay that prevents both the filing of any new lawsuits and the continued prosecution of existing lawsuits against the bankrupt party. If the contractor is a secured creditor, it can petition the court for relief from the stay in order to foreclose on the lien. When the property is sold, the contractor's rights depend on the priority of its lien. If the proceeds of the sale exceed the total of the secured debt, the excess goes into the bankrupt estate;

if the proceeds are not enough to cover the debt, the secured creditors become unsecured creditors for the amount of any deficiency.

17.9 TRUST FUND STATUTES

In addition to allowing subcontractors and suppliers to file mechanic's liens, a number of states have trust fund statutes. Although these laws vary from state to state, they commonly provide that money paid to a prime contractor for work or materials furnished by a subcontractor or supplier is held in trust for the subcontractor or supplier. The statutes allow subcontractors and suppliers to make a direct claim on monies paid to the contractor without going through the procedure for a mechanic's lien; some also provide subcontractors and suppliers with expanded remedies such as attorney's fees and interest. Funds held in trust are typically exempt from the claims of the contractor's other creditors if the contractor files for bankruptcy. Contractors that mishandle such funds may be subject to both civil and criminal penalties.

17.10 STOP NOTICES

A few states have adopted statutes providing for so-called stop notices, sometimes called *notices to withhold*. These statutes create an equitable garnishment of the construction loan funds. They allow an unpaid party such as a subcontractor to stop (freeze) construction funds by giving a notice of claim to the entity holding these funds—typically, the owner or lender. The lender or owner must then either withhold the amount claimed from its disbursement or disburse the money directly to the claimant. Some statutes impose personal liability on the entity holding the funds if it does not comply with the requirements of the statute.

Stop notices are useful for small claims, where the time and expense required to foreclose a mechanic's lien might not be justified. Stop notices also provide additional protection to subcontractors and suppliers in states where mechanic's liens do not have priority over mortgage liens. The claimant must strictly comply with timing and service requirements in order to enforce a stop notice and receive funds, however. Some statutes also require the claimant to post a bond, in the event the claim is determined to be fraudulent.

17.11 LIENS ON PUBLIC PROPERTY

Ordinarily, government property (public property) is not subject to either the claims of private parties or forced sale. Because mechanic's liens arise under state law, they are never valid on federal property. Mechanic's liens on property owned by the state or its administrative subdivisions (cities and counties) are contrary to public policy and therefore unenforceable unless specifically provided for by state law. However, some states distinguish between public works and publicly owned property. *Public works* refers to property that is being used for the benefit of the public; *publicly owned property* is government property that is being used for a private purpose—for example, a government-owned building that is leased to a private tenant. Although public works cannot be liened, some states allow liens on publicly owned properties.

Since subcontractors and suppliers on federal projects cannot file mechanic's liens, the Miller Act (40 U.S.C. §§ 3131–3134) requires contractors on federal contracts exceeding $100,000 to provide a surety bond that guarantees payment for work done in accordance with the terms of the subcontract. Many states have "little Miller Acts" that require contractors on state and municipal government projects to furnish similar payment bonds.

Trust fund and stop-notice statutes are typically valid on public projects. In addition, many states allow subcontractors to lien funds owed to the contractor by a government agency. To perfect a lien against such funds, the subcontractor must give written notice of the claim to the agency; the agency is then required to withhold any funds due to the contractor. The subcontractor must usually file suit to foreclose the lien with a certain number of days of giving notice; otherwise, the agency can release the funds to the contractor. Ordinarily, the agency does not have to be made a party to the suit; the suit is against the contractor for breach of contract.

18

CONSTRUCTION INSURANCE

Risk is an inherent part of any construction project. On most projects, the inherent risk is exacerbated by the interdependence of the project participants; if one participant runs into financial difficulty, it is likely to impact the entire project. As a result, construction contracts typically require the project participants to carry insurance, which reduces the risk that they, and thus the other participants, are exposed to.

By purchasing an insurance policy, the insured party shifts some of its risk to the insurance company. If the insured party suffers a loss that is covered by the policy, the insurance company must indemnify (reimburse) the party up to the amount of coverage. The insurance company is obligated to pay a valid claim and has no recourse against the insured party until the policy comes up for renewal. At that point, the insurance company can increase the premium or refuse to renew the policy. In some cases, the insurance company may be able to recover the amount it was obligated to pay, from whoever was responsible for the loss.

18.1 TYPES OF INSURANCE

There are two distinct categories of insurance: first-party insurance and third-party insurance. Under first-party insurance, the insured party contracts for coverage in the event of injury or loss to itself or its own property. Property insurance and health insurance are examples of first-party insurance. Under third-party insurance, the insured party contracts for coverage in the event it causes injury or loss to someone else (a third party) or the third party's property. Many insurance policies include both first- and third-party insurance; vehicle insurance is a common example of such a policy.

Insurance is regulated by state law; the power to regulate the insurance industry was explicitly given to the states by Congress in 1944 under the McCarran-Ferguson Act (15 U.S.C. §1011). Nevertheless, the insurance obtained for construction projects is generally the same in all states. The participants in a construction project typically have several policies, and each policy covers a specific risk or risks. Contractors and subcontractors usually carry commercial general liability insurance, workers' compensation, and auto insurance. The contractor may also carry builder's risk insurance on the project, but since the cost of the policy is passed through to the owner, many owners prefer to purchase the builder's risk policy themselves. The A/E may carry professional liability insurance, as well as workers' compensation and auto insurance.

18.2 COMMERCIAL GENERAL LIABILITY

Much of the coverage that contractors are required to obtain is provided by a commercial general liability (CGL) policy that covers the contractor's liability to third persons. The policy covers the costs incurred in defending against a claim as well as the claim itself. If the contractor is found liable for a claim, the insurance company will cover the claim up to the limits of the policy.

Most CGL policies are written on a standard form developed by the Insurance Services Office (ISO), an insurance industry trade association. A typical CGL policy consists of a declarations form, a coverage form, and any special endorsements adding or restricting coverage. The declarations form identifies the policyholder (the "named insured") and any additional insureds. It also states the policy period and territory, and indicates the dollar limits for each type of coverage provided.

The coverage form consists of five sections: Coverages, Who Is an Insured, Limits of Insurance, Conditions, and Definitions. In a standard CGL policy, the Coverages section includes three types of coverage: Coverage A—Bodily Injury and Property Damage Liability, Coverage B—Personal and Advertising Injury Liability, and Coverage C—Medical Payments. Within the subsection for each coverage, there is an insuring agreement that lists the hazards that are insured against. There is also a list of exclusions that indicates the circumstances under which a risk that is otherwise within the scope of the agreement will not be covered and any exceptions to these exclusions.

The Conditions section of the coverage form states the insured's obligations to the insurer in the event of a claim. These include providing prompt notice of a claim and cooperating in the defense of a claim.

18.2.1 Bodily Injury and Property Damage

Claims on a construction project typically arise under Coverage A—Bodily Injury and Property Damage Liability. Coverage A covers claims for bodily injury or property damage resulting from an occurrence. An *occurrence* is defined as an accident that is neither expected nor intended from the standpoint of the insured; property damage is defined as physical injury to tangible property or loss of use of property that is not physically injured.

Under the current ISO form, CGL policies are written on an "occurrence basis," which means that coverage is not triggered unless the injury or property damage occurs during the policy period. Because the date of the occurrence may determine which of several policies covering the property was in effect at the time of the injury or damage, there has been considerable litigation with respect to what constitutes an occurrence. Disputes are particularly common when the damage may have occurred over several years, such as water damage that was covered by other construction and thus not immediately noticed.

18.2.2 Exclusions to Coverage

A CGL policy is not intended to reimburse the contractor for damages incurred because the contractor furnished defective material or services; these are considered business risks that can and should be controlled by the contractor. Thus, most CGL policies contain a *work product* exclusion that precludes coverage for the cost of repairing or replacing one's own defective work. However, the current CGL policy forms contain an exception that provides coverage for work done on the insured's behalf by a subcontractor.

Claims for impairment or diminution in value because of defective construction are not covered if there is no physical injury or damage, even when the work was done by a subcontractor. An example of an impairment without physical injury would be a building that could not get a certificate of occupancy because the wrong type of sprinkler heads had been installed. Unless the sprinkler heads were in some way defective or had caused damage to the structure, there would be no physical damage, and the cost to install the correct sprinkler heads would not be covered by the contractor's CGL policy.

Under most CGL policies, coverage is limited to the insured's liability to other parties; damage to the contractor's property, such as equipment or materials stored on-site, is covered by builder's risk insurance. In addition, most, if not all, CGL policies exclude damage that the insured causes to someone else's property while the property is under the insured's "care, custody or control." The care, custody, or control exclusion arises most often with rental equipment; typically, damage to rental equipment would be covered under builder's risk rather than CGL insurance. However, in some cases courts have found that there was coverage under the contractor's CGL policy when the contractor damaged rental equipment that was not under its control. An example of rental equipment not under the contractor's control is a crane rental where the crane owner's employees operated, fueled, maintained, and repaired the crane.

Almost all CGL policies exclude coverage for contractually assumed liability. An example of a contractually assumed liability would be a clause in the construction contract that required the contractor to indemnify the owner for certain damages, whether or not the contractor was at fault. A claim based on such a clause would typically not be covered by the contractor's CGL policy.

18.2.3 Additional Insured Status

Contractors and subcontractors are often required to list both the owner and the A/E as "additional insureds" on their CGL policies. Subcontractors may be required to list the contractor as well as the owner and the A/E. This is done by an endorsement (written amendment) to the underlying policy. Additional insureds are covered for both defense costs and liability up to the limits of the policy. However, under most policies, additional insured coverage is limited to claims that arise during construction; it does not cover claims that arise after the project is complete.

Insurance companies typically issue *certificates of insurance* to the additional insureds as proof of their coverage. These certificates identify the additional insured and show the coverage limits. The insurance company is required to provide an additional insured with 30 days' notice if the policy is canceled or not renewed.

Certificates of insurance may also be issued to individuals or entities that are not additional insureds but have requested proof of the named insured's coverage. These certificate holders are not provided with any coverage under the policy, but they must be notified if the policy is canceled or not renewed.

It should be noted that an additional insured is not the same as an "additional named insured." An additional named insured is usually affiliated with the primary insured and may be liable for premium payments. In addition, there are some coverage exclusions that apply to an additional named insured but not to an additional insured.

18.3 BUILDER'S RISK INSURANCE

Builder's risk is property insurance that protects against fortuitous (accidental) damage to a project while the project is under construction. In addition to the actual structure, builder's risk policies generally provide coverage for foundations, underground pipes, and temporary structures such as scaffolding while they are at the insured location. Construction equipment and stored materials that have not yet been incorporated into the structure are also covered.

Fortuitous loss means that the loss is a matter of chance and not something like depreciation or ordinary wear and tear that is certain to occur. Losses from intentional misconduct are also excluded. Losses caused by the negligence of the contractor or its subcontractors are considered fortuitous, however, as negligence is by definition unintentional.

Builder's risk policies are typically "all risk" policies, which means that they cover all causes of loss that are not expressly excluded. Losses resulting from design defects or faulty workmanship are typically excluded, as are losses due to equipment breakdown. Many policies also exclude acts of nature such as earthquakes, floods, and freezing, as well as indirect losses such as loss of use caused by delay. Coverage for excluded losses can sometimes be obtained by endorsements to the standard policy.

Because builder's risk coverage only applies while the project is under construction, there can be disagreements over what constitutes the start and end of construction. Materials stored on-site are typically not covered before the start of physical work on the project. Likewise, if the policy states that coverage ends once the property is occupied or put to its intended use, damage that occurs while punchlist items are being completed may not be covered. Even during construction, the amount paid for a covered loss can vary considerably, depending on how the policy values the project at the time of the loss.

18.4 WORKERS' COMPENSATION INSURANCE

Workers' compensation insurance is designed to cover workers who are injured in the course of their employment. Workers are entitled to compensation without regard to fault and without having to resort to litigation. In exchange for guaranteed compensation, workers give up their right to sue their employer for employment-related injuries. The amount received for an injury under workers' compensation is likely to be considerably less than what would be awarded in a lawsuit, however. As a result, injured construction workers may try to prove that the A/E or a contractor other than their employer was responsible for their injury; workers' compensation statutes do not provide any protection to the A/E or other contractors.

Workers' compensation is administered by state agencies that provide a forum for resolving disputes about an employee's right to payment, the amount and duration of benefits, and any defenses the employer might have. Most states require any employer with more than a minimum number of employees to provide workers' compensation coverage. The insurance can typically be purchased from a commercial insurer or provided through a program of self-insurance.

18.5 PROFESSIONAL LIABILITY INSURANCE

Design agreements often do not require the A/E to carry insurance; nevertheless, many A/Es carry both commercial general liability and professional liability insurance. Professional liability insurance, also known as *errors and omissions* (E&O) insurance, covers damages caused by the A/E's failure to perform in accordance with the standard of care applicable to its profession. Failure to perform in accordance with the applicable standard of care constitutes negligence; to control against the "moral hazard" of being able to insure against negligence, E&O policies typically require a relatively high deductible.

Like CGL polices, E&O polices provide coverage for the cost of defending claims. However, unlike CGL policies, E&O policies are "wasting policies," which means that the defense costs are deducted from the policy limits. Unless this is taken into account when selecting policy limits, the A/E may end up with significantly less coverage than expected.

E&O policies also differ from CGL policies in that they are typically written on a claims-made basis rather than an occurrence basis. Under a claims-made policy, the policy in force when the claim is asserted is the only one that will cover the claim, regardless of when the damage occurred. To ensure that any claims on a project are covered, an owner will often require the A/E to maintain E&O coverage for several years after a project has ended. Most policies provide coverage as long as the insurer was notified of a potential claim while the policy was in force; the claim does not actually have to be filed before the policy expires.

The 2007 versions of the AIA owner-architect agreements (the B Series) require the architect to maintain commercial general liability, automobile liability, workers' compensation, and professional liability insurance. However, if the type of insurance or the coverage limits required by the owner exceed what the A/E normally maintains, the owner must reimburse the A/E for the additional cost.

18.6   WRAP-UP INSURANCE PROGRAMS

Typically, the contractor, the subcontractors, and the A/E buy their own insurance and pass the cost along to the owner as part of their contract price. On large projects, the owner can often save a substantial amount of money by purchasing insurance under an *owner-controlled insurance program* (OCIP), also known as *wrap-up insurance* or *project insurance*. With an OCIP, the owner's insurance covers all project participants that enroll in the program under whatever policies are included in the OCIP. To the extent that the OCIP covers a party's contractual insurance requirements, the party must reduce its contract price by the amount included for insurance. A contractor-controlled insurance program (CCIP) functions in a similar manner; even though it is controlled by the contractor, the cost savings pass to the owner.

The main benefit of both OCIPs and CCIPs is the cost savings, but there can also be an improvement in risk control and claims recovery. In addition, project participants may benefit, as the insurance limits may be higher than what they could obtain under separate policies. OCIP and CCIP programs are typically only used on large projects, however, because the costs to administer them are fairly high.

18.7   WAIVER OF SUBROGATION

Subrogation is a legal theory under which one entity has the right to "stand in the shoes" of another person or entity and claim whatever rights that other person or entity has. Under the theory of subrogation, if an insurance company has paid on a claim, it can pursue the rights of the insured against the party responsible for the damages. For example, if the contractor's insurer was forced to pay the owner for damage caused by a subcontractor, the insurer could sue the subcontractor for reimbursement.

Because subrogation defeats the objective of transferring project risk to the insurance company, many of the industry standard forms require the parties to waive their right of subrogation. AIA A201 requires the owner and the contractor to waive their subrogation rights against each other and also requires them to include waivers of subrogation in their other contracts. Since a waiver of subrogation cuts off the insurer's rights to recoup a loss, it can substantially increase the insurer's risk; thus, it is likely to mean a higher premium. Most insurance policies do not allow the insured to waive subrogation rights without the insurance company's approval.

19

SURETY BONDS

A surety bond is an instrument issued by a surety on behalf of another party (the principal), which guarantees that the principal will fulfill its obligations to a third party. The third party is referred to as the *bond obligee*; the bond is said to *run to* the obligee. There may be more than one obligee on a bond, and, depending on the amount of the bond, there may be more than one surety.

If the principal fails to fulfill its obligations, the principal and the surety are jointly and severally liable on the bond. *Joint and several liability* means that either the principal or the surety, or both, may be sued on the bond, and the entire liability may be collected from either party.

19.1 USE OF SURETY BONDS IN THE CONSTRUCTION INDUSTRY

The bonds used in the construction industry are referred to as contract bonds; the bonds guarantee the obligations in the underlying contract. The principal is usually the general contractor, but subcontractors are sometimes required to post bonds as well. The obligee is usually the owner, but when the principal is a subcontractor, the obligee may be the owner, the general contractor, or both. The bonds required most often are bid bonds, payment bonds, and performance bonds.

The amount in which a bond is issued is referred to as the *penal sum* of the bond. Unless the surety breaches its own obligations under the bond, the penal sum is typically the maximum amount of money that it will be required to pay if the principal defaults. This allows the surety to assess the risk involved in providing the bond and determine an appropriate premium. The surety may be discharged from its obligation under the bond if the obligee impairs the surety's rights, such as by substantially modifying the principal's obligations or allowing someone other than the principal to perform the principal's obligations.

The bond premium (cost) depends on both the amount of the bond and the contractor's credit rating and financial history. Contractors with poor credit may be limited in the amount of the bond they can qualify for and may end up paying an extremely high premium.

19.1.1 Bid Guarantees

Bid guarantees are intended to ensure that the bidder will honor its bid, will sign the contract documents if awarded the contract, and will furnish performance and payment bonds. If the bidder refuses to honor its bid, the bidder and the surety are liable for any costs the owner incurs in reletting the contract. In most cases, this is the difference in dollar amount between the low bid and the second-lowest bid. Any federal project that requires a performance or payment bond will also require a bid guarantee; the amount is typically 5 percent of the bid amount.

Bid guarantees are often provided in the form of bonds, but they may also be money orders, certified checks made payable to the owner, or irrevocable letters of credit. A contractor that can afford to put up its own funds as the bid guarantee may prefer to do so, thereby saving the cost of a bond. When a bid guarantee is something other than a bond, it is typically returned to the unsuccessful bidders after the bids are opened. The successful bidder's guarantee is returned after all contractually required documents and bonds are executed.

A requirement for a bid guarantee helps prevent frivolous bids. In addition, sureties generally only issue bid bonds to contractors that will qualify for the required performance and payment bonds. Since many bidders put up bonds as their guarantee, a requirement for a bid guarantee helps restrict bidders to firms that can satisfy performance and payment bond requirements.

Courts sometimes allow a contractor to withdraw a mistaken bid without forfeiting its bid security. However, a contractor can only withdraw its bid if the mistake was one of fact, such as a clerical error, a numerical miscalculation, or the inadvertent omission of part of the project advertised for bid. Mistakes in judgment such as underestimating costs are not grounds for withdrawing a bid. The mistake must also be substantial enough that it would be unfair to enforce the bid. Some states require that the mistake be such that the owner would have reason to suspect a mistake by looking at the amount of the bid.

19.1.2 Payment Bonds

Payment bonds, sometimes referred to as *labor and material bonds*, guarantee that the contractor will pay its subcontractors and suppliers. The language of the bond determines who has a right to make a claim on the bond. Subcontractors and suppliers that provide labor, materials, and equipment to the principal are generally granted rights on the bond. Lower-tier subcontractors and those supplying materials and equipment to subcontractors may also be granted rights, but the more remote the supplier, the harder it is to show that the materials were actually used on the project. This is especially true when the material is fungible (a standard, interchangeable commodity like drywall or shingles). Suppliers to a subcontractor may be able to claim on the bond if they can prove their materials were custom-fabricated for the job or were shipped directly to the job, as opposed to being shipped to the subcontractor.

CASE STUDY—FORFEITURE OF BID BOND

A contractor was the low bidder on a contract for a portion of a water treatment facility. Before the contract was awarded, the contractor notified the owner that it had made a clerical error and its $700,000 bid was $73,000 too low. The owner did not allow the contractor to withdraw its bid and awarded it the contract. When the contractor refused to proceed with the contract, the owner awarded the contract to the next-lowest bidder and brought suit against the contractor, seeking forfeiture of its bid bond.

The court held that the owner was entitled to keep the bid bond and established three requirements as a condition for allowing a bidder to withdraw a mistaken bid. The mistake must relate to a material feature of the contract, it must have occurred despite the exercise of reasonable care, and the other party must not be put at advantage (i.e. it must be in a position to accept the next lowest bid.) The court found that the contractor's error was more than ordinary negligence; thus, the contractor had not exercised reasonable care in preparation of its bid.

City of Florence v. Powder Horn Constructors,
716 P.2d 143 (Co.App. 1985)

Under AIA's combination performance bond and payment bond, AIA A312, claimants are limited to those who have a direct contract with either the bond principal or a subcontractor to the principal. Thus, if the principal is the general contractor, claimants are limited to subcontractors and suppliers that furnish labor and materials to the general contractor or a subcontractor.

Because mechanic's liens cannot be imposed on public property, payment bonds are typically required on public projects. The fact that payment is backed by a guarantee is also thought to encourage more competitive bidding from subcontractors and suppliers. The penal sum of a payment bond is usually 40 to 50 percent of the contract price. The cost of the bond depends on the penal sum, the type of project, and the contractor's bonding capacity, but it is generally 1 to 2 percent of the project cost.

19.1.2.1 *Filing Suit on a Payment Bond*

Subcontractors and suppliers that have a right to make a claim on a payment bond are referred to as *beneficiaries under the bond*. Depending on the language of the bond, claims must typically be brought within one year of the principal's last day on the project, or one year of the claimant's last day of supplying materials or labor to the project. Claimants are generally entitled to file suit if they have not been paid within a certain number of days after their last day of work on the project.

Claimants that do not have a direct contract with the principal (i.e., second-tier subcontractors) must usually give written notice to the principal and the surety before they can bring a claim. The adequacy of notice and the timeliness of action on the bond are common subjects of dispute. Court decisions have varied as to whether punchlist or warranty work restarts the clock on the period of time for bringing an action.

19.1.3 Performance Bonds

A performance bond assures the owner that the contract will be completed according to its terms. If the contractor is terminated for default, the surety must ensure that the contract is completed. Many performance bonds give the surety the option of taking over the project and completing it with another contractor, selecting a new contractor to contract directly with the owner, or negotiating a cash settlement. The surety will often negotiate a cash settlement when the owner agrees to arrange for completion and its damages are readily quantifiable. This might be the case if the contractor has not yet begun work and other bidders for the original contract are still available, or the work is nearly complete and the remaining work can be valued fairly accurately.

Some bonds require the surety to take over and complete the principal's performance if requested to do so by the obligee. Although the penal sum of the bond is usually the amount of the contract, depending on the bond language, the surety's costs may not be capped at the penal sum if it takes over the contract.

When the principal is the general contractor, the owner is typically the only party that can sue to enforce the performance bond; the suit must be brought within a specified time from the date that final payment is due under the contract. The performance bond usually requires the owner to provide the surety with written notice before declaring the contractor in default. When the contractor is struggling because of financial problems, the surety may prefer to help the contractor avoid default, so that it is not required to take over the project. If the owner consents, the surety can provide the contractor with the funds it needs to complete the project.

19.2 RIGHTS AND REMEDIES OF SURETIES

A surety that is required to pay on a bond is subrogated to the rights of its principal against the obligee and any others that it pays, to the extent of its payments. In defending against a claim on a bond, the surety can assert any defenses that the contractor has against the subcontractor or supplier—for example, that the work or material was not paid for because it was defective. The surety can also assert counterclaims against the subcontractor or supplier.

The surety is also subrogated to its principal's rights for purposes of determining the relative priorities among competing creditors. A surety that has paid on a performance bond is typically entitled to any money due to the principal under the contract, including retainage. The surety usually has priority over both the lender and any taxing authorities that have tax liens against the principal's assets.

19.2.1 Indemnity Agreements

Although the surety is sometimes an insurance company that provides the bond in exchange for payment of a premium, a surety bond is not an insurance policy; it is a guarantee that the principal's obligations will be performed. Unlike an insurance policy, where the insurance company expects to sustain some losses, a surety does not expect to suffer a loss on a bond.

Sureties generally do not issue bonds unless the contractor and often the individual owners of the contracting company have executed indemnity agreements and pledged assets as collateral for the bonds. The indemnitors (the contractor and individuals who have pledged their assets) must agree to completely reimburse (indemnify) the surety for any liabilities, attorney's fees, expenses, or damages that the surety incurs as a result of its issuance of the bond. Before issuing a bond, the surety must be satisfied that the indemnitors have sufficient assets to protect the surety from any claims that may be made against the bond.

Typically, the parties enter into a general agreement of indemnity (GAI) covering any bonds that the surety issues to the contractor. If a surety makes payment to the owner, a subcontractor, or a material supplier as a result of an obligation incurred under a bond, the surety will pursue indemnification from the contractor and any individual indemnitors who executed the GAI.

19.2.2 Discharge of the Surety's Obligations

An owner may feel compelled to advance construction payments when the contractor is facing cash flow problems. Such payments carry a number of risks for the owner, however. If the original contractor is unable to complete the project, there will be less money available for the contractor that takes over the project. In addition, if there is a performance bond, the surety may claim that the advance payments have materially altered the underlying contract and, thus, discharge the surety's obligations under the bond.

When a surety issues a performance bond, the surety becomes jointly and severally liable for the contractor's performance of its obligations to the owner under the contract. If the owner and the contractor alter their contract, it alters the surety's obligation; an unauthorized payment in violation of the contract may be considered a material alteration. Most bond agreements do not allow material contract alterations without the surety's consent. A surety may also claim to be discharged from its obligations if the owner accepts defective work or fails to make required inspections before making payments.

19.3 BONDING REQUIREMENTS

Under the Miller Act, 40 U.S.C. §§3131–3134, payment and performance bonds are required for prime contractors on all federal government construction projects where the contract price exceeds $100,000. In addition, every state requires performance and payment bonds for state government construction contracts. These state statutes are often called "little Miller Acts" because most of them are modeled after the federal Miller Act.

Surety bond requirements on federal projects can be satisfied through bonds issued by an approved corporate surety or bonds issued by an individual who pledges certain types of assets. Bonds issued by individuals acting as sureties must be supported by cash, readily marketable assets such as stocks traded on public exchanges, or an irrevocable letter of credit from a federally insured financial institution. Allowing individuals to act as sureties theoretically increases competition in bidding, because it allows contractors that would not qualify for bonds from an approved corporate surety to bid.

Private (nongovernment) owners sometimes require the general contractor to post bonds, particularly on large projects. However, since the cost of the bonds is passed along to the owner, private owners often do not require either a payment or a performance bond unless they are a condition of the loan.

20

LIABILITY FOR DEFECTIVE CONSTRUCTION

Construction may be defective for any of a number of reasons. Examples of defective construction include the following:

- The material or equipment was not of the quality required by the contract.
- The work did not conform to the requirements of the contract.
- The work was executed in a manner that was inconsistent with industry standards.
- The design violated applicable building codes.
- The project failed to meet performance requirements stated in the contract.

The fact that the owner was dissatisfied with the result of a project does not necessarily mean the construction was defective, however. The owner does not have a valid claim for defective construction unless the work falls below the standard that was promised or reasonably expected.

Likewise, the existence of an apparent problem does not necessarily mean someone can be held liable to the owner for damages. The owner only has a legal remedy for damages if the problem is the proximate (legal) result of another party's failure to perform its work in accordance with its legal obligations. These obligations may have arisen from the contract between the parties, from common-law doctrines such as implied warranties that have been developed by the courts, or from government requirements such as building codes.

20.1 DETERMINING LIABILITY

In evaluating claims of defective construction, it is important to distinguish between manifestations and defects. A *manifestation* is simply a condition that may indicate a defect. It is often not possible to determine what type of defect exists, or even whether there is a defect, simply on the basis of a manifestation.

An example of a manifestation would be a discolored ceiling tile. The discoloration could have resulted from a variety of defects. There could be a penetration in the roofing membrane, a leak around a skylight, a broken pipe, or a faulty sprinkler head. Alternatively, a discoloration could simply be a natural variation in the tile color, or a variation that was not natural but existed at the time the tile was installed and was accepted by the owner.

Likewise, it is often difficult to determine which party is responsible for correcting a problem. The problem may be the result of several defects, none of which would have individually caused a problem. In some cases, the liability of the party that was primarily responsible may be limited by the terms of its contract. In other cases, the party's liability may be reduced, or even discharged, because another party failed to comply with its contract or because the claim was not filed in time.

20.2 OWNER CLAIMS AGAINST THE CONTRACTOR

The contractor's primary obligation under the contract is to perform the work in accordance with the contract documents. The contractor is required to correct any defective work that is brought to its attention, either during construction or during the callback (correction) period. In addition, most contracts require the contractor to review the bid documents and notify the owner of any errors or omissions. Failure to comply with the plans and specifications, failure to correct defective work, or failure to notify the owner of errors in the bid documents could all be considered a breach of the contract.

20.2.1 Warranties

Most construction contracts require the contractor to warrant the quality of the work. An example of such a warranty is §3.5.1 of AIA A201:

> *The Contractor warrants to the Owner and Architect that materials and equipment furnished under the Contract will be of good quality and new unless the Contract Documents require or permit otherwise. The Contractor further warrants that the Work will conform to the requirements of the Contract Documents and will be free from defects, except for those inherent in the quality of the Work the Contract Documents require or permit.*

In addition to this general warranty, most contracts require the contractor to correct any work that is not in accordance with the contract documents within one year of substantial completion. The AIA documents refer to this one-year period as the *correction period*; other industry standard forms refer to this period as the *callback period*. Although it is also referred to as the *warranty period*, it should not be confused with the contractor's general warranty of quality, which lasts until the end of the applicable statute-of-limitations period. Work that is not in accordance with the documents is not necessarily defective and the owner may choose to accept the work.

The law can also impose implied warranties on the contractor. For example, most states hold that the contractor implicitly warrants that the work will be performed in a "workmanlike manner," where *workmanlike* means the work will be performed by one who has the necessary knowledge, training, and experience, and in a manner generally considered proficient by those capable of judging such work. In evaluating the work, courts look at whether the quality is what would be expected of a reasonably skilled and experienced contractor in a similar situation. The contractor's warranties do not extend to damage caused by improper maintenance or operation, however. In addition, the contractor has no obligation to correct damage due to normal wear and tear.

20.2.2 Notice Requirements

When defective work is discovered prior to final completion, the owner must typically give the contractor an opportunity to cure the defect. AIA A201 §2.4 requires the owner to give the contractor written notice of the defect. If the contractor fails to correct the work within ten days, the owner can carry out the work and backcharge the contractor for its expenses, including any additional compensation owed to the A/E for the defective work. The owner must also notify the contractor when defective work is found during the correction (callback) period. If the contractor fails to correct the work within a reasonable time, the owner may carry out the work itself and file a claim against the contractor.

After the callback period has passed, the owner is usually not required to notify the contractor but may proceed to fix the defect and bring a claim against the contractor. However, after the end of the callback period, the owner must rely on the contractor's general warranty of quality. To prevail on its claim, the owner must show that the defect is not simply the result of normal postconstruction changes or deterioration. This may be difficult to prove, as it is recognized that most materials have a finite useful life. Deterioration over time is to be expected and is not considered a defect.

20.2.3 Tort Claims

In most states, the owner is required to bring its claims against the contractor under contract law rather than tort law, at least where the claims arise out of the contractor's performance of the contract. In some cases, however, the owner may want to bring a negligence claim against a subcontractor or supplier that it does not have a contract with. Depending on how the state interprets the economic loss doctrine, negligence claims may not be allowed unless there was physical damage outside the scope of the allegedly negligent party's work.

20.3 THE SPEARIN DOCTRINE

Under the traditional design-bid-build project delivery system, the owner contracts with the A/E to develop plans and specifications for the project. The owner then provides these plans and specifications to the contractor. If the contractor's work is in accordance with the plans and specifications, but the project is ultimately defective because the drawings or specifications were defective, there is likely to be a dispute over liability.

This issue was addressed in the case *United States v. Spearin*. In *Spearin*, the government contracted with Spearin to build a dry dock in accordance with government-furnished plans and specifications. The work required that a sewer line be relocated before construction began. Spearin complied with the contract requirements for relocating the sewer, and the government accepted this work as satisfactory.

During a subsequent heavy rain, a dam that was not shown on the plans diverted the backflow, breaking the relocated sewer and flooding the dry dock. Spearin refused to resume construction until the government assumed responsibility for the damage and either made changes to the sewer system or assumed responsibility for future damage. The government, however, insisted that Spearin was responsible for remedying existing conditions. The government annulled the contract and completed the work with another contractor.

Spearin sued the government for the balance due for work done under the contract and for damages resulting from the annulment of the contract. The case ultimately went to the Supreme Court, which held that the government's breach of its implied warranty of the plans and specifications, followed by the government's denial of responsibility, justified Spearin's refusal to resume work. The holding in *Spearin* was that:

> *"When the Government provides specifications directing how a contract is to be performed, the Government warrants that the contractor will be able to perform the contract satisfactorily if it follows the specifications."*

The holding has become known as the Spearin doctrine and is one of the fundamental doctrines used to allocate responsibility for construction defects.

20.3.1 Application of the Spearin Doctrine

Because the *Spearin* case involved federal law, the holding itself only applies to contracts with the U.S. government. The Spearin doctrine has been adopted by most states, however, and is applied to both private and public construction. Under the Spearin doctrine, the party who supplies the drawings to the contractor (typically, the owner) implicitly warrants that the plans and specifications are adequate for their intended purpose. Contractors can use the Spearin doctrine as a defense against the owner's claims of defective construction or delay damages. Contractors can also use the Spearin doctrine as a basis for a claim against the owner if the defective drawings or specifications result in increased costs or delays.

If a contractor attempts to claim damages for defective plans and specifications, it must show that its reliance on the plans and specifications was reasonable. The specifications are not warranted when there is an obvious (patent) error or omission; if there is an obvious error or omission, the contractor has a duty to inquire. In addition, the specifications at issue must be design specifications; the Spearin doctrine does not apply to performance specifications. In other words, the specifications at issue must set forth detailed and precise requirements for the materials, equipment, and tolerances.

The contractor must show that it substantially complied with the plans and specifications, and that the damages were a consequence of this compliance. A contractor that has not complied with the plans and specifications cannot allege that the damages would have occurred even if the plans and specifications had been complied with; any deviation must have been entirely irrelevant to the alleged damage. The requirement for substantial compliance is waived if the defect is such that compliance is impossible.

CASE STUDY—PATENT ERROR IN DESIGN

A contractor entered into a contract with the Army Corps of Engineers to build a launching area. The launching area consisted of a pit with block walls that were to serve as forms for subsequent cast-in-place concrete walls. There was a heavy rain during construction, and two walls of the block walls collapsed. The contractor contended that the walls were constructed in strict compliance with the plans and specifications and that their collapse was due to their defective design.

The court held that the contractor was not entitled to recover the additional costs of rebuilding the walls. Even if the walls were erroneously designed, this was obvious, and the contractor therefore knew, or should have known, that unless they were properly supported, they would collapse if there were heavy rains. Accordingly, it was the contractor's clear obligation to take appropriate protective or precautionary measures to prevent a collapse from happening.

Allied Contractors, Inc., v. United States,
381 F.2d 995 (Ct.Cl. 1967)

20.3.2 Limitations on Spearin

The implied warranty of the plans and specifications will supersede general contract clauses that require the contractor to thoroughly check the drawings and examine the project site. The contractor does not have a duty to verify that the plans are adequate to accomplish their stated purpose, unless this is specifically required by the contract. Likewise, the contractor is generally not liable if the defect occurred because an improper material was specified.

Nevertheless, implied warranties are not favored by the courts, and they are interpreted narrowly, so as not to infringe on the parties' agreement. If the contract states that the contractor explicitly affirms the adequacy and sufficiency of the plans and specifications, courts may consider this to be a disclaimer of the Spearin warranty. If the contract contains a no-damages-delay clause, the contractor's remedy for defective plans and specifications will be limited to an extension of time.

In addition, the Spearin doctrine typically applies only to circumstances where there was a fundamental design defect. Numerous small defects that require a large number of RFIs generally do not constitute a fundamental defect, even if the cumulative effect of the defects is substantial.

CASE STUDY—WARRANTY OF PLANS

The roofing contract for a school building stated that the roofing subcontractor agreed to maintain and repair the roof for a period of five years after substantial completion of construction, without regard to the cause or the nature of any leaks or defects. The roof subsequently began to leak because of defects in the design, but the roofing contractor refused to make repairs, claiming that it had no liability for defective design.

The court held that the subcontractor's specific warranty overrode the owner's implied warranty against defects in the plans and specifications. The roofing contractor was thus held liable for the repairs.

Burke County Public Schools v. Juno Construction Corp.,
273 S.E.2d 504 (N.C. App. 1981)

20.4 THE A/E'S LIABILITY FOR DEFECTIVE CONSTRUCTION

During contract administration, the A/E is generally required to interpret the contract documents, review contractor submittals and shop drawings, make site visits, and reject work that does not conform to the contract requirements. These obligations raise an issue as to the A/E's liability when it fails to discover nonconforming work.

Whether the A/E can be held liable for failing to identify and reject nonconforming work depends in part on the A/E's contract, including whether the A/E has contracted to provide general supervision or is providing continuous inspection through a full-time on-site project representative (clerk of the works). Although general supervision creates less of a duty than an on-site representative, courts have not been consistent in their interpretations of the A/E's obligations under general supervision. Courts have sometimes held the A/E liable for defective construction, even though the design agreement specifically stated that the A/E did not guarantee the contractor's performance. In addition, courts typically hold the A/E liable if it actually knew, or should have known, of a defect and failed to notify the owner in time for the owner to take appropriate action.

20.5   AFFIRMATIVE DEFENSES

When a claim for defective construction is filed, the party being charged can deny liability by raising any applicable affirmative defenses. An affirmative defense does not consider whether the facts of the claim are true; it presents facts that attempt to justify or excuse the behavior on which the lawsuit is based.

Two affirmative defenses that are significant in the context of claims for defective construction are statutes of limitations and statutes of repose. Both statutes are state laws that specify the period of time within which a lawsuit must be filed. The statutes protect against so-called *stale claims*, where loss of evidence due to the death or disappearance of witnesses, fading memories, and lost documents can make it difficult to defend against a claim. Such statutes also promote the goal of certainty and finality in the administration of commercial transactions by terminating liability at a set point in time. Public policy dictates that there should be a point in time when people are no longer burdened by the possibility of litigation arising from past acts.

20.5.1   Statutes of Limitation

Statutes of limitation require that an injured party file suit within a specified period after the cause of action accrues. Although the statutory limitation period for both tort and contract claims varies widely from state to state, the limitations period for a tort claim is usually shorter than the limitations period for a contract claim. In many states, the limitations period for a contract claim is six years, while the limitations period for a tort claim is three or four years. However, the limitations period for a contract claim on a construction project usually begins at substantial completion, whereas the limitations period for a tort claim may not begin until the injury or damage is sustained.

20.5.1.1   Discovery Rule

The fact that the limitations period for contract claims begins at substantial completion can be a problem for construction defects, as a defect that is hidden by other construction may not be discovered until after the limitations period has run out. Because of the unfairness of a claim becoming time-barred before it is even discovered, many states have adopted the so-called discovery rule. Under the discovery rule, the limitations period does not begin until the injured party becomes aware, or should have become aware, of the defect.

Some states have explicitly adopted the discovery rule by statute; in other states, it has developed through case law. Some states apply the discovery rule only for tort claims; others apply it for both tort and contract claims. Even when the discovery rule applies, however, the injured party cannot ignore signs of a possible defect. The limitations period begins to run when there are signs of a defect, even if the injured party fails to investigate further and actually discover the defect.

Parties to a contract can agree to modify the limitations periods for claims arising out of the contract; in particular, they can change both the length of the limitations period and the date on which it begins. For example, the parties can agree that the limitations for contract actions related to the project will begin upon substantial completion. This agreement will be upheld in court, even if the state follows the discovery rule.

CASE STUDY—STATUTE OF LIMITATIONS

The construction contract for a housing project included a clause specifying that all claims had to be filed within one year of substantial completion of the project. The contractor brought a claim after the one-year period had expired, stating that the claim should be allowed because it was within the period of limitations allowed by state statute.

The court upheld the one-year limitation and dismissed the claim. The court relied on previous holdings that the statutory limitation period for contract actions could be waived by the express agreement of both parties. As long as the period that the parties agreed to was reasonable and did not violate public policy, clauses that shorten the limitations period are valid.

A.J. Tenwood v. Orange Senior Citizens Hous. Co.
491 A.2d 1280, 200 N.J. Super. 515 (N.J. Super. Ct. App. Div. 1985)

20.5.2 Statutes of Repose

In states that apply the discovery rule, both the A/E and the contractor can be sued many years after a project is completed. In addition to creating lingering uncertainty, this open-ended liability can affect the availability and cost of the parties' insurance. Statutes of repose address this issue by placing an absolute time limit on claims. These statutes are a legislative response to the A/E's and contractor's protracted vulnerability to lawsuit when the limitations period is based on discovery of the defect.

Almost every state that follows the discovery rule has adopted a statute of repose for claims arising out of construction projects. The period of repose is longer than the period of limitations but begins to run regardless of when the injury occurs, or whether the injury has manifested itself, or whether the injured party is aware of the injury. Unless the defect is discovered before the end of the period of repose, the injured party has lost its right to bring a claim.

Like statutes of limitation, statutes of repose vary widely from state to state with respect to both the length of the period of repose and the date it begins to run. The period of repose usually starts when the owner takes possession of the work, but the start date may also be tied to issuance of the certification of occupancy, or a filing that indicates the owner's acceptance of the work. If a defect is discovered during the period of repose, the claim must then be brought within the time specified in the statute of limitations.

In some states, the statute of repose applies only to tort claims, so there is no absolute time limit on bringing a contract claim. In some states, the statute of repose applies only to claims brought against the A/E; there is no period of repose for claims against the contractor.

21

CALCULATIONS OF DAMAGES

The amount of money awarded to a plaintiff who has prevailed on a claim of loss or injury is referred to as the plaintiff's *damages*. Most claims on construction projects are for breach of contract, and the damages are compensatory, which means they are designed to put the nonbreaching party in as good a position as it would have been in if the contract had been performed according to its terms. The rationale used to determine appropriate damages is referred to as the *measure of damages*.

Typically, the measure of damages for breach of contract is the nonbreaching party's expectation interest—in other words, how the party expected to benefit from the contract. Courts also refer to this as the party's *benefit of its bargain*. A party is entitled to have the benefit of what it contracted for; when one party has lost the benefit of its bargain because the other party breached the contract, a court will try to restore that benefit. Generally, the rights of the parties are fixed at the time the contract was breached, and damages are measured as of that time.

21.1 COMPENSATORY DAMAGES

Compensatory damages for a breach of contract can include both direct costs and consequential costs that were reasonably foreseeable at the time the contract was executed (signed). Direct costs are typically costs that can be identified with and charged to a particular cause. For example, if the owner improperly rejected work, the contractor's direct damages would be the cost to redo the work. Likewise, if the owner had to hire another contractor to repair defective work, the cost of the repair would be a direct cost. Proof of damages does not necessarily require exact calculations; it is usually acceptable to perform a reasonable estimate.

21.1.1 Consequential Damages

Consequential damages, also known as *special damages*, are damages that were caused by the breach of contract but cannot be traced to the breach as easily as direct damages. Consequential damages are often economic losses and can be considerably greater than the direct damages. If the contractor breached the contract by not completing construction by the contract date, the owner's consequential damages could include lost rents, lost profits, and additional financing costs. If the owner breached the contract by failing to make payment in accordance with the contract terms, the contractor's consequential damages could include loss of business, late charges, and loss of bonding capacity because of late payments to creditors.

Although consequential damages resulting from a breach of contract are recoverable if they were reasonably foreseeable and within the contemplation of the parties at the time of their agreement, many construction contracts contain a mutual waiver of consequential damages.

CASE STUDY—CONSEQUENTIAL DAMAGES

An owner hired a contractor to construct two roadside rest areas. Although the contract stated that the owner would make regular progress payments, payments were sporadic. The contractor experienced a cash flow problem and borrowed the money it needed to complete the project from its bonding company. The bonding company subsequently sold off much of the contractor's equipment to recover the money; the contractor eventually went out of business as a result.

The contractor sued the owner for consequential damages, alleging that the owner had breached the contract by not making regular progress payments and that this had destroyed the contractor's business. The court held that destruction of a business was not a foreseeable result of the failure to make progress payments on time. The claim was thus denied—in order to be recoverable, consequential damages must be reasonably foreseeable to the parties at the time they signed the contract.

Department of Transportation v. Cumberland Construction Co.,
90 Pa. Commonwealth Ct. 273 (1985)

21.2 PUNITIVE DAMAGES

Punitive damages are intended to punish malicious wrongdoers and deter others from behaving in a similar fashion. Punitive damages are rare in the construction industry because most states do not award punitive damages for breach of contract. To recover punitive damages, there generally must be an independent tort or the conduct accompanying the breach must be outrageous.

Punitive damages are sometimes awarded for breach of contract when there is a special relationship between the parties. These are typically fiduciary relationships such as guardianships, however, and the parties to a construction contract are seldom considered to have such a relationship.

21.3   DUTY TO MITIGATE DAMAGES

When there has been a breach of contract, the nonbreaching party always has an affirmative obligation to mitigate its damages. This means that once it becomes aware of the other party's breach, the nonbreaching party must take reasonable steps to minimize the damages it will suffer. As an example, if the contractor is unable to perform scheduled work because the owner has made a design change, the contractor must try to do other work, if this can be done reasonably. A party usually cannot recover damages that it could have avoided through a reasonable attempt at mitigation.

21.4   OWNER'S DAMAGES

When the contractor has breached the contract, the measure of the owner's damages is the amount of money that would put the owner in the same position it would have been in if the project had been completed for the contract amount, by the agreed-upon completion date, and with the quality specified in the contract.

In applying the benefit of the bargain principle to the cost element of a contract, a court compares the actual cost of construction to the contract amount. The owner is entitled to recover its additional expenses if it must hire another contractor to complete work that was left unfinished. Similarly, if the contractor's breach forces the owner to spend more on design fees, the owner is entitled to recover those additional costs.

21.4.1   Owner's Damages for Late Completion

Time is a critical element on most construction projects. If substantial completion is not achieved by the agreed-upon completion date, the owner will likely incur additional costs for project administration, such as the salaries of project personnel, and insurance. Such costs are generally considered direct costs and are fairly easy to prove.

The owner's direct costs for a delay are usually much less than its consequential damages, however. Consequential damages can include loss of rental income, loss of use of the facility (if the project is being constructed for the owner's use), or loss of interest on the profit (if the project will be sold once it is completed). Other consequential damages could include additional financing costs and a decrease in employee productivity as well as liability to third parties such as future tenants.

Unless the contract waives consequential damages, the owner is entitled to recover these expenses when the delay was caused by the contractor. Loss–of-use damages can be difficult to prove, however, as they raise issues of whether the claimed costs were foreseeable. Loss of profits for a business raises issues about the speculative nature of profits, particularly for a new business. Generally, an owner can only recover lost profits if it can show what the profits would have been with reasonable certainty. Proving a loss due to a delayed sale presents similar issues of foreseeability and speculation.

21.4.1.1 Liquidated Damages

In lieu of requiring the owner to calculate and prove actual delay damages, the contract may contain a liquidated damages clause, which provides that the contractor will be charged a specified amount per day of delay. Although many of the standard industry form contracts include a mutual waiver of consequential damages, the waiver typically does not preclude an award of applicable liquidated damages. To the extent that the liquidated damages specified for a delay in project completion include consequential damages, such damages are recoverable even when the contract includes a waiver of consequential damages.

CASE STUDY—ECONOMIC WASTE

The county hired an architect to design a concrete slab that was to be the roof of an underground parking garage. The top of the slab was landscaped with dirt, rock, shrubs, grass, and benches. After construction was complete and had been accepted by the county, water began dripping into the garage. Evidence showed that the major cause of the leakage was an admixture specified by the architect that was causing conduit embedded in the slab to rust; the architect was therefore held liable for the cost of the repair.

The cost to remove the landscaping, apply a waterproofing membrane, then replace the landscaping was estimated as $350,000 to $500,000. The court determined that an acceptable alternative would be to install cathodic protection to prevent further corrosion on the conduit and install drip pans to collect the leakage. As the total for this approach was approximately $107,000, the court held that it would be economic waste to remove the landscaping and apply a waterproofing membrane.

County of Maricopa v. Walsh and Oberg Architects, Inc.,
16 Ariz. App. 439, 494 P.2d 44 (1972)

21.4.2 Economic Waste

In applying the benefit of the bargain principle to the quality element of a contract, a court tries to ensure that the owner receives the quality agreed to in the contract documents. The measure of the owner's damages for defective work by either the A/E or the contractor is typically the cost of the repairs required to bring the construction in accordance with the contract. However, in some cases, the cost of the repairs would be excessive when considering the nature of the damage, the value of the project, or the diminution in the project's value. In such cases, the court considers a repair to be economic waste and may instead award the diminution of value. Alternatively, the court may award the cost of reasonable repairs, plus an amount of money representing the difference in value between the repaired property and the construction that was contracted for.

21.4.3 Betterment

When the breach of contract involves defective construction, the owner's measure of damages is typically the cost of correction. However, if the owner paid less for the defective construction than it would have paid if the work had been performed correctly, the damages award will be adjusted accordingly. Courts will not put the nonbreaching party in a better position than it would have been in if there had been no breach, as to do so is considered betterment.

CASE STUDY—BETTERMENT

The owner of an apartment complex hired a general contractor to design and install a heating system. Problems arose soon after the heating system was turned on; after the second season of use, the owner hired a mechanical engineer to inspect the system and make recommendations regarding any deficiencies. The engineer suggested a number of changes that would improve the efficiency of the system. A second engineer proceeded to make these changes and also replaced all of the control valves, even though only some of the valves were defective.

The owner subsequently sued the general contractor for the cost of these changes. The court held that the contractor was liable only for repairs to the parts of the system that were defective. Requiring the contractor to pay for a system that was more efficient than what was required by its contract would constitute betterment. The owner was not entitled to an optimum system such as might have been designed by an engineer.

Oakwood Villa Apartments, Inc., v. Gulu,
9 Mich.App. 568, 157 N.W.2d 816 (1968)

As an example, an error in the plans may have caused the contractor to install an item that was not allowed by the applicable building code. If the error was such that the A/E was found to have violated the required standard of professional care, the A/E would be liable for the cost to correct the defect, that is, the cost to remove the item that was installed and install the required item. If the required item was more expensive than the incorrect item, the A/E's liability would be adjusted to account for the difference in price; providing the owner with an item more costly than the item it had paid for would result in betterment.

21.5 CONTRACTOR'S DAMAGES

On a fixed-priced contract, the contractor's expectation interest is the right to complete the contractual scope of work within the time permitted under the contract, and without interference from the owner or the owner's agents. In exchange for this work, the contractor is entitled to receive the contract sum, as adjusted by any change orders.

The contractor's damages for an owner-caused breach of contract are generally direct costs. If the breach occurred because the owner requested work that was not required by the contract, actual damages may be fairly easy to calculate. It is typically more difficult for the contractor to prove the damages it has incurred because of owner-caused delays or disruption. The contractor's damages for a delay may include costs for idle equipment, overhead, price increases, and loss of productivity. While equipment costs, overhead, and price increases can often be estimated with reasonable accuracy, proving loss of productivity typically presents more of a challenge.

21.5.1 Equipment Costs

The contractor will generally claim damages if it has equipment on-site and cannot use this equipment because of an owner-caused delay. When the equipment is leased, the contractor can prove its costs by submitting an invoice from the rental company and showing that it could not mitigate its damages by using the equipment on another project.

When the contractor was using its own equipment, its damages would be based on its cost of ownership. If the contract includes an equipment schedule for pricing change orders, courts often allow the contractor to use this schedule to establish damages for equipment that could not be used because of a delay. When the scheduled rates include the cost of consumables such as fuel, there would need to be an adjustment to account for the fact that the equipment was not being used. If the contract does not include an equipment schedule and the contractor's record keeping is such that it is difficult to determine ownership costs, the contractor may be allowed to use either local rental rates or typical ownership costs, as determined by an industry trade association.

21.5.2   Home Office Overhead

On most jobs, the contractor has overhead costs such as a job site office trailer, site utilities, site security, and supervision. Such costs are usually considered to be direct costs and are thus recoverable when the owner is responsible for a project delay. Contractors that are large enough to work on several jobs at the same time may also have a home office, where administrative functions like payroll and accounts payable are handled. Overhead costs for a home office may include rent, utilities, office equipment, and the salaries of management, estimators, and office personnel. The contractor expects to absorb these costs through the overhead margin on its job billings. When a job is delayed and the contractor cannot take on other work, the reduction in billings means that some of the home office overhead will be unabsorbed.

Home office overhead is typically considered to be a foreseeable consequential cost, so if the contractor has not waived consequential damages, the contractor's damages for an owner-caused delay can include its unabsorbed home office overhead.

21.5.2.1   Eichleay Damages

There are several methods for calculating unabsorbed home office overhead. The most common method is the Eichleay formula, as set out in the *Eichleay Corporation* case.[1] *Eichleay* was brought before the Armed Services Board of Contract Appeals and involved a contract with the federal government. Nevertheless, the Eichleay formula has been accepted by some state courts for both public and private construction.

The Eichleay formula requires three calculations. First, the contractor must determine the overhead associated with the delayed contract by multiplying its total overhead by the ratio of its billings on the delayed contract to its total billings during the time the contract was performed. A daily overhead rate for the delayed contract is then calculated by dividing the total contract overhead by the number of days of contract performance. Finally, the recoverable overhead is calculated by multiplying the daily overhead rate by the number of days of delay. To establish a case for recovery of home office overhead, the contractor must show that:

1. Performance of the contract was delayed due to the owner's actions;
2. The nature of the delay made it impractical for the contractor to either take on other work or reduce its home office overhead costs; and
3. The contractor suffered actual damages as a result of the delay.

The owner may be able to rebut the contractor's claim by showing that any loss that might have occurred during the delay was compensated for by the increased work activity following the delay.

---

[1] *Eichleay* Corporation, ASBCA No. 5183, 60-2 BCA 2688 (1960).

21.5.3 Cost Increases for Labor and Materials

When there is a lengthy delay or disruption to a project, work that is performed later than originally scheduled may cost more than originally anticipated because of an increase in wages or materials costs. When cost increases can be documented with reasonable certainty by establishing prices at the time the work should have been performed and those at the time work was actually performed, the contractor may be able to recover the difference in its costs as direct damages.

21.5.4 Methods of Estimating Loss of Productivity

Often, the contractor is not able to isolate the costs resulting from a particular owner-caused delay. This is true particularly if the delay has impacted a large number of activities and caused a loss of productivity. In such cases, the contractor may resort to a general method of estimating its damages.

21.5.4.1 Measured-Mile Approach

Under the measured-mile approach, the contractor compares its productivity on an unaffected portion of the project with its productivity on the portion that has been affected by an owner-caused disruption. The contractor must show that the affected and unaffected portions represent comparable work such that the only material variable is the disruption caused by the owner. The measured-mile approach is one of the preferred measures of proving inefficiency or loss of productivity because it uses actual data from the project. The drawback with this approach is that some portion of the work must be unaffected by the disruption. Consequently, it cannot be used if the owner-caused delay or interference has affected all of the work.

21.5.4.2 Should-Cost Estimates

When the measured mile approach cannot be used because all of the work was affected, the contractor may try to estimate what performance on the project "should have" cost by looking at performance of substantially similar work on other projects. Should-cost estimates are generally not considered a reliable means of proving damages, however. The contractor bears the burden of proving that the estimate is reasonable; given the number of factors affecting productivity, this can be difficult.

21.5.4.3 Industry Standards and Studies

If neither the measured-mile approach nor should-cost estimates can be used, the contractor may try to use industry standards or studies to prove a lack of inefficiency. Such studies often look at various weather conditions and estimate how they affect the productivity of certain types of work. For example, the contractor may allege that it had planned to do certain activities during the summer, but because of owner-caused delays, it was forced to perform that work during cold weather and thus suffered a 15 percent loss in efficiency.

In general, industry studies are not considered a reliable means of proof because conditions at a particular project may be considerably different from those assumed in the study. In addition, such studies are generally not designed to be used as a means of quantifying damages. Industry studies are typically only allowed when it is clear that there have been some damages and there is no more exact means of proving them.

21.5.4.4 *Total Cost Method*

If the contractor cannot determine how much of its cost increase was due to delay damages, and how much was due to changes in the work, it may file a claim for its total damages without distinguishing the causes. The simplest, but also least accepted, method of estimating total damages is the total cost method. The total cost method calculates the contractor's damages as the difference between the bid amount and the actual costs incurred plus overhead and profit. This assumes that the entire cost overrun is attributable to the owner. By making this assumption, it is further assumed that the contractor's original bid was reasonable and the work could have been completed for the bid amount, if not for the owner's actions.

While the simplicity of this approach is appealing, courts typically reject the assumption that all cost overruns are the owner's responsibility. The contractor's costs may have increased because of its own inefficiencies and errors. Furthermore, its bid may have been unrealistically low. A contractor seeking damages through the total cost method must prove that:

- The nature of the losses makes it impossible to determine them with a reasonable degree of accuracy;
- The contractor's original bid was realistic;
- The contractor's actual costs were reasonable; and
- The contractor was not responsible for any of the cost overruns.

Courts usually consider the total cost method appropriate only if there have been so many changes to the project that it is impossible to isolate how a particular change affected the contractor's costs.

21.5.4.5 *Modified Total Cost Method*

The modified total cost method attempts to reduce the amount of damages calculated under the total cost method by any bid errors, any costs attributable to the contractor, and any costs attributable to parties other than the owner. The contractor is required to analyze its bid and make adjustments for any errors.

It is also required to analyze both its performance and the performance of its subcontractors, and take responsibility for any inefficiencies that were not factored into the bid. In addition, the contractor must determine whether any of the cost overruns were due to third parties that the owner had no control over; the owner is not held responsible for these costs.

21.5.4.6 Jury Verdict Method

Despite its name, the jury verdict method of determining damages is actually used by arbitration panels or courts acting without juries. It is essentially a process whereby damages are estimated from the available evidence because denying any recovery would be too unfair to the injured party. It takes its name from the fact that juries are often presented with evidence showing there was an injury, but damages cannot be easily determined.

This approach is not favored, however, and is only allowed when more exact methods cannot be applied. The contractor must show that there is clear proof of the injury, that there is no more reliable method of computing damages, and that the evidence is sufficient to make a fair and reasonable approximation of the damages.

21.6 LIMITATION OF LIABILITY

There are several methods by which a party can limit its exposure to damages that could result from negligent performance of a contractual obligation. These include exculpatory clauses, indemnity clauses, limitation of liability clauses, and waiver of consequential damages. Indemnity clauses are common in construction contracts, while limitation-of-liability clauses are common in design agreements. Waivers of consequential damages are common in both construction contracts and design agreements.

21.6.1 Exculpatory Clauses

An exculpatory clause is a clause under which one party agrees that it is not allowed to recover damages from the other party, even if the other party is at fault. Because the other party is protected from the consequences of its own actions, exculpatory clauses are not favored by the courts. For an exculpatory clause to be enforceable, the contract must relate solely to the private affairs of the contracting parties. It is not enforceable where any matters of public interest would be affected, as a party cannot be released from its responsibility to exercise reasonable care to the public. Each party must be a free bargaining agent, and the party seeking protection can only be relieved of liability for its own acts of negligence.

Any ambiguity is construed against the party seeking protection; the party seeking protection also has the burden of proving each of the conditions to enforcement of the clause. An example of an exculpatory clause is the no-damages-for-delay clause found in many construction contracts.

21.6.1.1 No-Damages-for-Delay Clauses

Because the contractor's damages for even a short delay can be considerable, many owners insist that the construction contract include a no-damages-for delay clause. A no-damages-for-delay clause limits the contractor's remedy for an owner-caused delay to an extension of the contract time. Although none of the industry standard form contracts includes such a clause, no-damages-for-delay clauses are often included in prime contracts and are even more commonly included in subcontracts. There is no standard wording for these clauses, but a typical clause in a prime contract might be:

> *No compensation shall be payable to the Contractor for delays due to any cause, including delays caused by the actions or omissions of the Owner, and Contractor's remedy for delay shall be limited to an extension of the contract time.*

In accordance with the general principle that parties are free to arrange the terms of their contracts, a no-damages-for-delay clause is usually enforceable in accordance with its terms. Nevertheless, no-damages-for-delay clauses are a frequent subject of litigation, and their use is controversial. Courts narrowly construe their application and will look closely at the wording of a clause to determine whether it applies in the particular circumstances. Several states have enacted legislation prohibiting enforcement of no-damages-for-delay clauses in contracts for public construction; some states prohibit them in all construction contracts.

Even in states where the clause is enforced, enforcement is subject to several well-established exceptions. No state will enforce a no-damages-for-delay clause if there has been fraud, misrepresentation, or bad faith by the owner. Other common exceptions to enforcement include owner-caused delays that are so long that they constitute abandonment of the project, delays caused by the owner's active interference with the contractor's performance, and delays beyond the contemplation of the parties at the time the contract was executed. The circumstances under which these exceptions are recognized vary widely from state to state, however, and some states enforce the clause in all but the most egregious circumstances.

21.6.2 Indemnification Agreements

In contrast to an exculpatory clause, where one of the parties waives its right to damages, an indemnity clause holds one party (the indemnitee) harmless from liability by requiring the other party (the indemnitor) to bear the cost of any damages the indemnitee may be liable for. Indemnity can be an important issue on construction projects. When an accident occurs, it may not be clear which party is responsible; often, several parties may be jointly responsible. Rather than having the issue of liability go to court after an accident, the parties may use indemnity agreements to apportion liability before an accident occurs. Indemnification clauses are common in both prime contracts and subcontracts. In a prime contract, the contractor generally indemnifies the owner and the A/E from liability for its acts. In a subcontract, the subcontractor typically indemnifies the contractor, as well as the owner and the A/E.

Indemnity agreements are often used to shift the burden of liability to the party whose actions were the cause of the damages. For example, if the owner holds the contractor liable for the subcontractor's deficient construction, an indemnification clause in the subcontract will allow the contractor to recover its damages from the subcontractor. When an indemnification clause shifts liability to the party that was responsible for the damage, it is generally enforceable. However, some indemnification clauses attempt to make the indemnitor liable for all losses, even those that are caused in whole or in part by the indemnitee.

Because of the potential unfairness and adverse social implications of such broad indemnity clauses, a number of states have statutes restricting their enforceability. These statutes, and the court's enforcement of the statutes, vary greatly from state to state, however. Some states invalidate clauses that indemnify a party against liability for a loss that was caused in part by that party's negligence. Others only invalidate clauses that indemnify a party even if they were solely responsible for the loss. Some states will not enforce agreements designed to indemnify design professionals from liability arising from their services.

21.6.3 Limitation-of-Liability Clauses

Whereas indemnity clauses attempt to contract away the liability arising from a party's negligence, limitation-of-liability clauses only limit the amount of damages the party may be required to pay for its negligence. Such clauses became common in the early 1970s, when the Associated Soil and Foundation Engineers (ASFE) developed a contractual provision that limited the geotechnical engineer's liability to the owner and the contractor.

Some states have prohibited such clauses in public contracts as against public policy, but they have become widespread in design agreements for private construction and are generally considered to be an acceptable way of allocating risk. A/Es view such clauses as reflecting a proper risk/reward analysis. On most projects, the A/E's fee is a small percentage of the potential damages. The owner receives the principal benefit from the project; thus, A/Es typically believe it is appropriate for the owner to bear most of the risk.

A limitation-of-liability clause is generally enforceable as long as the limitation is reasonable and does not absolve the protected party from meaningful responsibility for its own misconduct. In considering whether the limitation in a design agreement is reasonable, courts typically look at the A/E's expected compensation for the work rather than the alleged damages. An amount equal to or greater than the A/E's fee is often considered reasonable. Courts are most likely to find that a limitation of liability is enforceable if the parties are business entities that are dealing at arm's length, the limitation was freely bargained for, and there was no injury or property damage.

CASE STUDY—LIMITATION OF LIABILITY

A developer hired an engineer to do a feasibility study for a parcel of land that it was planning to purchase. The contract limited the engineer's liability to the greater of $50,000 or the engineer's fee, which was $7,000. The engineer's report stated that there were no height restrictions that would impair the developer's plan. Before closing on the purchase, however, the developer learned that there actually were height restrictions, and it would be unable to proceed with the proposed development.

The developer went ahead with the purchase and subsequently sued the engineer, seeking more than $2 million in damages as the result of the engineer's breach of contract, negligence, gross negligence, and negligent misrepresentation. The court upheld the clause limiting the engineer's liability to $50,000. Since the limit was seven times the engineer's fee, it did not insulate the engineer from the consequences of its actions. While the limit was nominal compared to the alleged damages, the other party's alleged damages are not the proper measure of whether a limit is appropriate.

Valhal Corp. v. Sullivan Associates, Inc.,
44 F.3d 195 (3rd Cir. 1995)

21.6.4 Waiver of Consequential Damages

Under contract law, consequential damages resulting from a breach of contract are recoverable if they were reasonably foreseeable at the time the contract was executed. However, many construction contracts, including the AIA documents, contain a mutual waiver of consequential damages between all parties.

The owner and the A/E waive their rights to consequential damages from the other party under §8.1.3 of AIA B101. The effect of the waiver is heavily weighted in favor of the A/E, however. The A/E's consequential damages are usually limited to the potential profits from any other projects it turned down. In contrast, the owner may suffer considerable consequential damages if the project is delayed because of the A/E's breach. As a result of this disparity in the potential effects of a waiver, the parties sometimes agree to a limitation on consequential damages rather than an outright waiver. For example, the owner may be limited to recovering the amount of the A/E's fee or the amount that can be recovered from the A/E's professional liability insurance.

The owner and contractor waive claims for consequential damages against each other under §15.1.6 of AIA A201. The owner waives all claims for rental expenses; loss of use, income, financing, business, or profit; loss of productivity; and loss of employee services. The contractor waives all claims for additional home office expenses including personnel stationed there; for financing, business, and reputation losses; and for loss of profit except anticipated profit arising directly from the project. As with the waiver between the owner and the A/E, these mutual waivers will likely penalize the owner much more than the contractor, particularly if the contractor does not have a home office. As a result, owners often alter or delete the waiver clause found in AIA A201 and other industry standard form contracts.

21.7 SPECIFIC PERFORMANCE

When there has been a breach of contract on a construction project, courts generally award only money damages. It is very rare for a court to require *specific performance*; in other words, courts seldom require the parties to perform the contract according to its terms. Specific performance is typically only required in sales contracts, when the subject of the transaction is something unique like a particular house or parcel of land.

It is also rare for a court to decide that the owner has the right to have the construction removed and the property restored to the condition that it was in before construction started. A court would only do so if the construction had no value because of the breach, and it was clear at the time the contract was executed that this would be the case if the contractor breached. For example, an owner may contract for construction of a temporary facility for a particular event. In such a case, the facility may have no value unless it is finished in time for the event. If the contractor did not complete the facility in time, through no fault of the owner, or the work was defective to the extent that the facility was unusable, a court might require the contractor to demolish the facility and restore the site to its preconstruction condition.

21.8 TORT CLAIMS

Although most claims related to construction projects are for breach of contract, tort claims alleging negligence sometimes arise. A project participant might be injured by another participant it has no contractual privity with. This would be the case, for example, if the contractor was delayed by the A/E's failure to review shop drawings within a reasonable amount of time. The contractor could not bring a breach-of-contract claim against the A/E but could possibly have a tort claim against the A/E for professional negligence. Alternatively, there may be contractual privity between the parties, but the injured party may not be able to bring a contract claim because the statute of limitations has passed.

The general measure of compensatory damages for tort claims is the same as the measure of damages for contract claims. It is the amount of money that will put the injured person in the same position it would have been in "but for" the negligence of the defendant. The damages calculation is similar to that used when determining breach-of-contract damages. However, the injured party may also be able to recover consequential damages that were not contemplated by the parties at the time of contracting. Depending on the circumstances, the injured party may be able to recover punitive damages.

If the damages are strictly economic—that is, there is no property damage or bodily injury—the injured party's ability to recover on a tort claim depends on the state's interpretation of the economic loss doctrine. If there is damage to other property or bodily injury, the injured party is entitled to bring a tort claim, whether or not there is a contract between the parties.

21.9 RECOVERY OF DAMAGES IN THE ABSENCE OF AN EXPRESS CONTRACT

Most contracts between the participants on a construction project are express contracts whereby the agreement is memorialized in a written form that both parties sign. If the contract is breached, the nonbreaching party is entitled to damages based on its expectation interest. In some cases, however, a court finds that a party is entitled to damages even without an express contract. Such claims may be brought under the legal theories of promissory estoppel, *quantum meruit*, or unjust enrichment.

21.9.1 Reliance Interest—Promissory Estoppel

In some cases, a promisee (the party receiving a promise) relies on the promise, anticipating that the promise will form the basis of a contract between the parties. The promisee may have a claim for promissory estoppel if the promissor (the party making the promise) subsequently refuses to honor the promise. The elements of a promissory estoppel claim are that the promissor made a promise that it expected the promisee to rely on; the promisee did, in fact, rely on the promise; and such reliance was detrimental to the promisee.

Because promissory estoppel claims arise when there is not an enforceable contract, a court is not seeking to protect the promisee's expectation interest. Instead, promissory estoppel protects the promisee's reliance interest in the promise. The measure of damages for promissory estoppel is typically the amount of money the promisee lost by relying on the promise.

In the construction industry, claims of promissory estoppel usually arise because the contractor has relied on a subcontractor's bid for its own bid and the subcontractor subsequently refused to honor its bid. In such cases, the contractor's reliance interest would be the difference between the subcontractor's bid and the amount the contractor had to pay another subcontractor. Promissory estoppel claims may also arise if the promisee made purchases or started work in anticipation of a contract that the promissor subsequently refused to carry through with.

21.9.2 Implied-in-Fact Contracts—*Quantum Meruit*

In addition to promissory estoppel, whereby a court may award damages for reliance even when a contract was not formed, courts may find that an implied contract has been formed by the parties' conduct, despite the lack of an express, enforceable contract.

Such a contract, where the parties have assented to the agreement by their conduct rather than by words, is referred to as an *implied-in-fact* contract. A court may infer the existence of an implied-in-fact contract based on one party's having performed services under circumstances in which both parties must have understood and intended compensation to be paid. The measure of damages is typically the reasonable value of the work and is referred to as *quantum meruit*, which is Latin for "as much as he deserves."

The basis for an implied contract is that if one accepts a benefit, knowing that it was not conferred as a gift, the law will infer that the recipient promised to pay the other party reasonable compensation. For example, if a contractor takes a piece of machinery into a shop for repair, without any agreement as to the cost of repair, the contractor implicitly agrees to pay a reasonable amount.

A contractor may file a claim under *quantum meruit* if it is not able to reach an agreement with the owner on the pricing of a change order. The contractor would then seek to prove the compensation it was entitled to, based on the value of the work. When a construction contract is wrongfully terminated, courts may allow the contractor to recover under *quantum meruit* rather than breach of contract. This can be to the contractor's advantage if it had underbid the project and the value of the work was greater than the contract amount.

A contractor is sometimes able to recover under *quantum meruit* if its contract with an owner is deemed unenforceable because it violated a statutory requirement—for example, if the contractor was not properly licensed. Courts are often reluctant to undermine statutory requirements, however, and courts in some states only allow a *quantum meruit* recovery if the contractor was not at fault for the violation.

21.9.3 Restitution Interest—Unjust Enrichment

In contrast to an implied-in-fact contract, the legal theory of restitution is not premised on an agreement between the parties. Instead, it is premised on society's interest in preventing a party from retaining a benefit without paying for it. Restitution is based on a *contract implied-in-law*, also referred to as a *quasi-contract*; the cause of action is often referred to as *unjust enrichment*.

A contract implied-in-law is not actually a contract, as there was no agreement between the parties. Instead, it is an obligation created by law to prevent an injustice. To recover under a contract implied-in-law, the claimant must show that a benefit was conferred on the other party, the claimant was not acting gratuitously, and it would be an injustice for the other party to retain the benefit without paying for it. In addition, the claimant must show that it has no other remedy based on contractual or statutory rights.

The remedy is referred to as *restitution* because the benefited party must make restitution for the amount of its gain. The court looks through the eyes of the recipient to determine whether the work does, in fact, constitute a benefit and, if so, the value of the benefit. Unlike promissory estoppel or *quantum meruit*, the court does not consider whether the compensation is fair to the claimant.

A claim of unjust enrichment sometimes arises because the party contracting for work defaulted and the benefit devolved to a party that has no legal obligation to pay for it. As an example, if a tenant hires a contractor to remodel leased space but goes bankrupt before paying for the work, the contractor may be able recover damages from the owner of the building. The measure of damages would not be the contract price or the contractor's costs, however, but the value of the work to the building owner. If the building owner is unable to lease the remodeled space to another tenant, the work may be of no value. The contractor is only entitled to seek damages from the building owner if recovery from the tenant is impossible. The fact that the tenant decides not to occupy the remodeled space does not, by itself, give the contractor the right to recover damages from the building owner.

A claim of unjust enrichment may also arise because of a mistake made by the party seeking compensation—for example, if the contractor did work at the wrong house or did work other than what was required by its contract. However, courts typically do not impose an obligation to pay for the benefit received unless the recipient of the services or materials was aware of the mistake and made no attempt to stop the contractor.

A contractor that has been terminated for default may be entitled to restitution if the benefit it has conferred is greater than the loss caused by the default. Although the court will not allow the contractor to benefit from its default, it will typically not allow the owner to be unjustly enriched. Likewise, a subcontractor that has not complied with the requirements for a mechanic's lien will not be able to enforce the lien. To prevent the owner from benefiting at the subcontractor's expense, some courts have allowed the subcontractor to recover on the basis of unjust enrichment. However, courts may refuse to create an implied-in-law contract when the claimant has lost its legal rights by failing to comply with statutory requirements.

21.9.4 *Quantum Meruit* versus Unjust Enrichment

It should be noted that the terms *quantum meruit* and *unjust enrichment* are not used consistently in either legal opinions or legal writing. *Quantum meruit* is sometimes used to refer to both implied-in-fact and implied-in-law contracts. *Quantum meruit* may also be used to indicate that the claimant is entitled to the fair value of its services, regardless of the type of claim it has made. Similarly, *unjust enrichment* may refer to the equitable remedy of imposing a legal obligation when there has been no agreement between the parties, but it may also be used as a general reference, to indicate that goods or services have not been paid for.

The confusion in terminology aside, there are two different causes of action that may be invoked to prevent a party from being enriched by materials or services that have not been not paid for. One cause of action applies when an implied contract was created by the parties' conduct, or an express contract was terminated through no fault of the claimant. In such cases, courts typically find that the claimant is entitled to the fair value of the goods and services provided (*quantum meruit*).

The other cause of action applies either when there was no contract between the parties, the contract was terminated because of the claimant's default, or the claimant lost its legal rights by failing to comply with contractual or statutory requirements. In such cases, a court may find that the claimant is only entitled to restitution of the value of the benefit to the recipient. If the value of the services provided is the same as the value of the benefit received, recovery will be the same, no matter how the claim is brought. However, in some cases, the value of the benefit to the recipient is considerably less than the fair value of the services provided.

22

THE ECONOMIC
LOSS DOCTRINE

Although business dealings are nominally governed by the contracts between the parties, tort law and its legally imposed responsibilities and remedies have crept into many areas of commerce, including construction. In some cases, this is because there is no contract between the parties, for example, when the owner wants to bring a claim against a subcontractor or the contractor wants to bring a claim against the A/E. In other cases, it is because the problem did not manifest itself until the warranties and other contractual remedies had expired. Under the economic loss doctrine, however, the injured party's ability to bring a tort claim may be limited unless there has been bodily injury or property damage.

22.1 TORT VERSUS CONTRACT LAW

Historically, plaintiffs who suffered injuries from defective products could only sue the manufacturer under a warranty theory; they could not sue on a tort theory such as negligence, because the manufacturer did not owe them any duty. An injured consumer who did not have a contractual relationship with the manufacturer (i.e., someone who was using a borrowed piece of equipment) was not covered by any warranty and thus did not have a remedy against the manufacturer.

This changed with the 1916 New York case *MacPherson v. Buick Motor Co.*[1] The court in *MacPherson* held that manufacturers have a duty to act reasonably. The duty exists even without a contract between the parties, and breaching this duty by selling defective products allows a tort action for negligence. *MacPherson* has been accepted in every state to provide a remedy to those who are injured by negligently made products.

A similar duty applies to services such as construction work. A contractor is liable in tort to all those who may foreseeably be injured by its negligent work.

---

[1] *MacPherson v. Buick Motor Co.*, 217 N.Y. 382, 111 N.E. 1050 (1916).

This applies not only to contractors that do construction but also to those that do repair work and those that install parts. When there is physical injury—either bodily injury or damage to other property—the injured party is allowed economic damages such as lost profits as well as its damages for the physical injury. Under a strict application of the economic loss doctrine, however, economic losses cannot be recovered under tort if there is no physical injury. The economic loss doctrine holds that when losses are just economic, they can be recovered only through contract law, such as by warranties.

22.1.1 Definition of Economic Loss

As its name implies, the economic loss doctrine focuses on the type of damages suffered by the injured party. *Economic loss* is monetary loss caused by a defective product or damage to the product itself, excluding loss resulting from bodily injury or damage to property other than the defective product. It includes the diminution in value of the product because the product does not work for the purpose for which it was sold, as well as the cost of repair or replacement of the defective product. Economic loss may be either direct or consequential (indirect). Direct economic loss is the loss in value of the product itself and any repair or replacement costs. All other economic loss caused by a defective product, including lost profits, is consequential.

22.1.2 Development of the Economic Loss Doctrine

The economic loss doctrine developed as a judicial response to the increased number of tort actions brought in contractual settings following the *MacPherson* decision. The doctrine's underlying rationale is that parties should protect against the risk of economic loss when they are negotiating the contract; they should not try to recover under tort law after a loss occurs.

The doctrine was first stated by the California Supreme Court in the 1965 case *Seely v. White Motor Co.*[2] The *Seely* court held that allowing a plaintiff to recover for purely economic loss outside the context of a warranty meant the manufacturer could be liable for unknown and potentially unlimited economic damages. The doctrine was subsequently adopted by the U.S. Supreme Court in the 1986 case *East River S.S. Corp. v. Transamerica Delaval, Inc.*[3] The court held that a manufacturer in a commercial relationship has no duty to prevent a product from injuring itself, and if the harm is purely economic, recoverability of damages must be determined by the contract between the parties.

Both of these cases involved liability for defective products, where the product damaged itself such that there were repair costs and lost profits, but no bodily

---

[2] *Seely v. White Motor Co.*, 63 Cal.2d 9, 18, 45 Cal.Rptr. 17, 23, 403 P.2d 145, 151 (1965).

[3] *East River Steamship Corp. v. Transamerica Delaval, Inc.*, 476 U.S. 858, 106 S.Ct. 2295, 90 L.Ed.2d 865 (1986).

injury or physical damage to other property. In subsequent cases, the doctrine has been extended to limit an injured party's ability to recover purely economic losses resulting from defective services.

22.1.3   Basis for the Doctrine

The economic loss doctrine preserves the fundamental distinction between contract and tort principles by recognizing that contract law rests on bargained-for obligations, while tort law is based on legal obligations created by the courts or by statute. The goal of contract law is to ensure that each party to a contract receives the benefit of its bargain. The parties' duties arise from the terms of their agreement. If one of the parties does not comply with its duties under the contract, the other party's remedy is determined by the contract.

In contrast, the goal of tort law is to protect people from unexpected and overwhelming misfortunes through the fault of others, and compensate the injured party when such misfortunes occur. Tort law imposes minimum standards of behavior on all members of society; these standards include the duty to take reasonable steps to protect others from being injured or having their possessions damaged. If this duty is violated, tort law requires that the injured party be compensated, provided the injury was foreseeable and proximately (legally) caused by the other party's wrong doing.

The economic loss doctrine helps to ensure predictability in commercial transactions by encouraging parties to address risks and costs during their bargaining. It also protects the parties' freedom to allocate economic risk via contract. Finally, the economic loss doctrine encourages purchasers to guard against the risks that a defective product could cause their business. Purchasers are better equipped than sellers to anticipate the economic loss that may result from a defective product; purchasers can guard against foreseeable economic loss through contractual remedies such as warranties or insurance.

22.1.4   Public Policy Considerations

Public policy considerations involved in the economic loss doctrine can be understood by looking at the case *532 Madison Avenue Gourmet Foods, Inc., v. Finlandia Center, Inc.*[4] This case, which came before the New York Court of Appeals, consolidated two cases, one that involved the collapse of an office tower at 532 Madison Avenue and one that involved the collapse of a construction elevator tower in Times Square. Both collapses resulted in street closures and caused considerable economic losses to nearby merchants. Several merchants subsequently filed suit to recover for those losses. The court unanimously held that the economic loss doctrine barred recovery by plaintiffs who had only

---

[4]*532 Madison Ave. Gourmet Foods v. Finlandia Ctr.* 96 NY2d 280 (2001).

suffered economic damages, because the plaintiffs constituted an indeterminate class of people to whom no tort duty was owed.

It is easy to see the indeterminate nature of the plaintiffs in these cases: anyone who was prevented from using a closed street could have been economically damaged. This would include not just residents and local shop owners but also those unable to access the services within the closed-off areas and those forced to detour around the closed-off areas. Likewise, anyone doing business with someone who was delayed by the closed streets could have been economically damaged. If all of these individuals were allowed to file suits for their economic losses, it would swamp the court system. Requiring the plaintiff to have suffered either bodily injury or physical damage in order to recover for economic loss thus serves as a means of creating a definable class of plaintiffs.

22.1.5   Strict Application of the Doctrine

In most states, the negligent performance of a contractual obligation, without more, is simply a breach of contract. Failure to perform one's contractual obligations does not support a tort action unless there is either bodily injury or damage to property other than the property that is the subject matter of the contract. This is true whether the contract is for the purchase of a product, installation of the product, leasing of equipment, or services. Under a strict application of the economic loss doctrine, if the parties are in privity of contract, there can be no tort recovery when the losses are only economic—the recovery must be pursued as a contract claim.

A strict application of the economic loss doctrine also precludes a tort claim when the parties do not have a contract and the losses are only economic, but the rationale is different. If there is no contract between two parties, neither party has any duty to prevent the other party's economic losses. Without such a duty, there can be no basis for a tort claim for these losses.

On a construction project, losses are often purely economic. In addition, many of the participants on a construction project are not in privity of contract with each other and thus cannot bargain for contractual remedies such as warranties. As an example, on a design-bid-build project, the contractor does not have a contract with the A/E. Thus, under a strict application of the economic loss doctrine, the A/E does not owe the contractor any duty to prevent economic losses. If the A/E's failure to review shop drawings within a reasonable amount of time delays the contractor and causes its costs to increase, the contractor must try to recover its damages from the owner. If the owner is held liable for the contractor's additional costs, the owner must pursue an action against the A/E to recover the costs.

22.1.6   Exceptions to the Economic Loss Doctrine

Because the economic loss doctrine can eliminate many valid claims for which there is no other remedy, courts have struggled with how to apply it. The doctrine is not applied uniformly from state to state, as various exceptions have been carved out. State courts carve out exceptions to legal doctrines based on public policies considered important in that particular state. Because public policies recognized by the courts vary from state to state, so do the exceptions to the doctrines. In some cases, the circumstances under which different states allow exceptions seem to be completely contradictory.

Many states treat claims based on defective products differently from claims based on defective services. Some states also distinguish between professional services, such as those provided by the A/E, and other services. The different applications of the doctrine have caused considerable confusion, particularly with respect to claims on construction projects.

22.2 CLAIMS OF DEFECTIVE CONSTRUCTION PRODUCTS

The economic loss doctrine is easiest to apply in the context of manufactured products liability cases. Courts uniformly hold that, as a matter of public policy, a consumer should not bear the risk of physical injury from a defective product. A consumer can file a tort claim if there has been bodily injury or damage to property other than the product itself. However, if the product simply does not work as desired, or does not work at all, the consumer must resort to a breach-of-contract case in accordance with any warranty that was provided. A manufacturer cannot be held to a customer's desired level of performance unless that performance has been implicitly or explicitly warranted.

In the manufactured products context, most states thus apply the economic loss doctrine to bar tort claims when the losses are just economic, whether or not the parties are in privity of contract. Only a few states allow negligence actions for economic losses against manufacturers of defective products when there has been no physical harm. Defective products are considered to be a disappointed economic expectation that can only be brought as a contract claim.

Limiting tort liability for economic losses when a contract exists between the parties is considered appropriate because the product's potential nonperformance can be addressed when the parties bargain over the terms of the contract. A buyer may choose to assume the risk that a product will not perform properly by accepting a lower quality in exchange for a lower product price. Alternatively, the buyer may choose to pay more and obtain a more extensive warranty.

Limiting tort liability for economic losses when there is no contract between the parties is considered appropriate because the party allegedly causing the loss typically owes no duty to the injured party. For example, a manufacturer does not owe a duty to the purchaser of a secondhand product that does not function as claimed by the seller; the manufacturer is only responsible for any warranty that may apply.

Nevertheless, the inherent complexity of the construction process creates difficulties in determining how the economic loss doctrine should be applied. There are many reasons why a product may not perform as required, and problems with performance may involve more than one identifiable reason. If a defective product was not installed correctly or was damaged by another contractor, the product warranties may be voided. In addition, the "damage to other property" exception is often difficult to apply because products typically do not remain in their as-purchased form but are incorporated into the structure during construction.

22.2.1 Damage to Other Property

A defective construction product will frequently cause damage to other parts of the structure. Common examples of such damage include ceiling damage from defective roofing and drywall cracks caused by a floor truss that deflects excessively under design loads. The economic loss doctrine allows claims for damage to property other than the product itself. If a plaintiff has sustained physical harm to other property, it may recover its economic losses along with the physical damages to the other property. States vary widely in what they consider the defective product versus what they consider "other property," however, and there have been completely opposite results in virtually identical cases.

Many states follow a broad "integrated structure" analysis and treat the entire structure as the product. Under this analysis, water damage to other parts of the structure caused by defective roofing would not be recoverable under tort, because the damage would not be to "other property." Damage to the structure is considered damage to the product; thus, the economic loss doctrine bars any recovery.

A number of states do not followed a strict integrated structure analysis, however, and allow tort recovery against a manufacturer when a defective product damages another identifiable component. Some courts have held that integrating building materials into a structure as intended by the manufacturer does not detract from the character of those materials as separate products. However, even when incorporated products are considered identifiable and separate, courts have disagreed on what constitutes "damage" to other property. Often, other components must be removed to repair a defective product, and the removed components may be damaged in the process. However, this may not be considered to fall within the "damage to other property" exception if the defective product did not actually damage the removed components.

In determining liability, courts sometimes look at the parties involved. When the contract was negotiated between what the court considers "sophisticated parties," the court may deny a tort claim, even if what appears to be "other property" was damaged. In such cases, the court may hold that such damages were contemplated by the parties' contract, and thus the claim must be brought as a contract claim.

22.3 CLAIMS OF DEFECTIVE CONSTRUCTION SERVICES

Some states only apply the economic loss doctrine to bar recovery of economic losses in product liability cases. However, most states have extended the economic loss doctrine to bar recovery against service providers such as contractors and subcontractors. These states hold that there cannot be a tort action for negligence against a service provider that simply fails to perform its contract properly, even if the failure to properly perform was negligent or intentional. Under such a holding, if the parties are in contractual privity, one party's breach of its contract obligations cannot support a tort action in negligence—the parties have already selected their remedies through the provisions of the contract.

A strict application of the economic loss doctrine also bars tort claims when the party suffering the loss does not have a contract with the provider of the defective work, but the defective work was part of the service provider's contract and no other work was damaged. Under such a holding, the owner could not bring an action against a subcontractor for defective work if there was no damage to any other work.

However, a tort action for negligence will be allowed when the economic loss results from damage caused to "other property" by defective services, whether or not the parties are in contractual privity. Damage to other property in this context generally means property unrelated to the service provider's work. In some states, the injured party may also be able to recover economic losses even without damage to other property if it can show that the service provider breached a tort duty that was independent of the contract. Several states hold that contractors owe an independent tort duty for any foreseeable losses and damages proximately caused by their negligent acts.

22.3.1   Claims of Defective Design Professional Services

Design professional services are those supplied by architects and engineers, and related consultants such as surveyors, hydrologists, and geologists. A structure's failure to meet expectations because of defective design typically results in claims that concern the quality, rather than the safety, of the building. Claims related to quality include increased operating costs, lost rents, the cost of remedying alleged defects, and diminution of value. Such claims are considered economic losses; most courts find that the owner must look to its contract with the design professional for resolution of such economic loss disputes.

Nevertheless, courts have recognized that some special relationships trigger an independent duty of care that supports a tort action, even when the parties have entered into a contractual relationship. Common examples of these relationships are the attorney-client relationship and the physician-patient relationship. Courts often hold that tort claims for physician and attorney malpractice can exist independent of the contract. Some courts have held that the relationship between design professional and client triggers a similar independent duty of care, since it is a professional relationship built on trust and confidence. If there is an independent duty of care, the existence of a contract does not, per se, bar a tort action for negligent design.

It should be noted that in many cases there is little difference between a tort action and a contract action for negligent design when the parties are in privity of contract. Most contracts require a design professional to use the professional standard of care for their work. Breach of contract would thus be based on breach of the professional standard of care, which is the same standard used for a tort claim. Although a tort action might allow punitive damages, such damages are only awarded when the breach of duty has been egregious.

22.3.1.1 Claims of Defective Design Professional Services without Privity of Contract

Courts vary widely in how they apply the economic loss doctrine in claims against a design professional when there is no privity of contract. Some states hold that the economic loss doctrine prevents a negligence action against a design professional only when the parties are in privity. However, a number of states also bar actions for economic losses by any party that is not in privity with the design professional on the basis that, since there is no contract, the plaintiff is not owed any duty by the design professional.

In contrast, some states hold that the design professional may be liable to the general contractor and its subcontractors for economic loss that results from a breach of a common-law duty of care. These courts hold that the duty of care arises from the relationship between the parties. A few states distinguish claims based on the type of the allegedly negligent professional services. California was one of the first states to hold that, while there is no duty to third parties for economic losses caused by design services prior to construction, an A/E performing contract administration has a considerable amount of power over contractors and, thus, owes them a duty of care.

Some states consider the construction industry differently from other industries. Illinois allows negligence claims for economic losses against accountants and attorneys if the parties are not in privity but does not allow such actions against architects or engineers. Virginia, on the other hand, requires privity of contract for economic loss claims against any type of professional.

22.4 POTENTIALLY DANGEROUS PRODUCTS (RISK OF HARM EXCEPTION)

One of the economic loss doctrine's major weaknesses in the construction context is that even when a defect creates a potentially dangerous situation, there can be no recovery for repair or replacement of the defective product until there has been bodily injury or property damage. Some states have recognized that it is unreasonable to require that a tragedy occur before a dangerous defect is repaired and have created an exception in cases where a defect can lead to a serious risk of harm.

As an example, Maryland courts have decided that the duty to repair a defective product depends on the risk generated by the defect. When there is risk of death or serious injury, Maryland courts hold that there has been a breach of the duty of care and allow recovery of the reasonable cost of correcting the dangerous condition; privity of contract is not a prerequisite to the existence of this duty. It is difficult to define what constitutes a risk serious enough to create this duty, however, and most states have declined to create such an exception.

22.5 NEGLIGENT MISREPRESENTATION

The economic loss doctrine can be difficult to reconcile with torts such as negligent misrepresentation that exist to provide remedies for harm that is almost always economic in nature. Most states hold that the economic loss doctrine does not preclude claims of intentional misrepresentation (fraud), because fraud is considered to be an independent tort; in most cases, both compensatory and punitive damages can be recovered for fraud. Fraud claims are difficult to prove, though, and are much less common than negligent misrepresentation claims.

22.5.1 Negligent Misrepresentation Claimants

In the construction industry, negligent misrepresentation claims are typically brought against the A/E as professional negligence, but they may also be brought against the owner. Since a strict application of the economic loss doctrine would bar many, if not all, of these claims, many states hold that such claims are not subject to the doctrine. In keeping with the different interpretations of the economic loss doctrine, however, states vary widely as far as the circumstances under which they allow negligent misrepresentation claims. Many states follow the view expressed in §552 of the Restatement (2nd) of Torts, which states that if an individual is negligent in supplying information for the guidance of others in the context of a business transaction, the individual is liable for losses caused by justifiable reliance on that information.

This allows an action whether or not there is privity of contract between the parties, but potential claimants are limited to those for whose benefit the information was supplied. To bring a claim of negligent representation against an A/E, for example, the claimant must have been an intended recipient of the information that was provided. A building tenant would typically not have a claim against the A/E for defective building plans unless the A/E's contract with the owner required it to provide plans to the tenant. The contractor and its subcontractors would generally be allowed to bring a claim, since they are the intended recipients of the information in the plans.

Under the Restatement view, the duty of care arises from the foreseeability of harm to the intended recipients of the information. A number of states reject this view as too broad and only allow claims for negligent misrepresentation when the parties are in contractual privity. Other states accept the Restatement view but limit the circumstances under which a claim can be brought by making fine distinctions. Under one such analysis, tort actions for defective plans are not allowed against design professionals because the structure being built is considered the product. The plans are considered incidental to the structure and thus cannot be the basis of a tort claim. Under another analysis, design professionals cannot be held liable for negligent misrepresentation because they are not in the business of selling information.

Many states hold that when the parties are in privity of contract and there are only economic damages, there is no need to allow a tort claim for negligent misrepresentation because there are contractual remedies. Some states do not allow negligent misrepresentation claims if there is any contract covering the work, even if the contract is not between the injured party and the party that allegedly caused the injury. In such cases, the contractor would not be allowed to bring a claim of negligent misrepresentation against the A/E for defective plans but must instead bring a contract claim against the owner.

22.5.2 Tort versus Contract Claims for Negligent Misrepresentation

Some states allow both contract and tort claims for negligent misrepresentation. If the contract does not have any limiting provisions such as a waiver of consequential damages, there may be little difference in recoverable damages for negligent misrepresentation under tort or contract theories. In such cases, most contractors pursue a contract claim against the owner rather than a tort claim, because the proof is easier. Proof of the tort of negligence requires proof of a duty of care, breach of that duty, foreseeability of the harm, "but for" causation, and proximate causation. Proof of a breach of contract simply requires proof that there was a contract and it was breached.

23

ALTERNATIVE DISPUTE RESOLUTION

Disputes are the rule rather than the exception on many construction projects, and quick resolution of disputes can be crucial to the success of a project. The uncertainty created by unresolved disputes can interfere with the progress of the project and cause major cash flow disruptions. In addition, postponing dispute resolution until the end of the project increases the difficulty and expense of establishing the relevant facts and events.

Alternative Dispute Resolution (ADR) is a general term for a range of dispute resolution techniques that are used as an alternative to litigation. Because these techniques often resolve disputes more quickly than litigation, the construction industry began using these techniques before many other industries. While arbitration is the best-known and most widely used alternative dispute resolution technique, there are a number of other techniques. There are also a number of techniques aimed at dispute prevention.

23.1 ARBITRATION

Arbitration is the voluntary submission of disputes to an independent third party for determination. A party cannot be compelled to arbitrate an issue unless it has consented to arbitration. In the construction industry, consent is typically given by an arbitration clause in the party's contract. Clauses requiring arbitration of disputes have been common in construction contracts for many years—arbitration was required by the first AIA contract documents in 1888. Arbitration continued to be required in subsequent versions of the AIA documents until 2007, but the parties were free to delete the clause. Arbitration is no longer required in the AIA contract documents, however, partly because the arbitration clause was often deleted or modified.

Despite being an alternative to litigation, arbitration is not completely separate from the judicial system—the federal and state governments have statutes that provide for judicial facilitation of the arbitration process. If a party refuses to act in accordance with its arbitration agreement, the other party can file a motion in court to compel arbitration. If a party fails to comply with the arbitral award, the other party can file a motion to confirm the award and convert it to an enforceable judgment. Courts rarely review arbitral awards, however, and will only overturn awards in extraordinary circumstances.

23.1.1 Arbitration Clauses

The parties have considerable leeway in defining the nature and scope of their arbitration agreement. Under a broad-form arbitration clause, the parties agree to submit all disputes related to the underlying contractual relationship to arbitration. Broad-form clauses cover disputes involving extras, delays, claims for retainage, claims of defective work, and liquidated damages. The American Arbitration Association (AAA) provides the following model broad-form provision that the parties can incorporate into their contract:

> *Any controversy or claim arising out of or relating to this contract, or the breach thereof, shall be settled by arbitration administered by the American Arbitration Association Rules, and judgment on the award rendered by the arbitrator(s) may be entered in any court having jurisdiction thereof.*

The parties can also agree to a more limited arbitration clause, under which only certain issues are submitted to arbitration. If the parties subsequently disagree over whether a dispute falls within the scope of the arbitration clause, the arbitration clause will be interpreted in accordance with the applicable arbitration statute (federal or state). The federal courts and the majority of the state courts hold that public policy supports arbitration as an economical means of resolving disputes and relieving overcrowded court systems. These courts generally attempt to interpret an arbitration clause as including all disputes. If the scope of the arbitration clause is ambiguous, the ambiguity is typically construed in favor of arbitration, especially if the arbitration clause was drafted by the party seeking to avoid arbitration.

Subcontracts often do not include arbitration clauses but merely incorporate the terms of the contract between the prime contractor and the owner by reference. Subcontracts incorporating arbitration clauses by reference may be held to bind the parties, even though the parties did not specifically agree to arbitration. Courts have not been consistent in their rulings on this issue, however.

23.1.2 Arbitration Statutes

The Federal Arbitration Act (FAA), enacted in 1925, expresses the strong federal support for arbitration and makes an agreement to submit disputes to arbitration irrevocable. Because the FAA is based on the commerce clause powers given to Congress in the U.S. Constitution, it applies only when the transaction between the parties involves interstate commerce or maritime affairs.

Transactions of the type involved in a large construction project typically satisfy the interstate commerce requirement and thus come within the scope of the FAA. State law applies in all other cases, even when the dispute is brought in federal court.

All 50 states and the District of Columbia have enacted their own arbitration statutes. Most of these statutes are based on either the FAA, the Uniform Arbitration Act of 1956 (UAA), or its successor, the Revised Uniform Arbitration Act of 2000 (RUAA). Like the FAA, the state statutes make an agreement to submit disputes to arbitration irrevocable, thereby abolishing the common-law rule that agreements to arbitrate were revocable by either party before an award had been made. In addition, these statutes define how and when a party to a contract with a valid arbitration clause can seek assistance from the courts.

When both a state arbitration statute and the FAA apply to a particular dispute, the FAA preempts state law by virtue of the Supremacy Clause of the U.S. Constitution, even if the suit is brought in state court. In particular, when the FAA applies, it preempts any state law that hinders enforcement of arbitration agreements. State laws that govern the arbitration process but do not affect enforcement of the agreement are not preempted by the FAA.

23.1.3 Arbitration Organization Rules

A number of dispute resolution organizations have emerged to serve as forums for hearing arbitrations. The American Arbitration Association (AAA) is the forum used most often for construction disputes. Other organizations include the International Institute for Conflict Prevention & Resolution (CPR) and JAMS. Each organization has promulgated rules governing matters submitted to the organization for arbitration. These rules, which typically specify the procedures for administrative matters such as selecting arbitrators, providing notice, and determining the hearing location, are valid to the extent they do not contradict applicable statutes. AAA has specific construction industry rules that were developed in conjunction with several construction trade associations.

23.1.4 Prehearing Activities

To initiate arbitration, a party must file a notice of its intention to arbitrate with the organization that the parties have agreed on and must pay fees based on the amount of the claim. The notice, also referred to as a *demand for arbitration*, must state the nature of the dispute, the amount of the claim, and the remedy being sought. The responding party must file an answer within the time specified by the organization and can also file a counterclaim (its own claim against the party that initiated arbitration). If the responding party has begun litigation with respect to the matter in dispute, arbitration statutes typically require the litigation to be stayed (suspended) pending completion of arbitration proceedings.

Unless specifically provided for by agreement or statute, discovery (the ability to obtain the other party's evidence) is not available in arbitration, as arbitrators have no power to order discovery. However, the FAA allows arbitrators to subpoena individuals to appear as witnesses at the hearing and produce documents deemed material evidence in the case; many state statutes also empower arbitrators to issue subpoenas. The parties can agree to voluntarily exchange information and will usually engage in a limited examination of the opposing party's witnesses and documents before selection of the arbitration panel.

23.1.5 Selection of Arbitrators

Arbitration is usually done by either a single arbitrator or a three-member panel; three-member panels generally render their decisions by majority vote. Although the parties are free to specify their own procedures for arbitrator selection, the procedures set forth in the AAA Construction Industry Arbitration Rules are often used. The AAA procedures provide for selection of either one or three arbitrators by having the parties rank a list of arbitrators in order of preference and choose the arbitrator or arbitrators with the highest ranking. An alternative to the AAA procedures is for each party to select an arbitrator and then for these two to select a third arbitrator that is acceptable to both parties. This essentially makes the third arbitrator the swing vote that decides the arbitration.

Under the FAA, if the parties have not specified a method of selecting an arbitrator, the default is a single arbitrator that is acceptable to both parties. Most arbitration statutes authorize courts to appoint arbitrators and fill vacancies when one party will not designate an arbitrator or an arbitrator has withdrawn or is unable to serve.

23.1.6 The Arbitration Hearing

Arbitration proceedings are not as formal as court proceedings, but the fact that the arbitral award can be enforced in court means that there must be procedural safeguards to guarantee the integrity of the proceedings. Each party is entitled to present its case at a hearing attended by the other party unless this right is waived, either by agreement or by conduct. If the location for the hearing is not specified in the arbitration clause, and the parties cannot agree on a location, the arbitrator will typically select a venue convenient to both parties, such as the city nearest the project site.

The hearing is essentially a mini-trial where each side presents its evidence and witnesses; the parties are entitled to cross-examine the other party's witnesses. Neither federal nor state rules of evidence apply to arbitrations, and arbitrators are generally fairly liberal in their acceptance of evidence; the AAA rules encourage arbitrators to accept any evidence they consider relevant to the dispute.

23.1.7 The Award

Arbitrators have considerable latitude in their conduct of hearings and rendering of awards. Unless the arbitration agreement states otherwise, arbitrators are free to determine the damages that result from the issues being considered, with the amount of the award limited only by fairness. Although arbitrators cannot award punitive damages, liquidated damages can be awarded as long as they bear some relationship to the actual damages incurred. Consequential damages can be awarded unless the party has waived its right to consequential damages.

Arbitration statutes typically require the arbitrator's fees and expenses to be included in the award. However, attorney's fees are only recoverable if they are expressly authorized by the arbitration agreement. In addition, attorney's fees cannot be included in the award; the party in whose favor the award was made must go to court for a judgment. The court then enters an order for a judgment in conformity with the award and adds what it determines to be reasonable attorney's fees.

23.1.8 Appealing the Award

In litigation, the losing party always has the right to appeal the verdict and award. By contrast, the right to challenge an arbitral award is extremely limited. Courts generally hold that if the parties have agreed to arbitrate, they are bound by the result, except in extraordinary circumstances. The parties cannot tailor their arbitration agreement to expand the grounds for which a court will review the award.

Unless explicitly allowed by statute, an arbitrator who has rendered an award does not have authority to modify the award. Likewise, a court's power to review the arbitrator's findings of fact and application of the law is generally limited by statute. Courts typically cannot substitute their judgment for that of the arbitrators, even if the arbitrators' findings appear erroneous, and courts will not set aside an arbitrator's decisions on grounds such as newly discovered evidence. Even though the parties often present legal precedent as part of their case, arbitrators are not bound by case law. Furthermore, arbitrators have no obligation to provide a rationale for their decision, as there is a presumption of correctness.

Under the FAA, the grounds for vacating an award are limited to circumstances where the award was procured by corruption or fraud, there was obvious arbitrator partiality, the arbitrators refused to hear pertinent evidence, or the arbitrators exceeded their power. Under most state arbitration statutes, an award can only be vacated if it was improperly procured, the arbitrators acted improperly such that the rights of one of the parties were prejudiced, or the arbitrators exceeded their power. An award can be modified only if the modification is necessary to accomplish the intent of the award—for example, if there was an obvious miscalculation of figures or the arbitrators calculated the award based on information not submitted at the hearing. A motion to vacate or modify an award must be filed within the time required by the applicable statute. Under the FAA, the time limit is three months after the award. Failure to file a motion within the prescribed period precludes any future challenge of the award. If an appeals court vacates an award for reasons other than an invalid arbitration agreement, it typically will remand (send back) the case for a new hearing. A new arbitration panel must be appointed if the award was vacated because of fraud. Otherwise, the remand may be to either the original panel or a new panel, at the court's discretion.

23.1.9   Costs of Arbitration

Although the costs of an arbitration ultimately depend on the parties and the scope and complexity of the issues, the fact that arbitration is generally much quicker than litigation typically means it is also less expensive. There are certain costs that cannot be avoided, however. These include the costs incurred in preparing for the hearing such as each party's examination and analysis of its own documents, legal research, expert witnesses, the development of demonstrative evidence, and limited discovery of the other party's evidence.

There are also costs that are unique to arbitration, such as the arbitrators' fees and expenses, administrative fees such as filing fees, and the cost of meeting rooms. The filing fees for arbitration are usually considerably higher than the costs of filing a lawsuit. The AAA, for example, charges a filing fee of $775 and a case service fee of $200 for claims up to $10,000. The fees increase in proportion to the claim, with a maximum case service fee of $6,000 and a maximum filing fee of $12,800 plus .01 percent of the amount in excess of $10 million.

The cost of an arbitration can increase significantly if the responding party refuses to cooperate or challenges the scope or validity of the arbitration agreement in court. Nevertheless, the brevity of the arbitration proceedings and the savings that result from limiting discovery make arbitration less expensive than litigation in most cases.

23.1.10   Typical Schedule for Arbitration

A standard arbitration usually takes between three and four months once the arbitrator is selected. The hearing typically takes five to ten working days, but the hearing for a complex case can be much longer. The arbitrator is usually required to render a decision within 30 days of the hearing.

The AAA provides a fast-track procedure for claims up to $75,000. The fast-track procedure allows very limited discovery, requires the hearing to be within 30 days from the date the arbitrator is selected, and restricts the hearing to one day. The arbitrator must provide a decision within 14 days and generally charges a lower fee.

23.1.11   Joinder and Consolidation

Construction disputes often involve a number of parties. In some cases, parties that may be important to an arbitration proceeding are not in contractual privity with one another. This raises the issue of whether disputes having similar factual issues can be consolidated into one proceeding if some of the parties are not in privity. To avoid the issue, the arbitration clause may specifically allow consolidation. An example of such a clause is:

In the event that any dispute for which a demand for arbitration is made relates to the work or responsibility of the Owner, another contractor, or any subcontractor on this project, the parties hereto agree to a joint arbitration with the Owner, contractor, or subcontractor.

Historically, the AIA contract documents did not allow the owner to consolidate arbitrations with the architect and the contractor without consent from both parties. Consolidation of owner-contractor and contractor-subcontractor arbitrations was permitted, however, if there was a common question of fact or law. The explanation for the distinction was that different legal standards were involved. Architect-owner disputes generally involve the architect's professional standard of care, while both owner-contractor and contractor-subcontractor disputes typically center on whether performance was in accordance with the terms of the contract.

The prohibition against consolidation often put the owner in the position of having to defend the contractor's claim that the design was defective but not being able to compel the architect to join the arbitration as a party to assist in the defense. It also meant the owner bore the expense of duplicative arbitrations and risked inconsistent results. The owner could lose on the contractor's claim of a defective design in one arbitration but be unable to convince the second arbitration panel that the architect should reimburse the owner for the claim, despite the fact that the design had been found defective.

This was changed in the 2007 version of the AIA documents. Article 15 of AIA A201-2007 sets forth the requirements for arbitration when arbitration is selected as the method of binding dispute resolution. A201 §15.4.4.1 provides that both the owner and the contractor may consolidate all arbitrations to which it is a party as long as the agreements governing the arbitrations permit consolidation and the arbitrations involve common issues of law or fact. In addition, A201 §15.4.4.3 states that parties to an arbitration may join (bring in) any entity or person substantially involved in common questions of fact or law when such joinder is necessary to provide complete relief, as long as the entity or person consents to joinder.

If the contract is silent on the issue of consolidation, it may be necessary to litigate the issue. Courts have varied in their decisions. An argument in favor of consolidation is that it reduces the cost of arbitration and avoids inconsistent results. An opposing argument is that arbitration is a voluntary agreement and consolidation could force a party to participate in the arbitration against its will. Even though consolidation is an expeditious means to resolve disputes, most courts do not require consolidation without express contractual authorization.

23.1.12 Waiver of Arbitration Rights

Because the right to arbitrate arises from the parties' contract, it can be waived, just as any other contractual right can be waived. Arbitration clauses and statutes generally do not state a precise time within which a demand for arbitration must be asserted. Nevertheless, a party can waive its right to arbitrate by failing to demand arbitration within a "reasonable time."

A party can also waive its right to arbitrate by conduct that appears inconsistent with an intention to arbitrate, for example, by commencing litigation. In addition, courts have held that a party waives its arbitration rights if it does not assert its rights when the other party files a lawsuit but instead files a response to the other party's complaint and allows the litigation to proceed. When determining whether there has been a waiver of rights, courts often look at whether the party alleging a waiver was prejudiced by the other party's actions.

The issue of waiver often comes up with respect to mechanic's liens. Courts are split on the question of whether seeking to enforce a mechanic's lien constitutes a waiver, but the tendency is to promote arbitration and find that arbitral rights have not been waived. However, a contractor that wants to retain its rights to a mechanic's lien without jeopardizing its right to arbitrate the dispute should first file a demand for arbitration, then file its mechanic's lien and complaint to foreclose the lien. In the complaint, the contractor should specifically reserve its right to arbitrate and should immediately move for a stay of the litigation pending arbitration.

23.1.13 Effect of Arbitration on the Surety

Courts decisions as to whether a surety is bound by an arbitral award against its principal when the surety was not a signatory to the arbitration agreement have varied. Some courts have held that a surety should not be bound by such an award, on the theory that, since an arbitration clause is contractual in nature, only signatories to the contract can be compelled to arbitrate and thus be bound by the arbitral decision.

However, other courts have held that a surety is necessarily liable when there is an arbitral award against its principal. These courts find that by executing a bond for a contract providing for arbitration, the surety has implicitly agreed that it will be bound by an arbitral award. Courts have also held that when a surety has notice of a claim against its principal and thus has the opportunity to appear and defend against the claim, it will be bound by the results, regardless of whether it participated in the proceedings.

23.2 LITIGATION VERSUS ARBITRATION

Arbitration was originally envisioned as a streamlined process that relied on individuals with industry experience to resolve disputes quickly and cost effectively. The speed with which a decision can be rendered is one of the major advantages of arbitration over litigation. In addition, both the matters discussed during the arbitration and the exhibits filed with the arbitrator remain private unless there is an appeal. This can be important to a party concerned that information such as financial statements, bidding strategies, or business plans will become public.

Over the years, arbitration has become more like litigation, with a corresponding increase in both time and costs. Nevertheless, arbitration is usually quicker and less expensive than litigation, particularly for smaller claims. This is largely because discovery is generally limited to examination of the other party's witnesses. The limited discovery makes it difficult to determine the relative strengths and weaknesses of the other party's position before the hearing, though. This can act as a deterrent to settlement negotiations and can also lead to a less focused hearing. The ability to take depositions and conduct extensive pretrial discovery may make litigation more cost effective on complex projects, particularly if it induces the parties to settle. In addition, there are generally no provisions for summary disposition of a dispute submitted to arbitration. Thus, if the parties are unable to settle their dispute, there will be a full arbitral hearing, even if the dispute has no merit.

One often-cited advantage of arbitration over litigation for a construction-related dispute is that the arbitrators are typically well-respected contractors, construction managers, or design professionals. Their expertise and familiarity with construction matters can expedite the proceedings and allow them to reach a decision relatively quickly. However, because these individuals are usually not trained in the law, they may consider evidence that would be inadmissible in court.

Legal defenses such as statutes of limitations, no-damage-for-delay clauses, and notice requirements are typically given less weight in arbitration than in litigation. This may complicate the hearing process and make the arbitration less predictable. In addition, joinder of parties and consolidation of disputes is generally more difficult in an arbitration than in a litigation.

23.3 MEDIATION

Many industry standard form contracts, including the AIA documents, require mediation before either litigation or binding arbitration. Mediation is a relatively quick process and is less costly than arbitration or litigation; the parties usually split the filing fees and the cost of the mediator. The mediator does not render a decision on the issues, however, and it cannot impose a settlement—it merely facilitates the process and tries to bring about a resolution that is acceptable to both parties.

For mediation to be successful, the parties must thus agree that a compromise is in their respective best interests. This typically means that they must appreciate the strengths and weaknesses of both their case and their opponent's case, as well as the time and costs that will be required to pursue the claim. If it is clear that the parties are merely going through the mediation process to get to the binding resolution stage, they can agree to waive mediation.

AIA A201 requires that disputes between the owner and the contractor be submitted to an Initial Decision Maker (IDM), who can be either the A/E or an independent neutral. The IDM must review the dispute, seek any additional information that it needs, then either render an initial decision or indicate that it is unable to resolve the dispute. The initial decision is binding on the parties but is subject to mediation. Either party can file for mediation; if mediation does not resolve the dispute, the parties can proceed to either arbitration or litigation. Either party can also limit the other party's right to file for mediation by demanding that the other party file for mediation within 60 days after the initial decision. If a demand for mediation is made and the party receiving the demand fails to file for mediation within the time allowed, the party waives its right to challenge the IDM's decision.

23.4 OTHER TYPES OF ALTERNATIVE DISPUTE RESOLUTION

Although mediation and arbitration are the most common forms of alternative dispute resolution, there are a number of other methods. These include med/arb, mini-trials, summary jury trials, and dispute resolution boards.

23.4.1 Med/Arb

Med/arb is a somewhat generic term for a process whereby mediation is followed by arbitration of the issues that were not resolved in mediation. Before proceeding with the arbitration, the parties typically sign an agreement that settles the issues resolved in mediation.

The parties can agree to have the mediator serve as the arbitrator. The advantage of such an arrangement is that the mediator will be familiar with the parties, the project, and the dispute, which can lead to a more efficient process. The disadvantage is that the mediator will likely carry any biases acquired during the mediation over to the arbitration. Typically, the mediator is only asked to be the arbitrator on small claims, when the parties want the dispute to be resolved quickly.

23.4.2 Mini-Trial and Summary Proceedings

In a mini-trial, the parties present their case to a neutral mediator and representatives from each party. The representatives are usually senior executives who are unfamiliar with the details of the dispute. After hearing the presentations, the representatives attempt to negotiate a settlement with the assistance of the mediator. Because the representatives have not been involved in the dispute, they are often able to view the facts more objectively than those who are more directly involved.

In a summary jury trial, the parties conduct an abbreviated trial before a judge and a mock jury. The trial typically lasts only a day; the jury then renders an advisory opinion, which is nonbinding on the parties. The purpose of a summary jury trial is to allow the parties to see the strengths and weaknesses of their respective cases and try to reach a settlement.

The parties may also engage in an informal summary arbitration in which representatives of the parties present their positions to a neutral third party, who is then asked to issue a nonbinding decision. A decision from a neutral third party may help the parties reach a settlement. Mini-trials, summary jury trials, and summary arbitrations are not required under any of the industry standard form contracts, and they are much less common than arbitration and mediation.

23.4.3 Dispute Resolution Boards

Dispute Resolution Boards (DRBs) were pioneered in the 1970s by engineers, contractors, and government owners working on tunneling projects. The use of DRBs has greatly expanded, and many state and local governments now require that owner-contractor disputes on public projects be taken to a DRB before litigation is allowed.

A DRB is usually composed of three members. The owner and contractor each select one member; these two then select the third member. The DRB members are selected early in the project and are provided with the contract documents. They receive periodic reports throughout the project and may occasionally attend job site meetings to get a feel for the project relationships.

The DRB is expected to be available on relatively short notice to help resolve any disputes that the parties are unable to resolve on their own. When called on to resolve a dispute, the DRB typically asks the parties to provide written position papers. The DRB then conducts a hearing, often at the project site, to allow the parties to present their positions and respond to questions from the DRB. The hearings are conducted informally and are typically attended by decision makers from both parties, as well as individuals with firsthand knowledge of the issues in dispute. After the hearing, the DRB will provide a written recommendation.

The existence of a preselected neutral board that is familiar with the project and the parties avoids many of the initial problems involved in selecting arbitrators after a dispute has arisen. The DRB also tends to reduce the number of disputes that arise. The availability of the DRB, the speed with which it can render decisions, and the fact that the DRB will hear all disputes that occur during the project gives the parties an incentive to deal with each other candidly. Even though there are some costs involved in selecting the DRB members, familiarizing them with the project, and keeping them informed, these costs are relatively minimal.

Unlike an arbitration decision, which can only be overturned under very limited circumstances, the DRB's decision is subject to a full appeal. The parties tend to accept the DRB's decisions as the basis for resolving disputes, however. The nature of the neutral review process encourages the parties to be more realistic and objective in their dealings with each other, while giving them an opportunity to construct their own solutions.

23.4.4 Standing Neutrals

In some cases, a single individual is used for dispute resolution. When there is only a single individual, the contractor and the owner select a mutually acceptable adviser who works as a neutral party to help resolve disputes. Like the DRB members, this individual, sometimes referred to as a *standing neutral*, is typically required to be available on short notice to hear disputes. The 2007 version of AIA A201 incorporates the concept of a standing neutral by allowing the parties to choose someone other than the A/E to be the Initial Decision Maker when there are disputes between the contractor and the owner.

23.5 DISPUTE PREVENTION

The escalating cost of litigating, and even settling, disputes provides the parties with an incentive to prevent disputes from arising. One means of dispute prevention is for contracts to allocate risk realistically by assigning a risk to the project participant that is best able to manage, control, or insure against the risk. When the contract allocates risks to project participants that are unable to handle them, even relatively minor problems can lead to disputes that jeopardize the project. The various industry standard form contracts attempt to incorporate the current industry consensus on realistic risk allocations.

Techniques such as project-specific partnering have also been used to foster an atmosphere of cooperation that helps prevent disputes. Project-specific partnering is a team-building effort developed by the U.S. Army Corps of Engineers in which the project participants establish cooperative working relationships through a formal strategy of commitment and communication. At the start of the project, project participants with leadership and management responsibilities usually attend a retreat with an independent facilitator who helps the attendees establish nonadversarial processes for resolving problems. Often, the attendees adopt a charter in which they make a formal commitment to cooperate. The retreat is typically followed by periodic meetings to ensure that communications and teamwork are continuing.

It should be emphasized, however, that partnering does not change contractual obligations. Partnering only establishes a framework under which project participants will work together. It does not eliminate contractual requirements such as the requirement for a written notice of differing site conditions even if the parties have provided such notices verbally.

APPENDIX A: LIST OF ABBREVIATIONS

AAA	American Arbitration Association
ADA	Americans with Disabilities Act
ADM	Arrow Diagramming Method
ADR	Alternative Dispute Resolution
AGC	Associated General Contractors of America
AIA	American Institute of Architects
AWCPA	Architectural Works Copyright Protection Act
BIM	Building Information Modeling
CCD	Constructive Change Directive
CCIP	Contractor-Controlled Insurance Program
CCN	Contemplated Change Notice
CD	Construction Documents
CGL	Commercial General Liability
CM	Construction Manager
CMAA	Construction Management Association of America
CMAR	Construction Management At-Risk
COAA	Construction Owners Association of America
COTR	Contracting Officer's Technical Representative
CPM	Critical Path Method
CPR	International Institute for Conflict Prevention & Resolution
DBB	Design-Bid-Build
DBE	Disadvantaged Business Enterprise

DBIA   Design-Build Institute of America

DCC   Design Criteria Consultant

DOT   Department of Transportation

DRB   Dispute Resolution Board

DSC   Differing Site Conditions

EJCDC   Engineers Joint Contract Documents Committee

E&O   Errors and Omissions Insurance

EPA   Environmental Protection Agency

EPC   Engineer-Procure-Construct

FAA   Federal Arbitration Act

FAR   Federal Acquisition Regulations

FCA   False Claims Act

FPPA   Federal Prompt Payment Act

GAI   General Agreement of Indemnity

GC   General Contractor

GMP   Guaranteed Maximum Price

ICC   International Code Council

IDM   Initial Decision Maker

IFB   Invitation for Bids

IPD   Integrated Project Delivery

LEED   Leadership in Energy and Environmental Design

MBE   Minority Business Enterprises

MOU   Memorandum of Understanding

MWBE   Minority and Women Business Enterprises

NOAA   National Oceanic and Atmospheric Administration

OCIP   Owner-Controlled Insurance Program

OMB   Office of Management and Budget

PCB   Polychlorinated Biphenyl

PDM   Precedence Diagramming Method

PERT   Project Evaluation and Review Technique

PMI	Project Management Institute
PPP	Public-Private Partnerships
RFI	Request for Information
RFP	Request for Proposal
RUAA	Revised Uniform Arbitration Act of 2000
SBA	Small Business Administration
SDB	Small Disadvantaged Business
SPV	Single-Purpose Vehicle
TIA	Time-Impact Analysis
T&M	Time and Materials
UAA	Uniform Arbitration Act of 1956
UCC	Uniform Commercial Code
U.S.C.	United States Code
VEQ	Variation in Estimated Quantities

APPENDIX B:
TABLE OF CASES

APPENDIX C: UNDERSTANDING CASE CITATIONS

Because previous case decisions often play an important role in resolving construction disputes, it is helpful to understand how cases are identified. Before a case is decided, it is identified by its docket number, which is the number assigned to it by the court. The format for docket numbers varies from court to court but often contains the year the lawsuit was filed, a letter or letters indicating the type of case (i.e., civil, criminal, small claims, probate), and a sequence number.

After a case is decided, it may be certified for publication. Published cases are collected in books called *reporters* that include cases from one or more court systems. As an example, the *Southern Reporter* contains published appellate court decisions for the state courts of Alabama, Florida, Louisiana, and Mississippi. Each reporter is published as a series, with the sequentially numbered volumes in a series containing a chronological compilation of decisions.

Volume numbers go up to 999; when the volume number for a reporter reaches 999, a new series is started and the volume number is reset to one. A "2d" in the name of the reporter indicates that it is the second series of the reporter. Similarly "3d" indicates the third series of the reporter. Depending on how many decisions the courts included in a particular reporter have published, the reporter may now be in its second, third, or fourth series of volumes.

The full citation to a published case indicates the parties, the reporter and volume in which the case was published, the page number on which the case starts, and the year of the decision. When the citation is to the original case (the trial), the first name in the citation is the *plaintiff*. When the citation is to an appeal, the first name in the citation is the *appellant* (the party who is appealing the lower court's decision). Some appeals refer to the appellant as the *petitioner* or the *appellant-petitioner*. The name following the "*v.*" or "*vs.*" (meaning "versus") in a citation is either the *defendant* (the party responding to the original suit) or the *appellee* (the party responding to the appeal). Courts that refer to the party appealing a decision as the petitioner typically refer to the other party as the *respondent*.

There are both official and unofficial reporters. Official reporters are those designated as such by a court system. Unofficial reporters are published by private companies that typically add commentary on the significant issues discussed in the case. One of the cases cited most often in construction litigation is *United States v. Spearin*, 248 U.S. 132 (1918). This was a Supreme Court case in which the government appealed the decision from the court of appeals. "U.S." is the abbreviation for the *United States Reports*, which is the official reporter of the U.S. Supreme Court. "248" is the volume number of the reporter; "132" is the page number in that volume where the opinion begins, and "1918" is the year in which the court rendered its decision.

CITATIONS TO FEDERAL COURT CASES

There are several unofficial reporters for U.S. Supreme Court decisions, including the *Supreme Court Reporter* (abbreviated in citations as "S.Ct.") and the *United States Supreme Court Reports, Lawyers' Edition* (abbreviated as "L.Ed."). A citation that lists more than one reporter is referred to as a *parallel citation.* For example, *United States v. Spearin*, 248 U.S. 132, 39 S.Ct. 59, 63 L.Ed. 166 (1918) is a parallel citation to all three Supreme Court reporters.

Although the *United States Reports* includes only U.S. Supreme Court decisions, most reporters collect decisions from several courts. The citations for cases in these reporters include the court inside the parentheses. For example, cases from all 13 of the federal courts of appeals are published in the *Federal Reporter.* An example of a citation in the *Federal Reporter*, which is currently in its third series, is *Fletcher-Harlee Corp. v. Pote Concrete Contractors, Inc.*, 482 F.3d 247 (3rd Cir. 2007).

Federal district court opinions are published in the *Federal Supplement*, now in its second series; however, very few federal district court opinions are actually published, as most do not address new or novel questions of law. The *Federal Reporter* and the *Federal Supplement* are actually unofficial reporters but have become the de facto "official" reporters of the lower federal courts because there is no official reporter.

CITATIONS TO STATE COURT CASES

Many states have official state reporters. For example, *Green v. Chi. Tribune Co.*, 286 Ill.App.3d 1 (1st Dist. 1996) is the citation for a case reported in the *Illinois Appellate Court Reports.* In addition to the official state reporters, there are seven unofficial regional reporters, each of which includes decisions from the courts in several states. *Berger v. Teton Shadows Incorporated*, 820 P.2d 176

(Wyo. 1991) is a case in the Wyoming Supreme Court that was published in the *Pacific Reporter* (abbreviated as P.)

There are separate unofficial reporters for California, Illinois, and New York, because of the large number of cases that come out of those states. Some state courts require parallel citations to both the official and the unofficial reporter when citing cases from a court in that state. A few of the smaller states have stopped publishing their own official reporters and have certified the regional reporter as their "official" reporter.

CITATIONS TO UNPUBLISHED CASES

When a case has been decided but not yet published in a case reporter, the citation indicates the volume it will appear in but leaves the page number blank, since the page number is not determined until the reporter is printed. For example, *Bowles v. Russell*, 551 U.S. ___ (2007) is the citation for a case that was subsequently published in volume 551 of the *United States Reports.* Published cases are identified by their reporter, even when accessed via online databases such as Westlaw and LexisNexis.

An increasing number of court decisions are not published in any case reporter. This is partly because judges only certify significant decisions for publication. In addition, most states have not expanded the judicial branch in proportion to the increase in lawsuits in recent decades. As a result, judges often write short decisions that address minor issues in one or two sentences. Such decisions typically are not published because the reasoning underlying the decision is not well explained.

Cases that are not published in a reporter are often available online through Westlaw and LexisNexis. The citations for these cases typically include the year the case was decided, an abbreviation indicating the database, and a document number. Citations to online databases also usually include the docket number for the case and the specific date on which it was decided.

An example of a citation to a case in an online database would be:

Fuqua Homes, Inc., v. Beattie, No. 03-3587, 2004 WL 2495842 (8th Cir. Nov. 8, 2004).

This is a case in the Westlaw electronic database, decided by the U.S. Court of Appeals for the Eighth Circuit. The citation includes the year of the decision, the database (WL for Westlaw), and the document number (2495842) as well as the case's original docket number (No. 03-3587) and the date it was decided.

Some court systems do not allow attorneys to cite unpublished cases as precedent. Others allow citations to unpublished cases when there is no published opinion that would adequately address the issue before the court. Many courts are now putting recently decided cases on their websites. However, the fact that a case has been put on the court website does not mean it has been published. A case is not considered published unless it is included in either an official or an unofficial reporter.

PIN CITES

Decisions can be quite lengthy and may contain more than one holding. A citation to a specific statement in a decision must include the page number on which the statement occurs. For example, a statement on the third page of the *Spearin* decision in the *United States Reports* (page 134 of the reporter) would be cited as *United States v. Spearin*, 248 U.S. 132, 134 (1918). Page citations are also known as *pinpoint citations* or *pin cites.*

GLOSSARY

Actual Authority   The authority that a principal confers on an agent.

Actual Causation   The plaintiff in a tort claim must prove actual causation by showing that the defendant's conduct was connected with the plaintiff's harm.

Agency   The relationship between a principal and an agent.

Agent   Under agency law, an agent is authorized by the principal to act on the principal's behalf. As long as the agent acts within the scope of its agency, its acts bind the principal as though the principal had acted directly.

Apparent Authority   The authority that exists when a principal's words or conduct lead a third party to reasonably believe that the principal consents to the acts performed on its behalf by the agent.

Arbitration   The process under which parties to a dispute agree to submit the dispute to a third party (the arbitrator) for determination, rather than pursuing their claims through litigation.

Assignment of a Contract   Transfer of rights arising from the contract.

Authority   Under agency law, the power that a principal confers on its agent to act on its behalf.

Bid   An offer to do specified work for a stipulated sum.

Breach of Contract   The failure to perform a contractual obligation in accordance with the terms of the contract.

Change Order   An owner's order authorizing a change in the work required by the contract, the contract time, and/or the contract amount.

Commercial General Liability Insurance   A broad form of liability insurance covering claims for injury to others (third parties) and their property.

Common Law   Principles of conduct based on usage, custom, or commonly held beliefs as interpreted by the courts. Common law is created by the courts rather than by statute, based on accepted standards of conduct. Common law is also referred to as *case law*.

Comparative Negligence   An allocation of damages according to the relative (comparative) fault of the parties. Some states require that comparative negligence be considered when awarding damages for negligence claims.

Compensatory Damages   Damages intended to compensate the plaintiff by granting a monetary amount equal to the loss or injury suffered. Compensatory damages can be either direct or consequential.

Consequential Damages   Compensation for loss or injury that is not directly attributable to the wrongful act alleged by the plaintiff but results from the consequences of the act.

Consideration   Something of legal value that induces parties to form a contract. Consideration can be money, the promise to perform work, performance of work, or the promise to refrain from doing something.

Constructive   A legal fiction that allows a court to treat a situation as if certain conditions had been satisfied. As an example, if an A/E should have known of a defect in the construction, it will be held to have constructive knowledge of the defect and may be liable if the owner suffers damages because of the defect.

Contract   A written or oral agreement between two or more parties with at least one legally enforceable promise.

Contract Disputes Act of 1978   A federal law that allows contractors to sue the U.S. government for monetary damages related to their contractual dealings.

Contribution   A principle in tort law under which a defendant that has paid the entire amount of a judgment can recover from other individuals whose negligence contributed to the plaintiff's injury.

Contributory Negligence   A type of negligence in which an injured person's own negligence contributed to the harm that was suffered.

Copyright   A right granted by statute to creators of original literary, artistic, and creative works. A copyright gives the creator an exclusive privilege to copy and publish the work.

Counteroffer   An offeree's response to an offer that does not accept or reject the offer, but proposes modifications. A counteroffer voids the original offer such that it can no longer be accepted by the offeree.

Damages   A measure of monetary compensation that a court or arbitrator awards to a plaintiff for the loss or injury the plaintiff has suffered.

Deed   A legal document used to transfer ownership of real property.

Defendant   The individual or entity against whom a claim or action is brought.

Defense   With respect to a lawsuit, a defense is a reason why a party should not be held legally responsible (liable) for the claims made against it. An affirmative defense is a defense that does not consider whether the facts of the claim are true but presents facts that attempt to justify or excuse the behavior on which the lawsuit is based.

Delegation   The transfer of duties under a contract to another party.

Differing Site Conditions   Unforeseen physical conditions at the project site that are not discovered until after the contract has been executed.

Direct Damages   Damages that can be expected to arise as a matter of course from a breach of contract.

Duress   Under contract law, duress occurs when one party is forced into an agreement by physical or verbal threats. The law will not enforce a contract signed under duress.

Duty   An obligation or standard of conduct established by statute, contract, or common law.

Easement   The right to use another's property in a particular way or for a particular purpose.

Encumbrances   A claim or liability against real estate that affects the title to the property. An encumbrance does not necessarily prevent the transfer of title, however. Encumbrances can include liens against the property, deed restrictions, easements, and encroachments.

Equity   The value of a business or property in excess of any mortgages, liens, or other charges and liabilities.

Escrow   Property (such as money or a deed) that is delivered by one party (the grantor) to a third party to be held until certain conditions are satisfied. When the conditions are satisfied, the third party releases the property to another party (the grantee).

Executed   Under contract law, a contract has been executed when it has been signed by both parties.

Express Authority   Actual authority that is explicitly given to the agent, either orally or in writing.

Express Contract   A contract that is formed when parties indicate, through written or spoken words, their agreement to be bound to the terms of the contract.

Express Warranty   A written or oral representation of fact or promise.

Fiduciary   One in whom the confidence and trust of another has been placed and who, as a result, owes a special duty to act in good faith and in the best interests of the other.

Fixtures   Goods that are permanently attached to, or embedded in, real property such that they are considered to be part of the real property.

General Conditions Guidelines that define the rights and responsibilities of both the owner and the contractor, and include the general procedures governing the performance of the work.

Implied Authority Actual authority that is implied from a principal's conduct or the express authority granted to the agent.

Implied-in-Fact Contract A contract that is formed when the parties indicate their intention to be bound to the terms of the contract through their conduct. The agreement is inferred from the parties' conduct rather than their words.

Implied Warranty A guarantee created not by explicit statements but through a promise that is inferred under the law to exist by virtue of the nature of the transaction or the circumstances between the parties, or by the relative position one party holds with respect to another.

Indemnify An obligation contractually assumed by, or legally imposed on, one party to protect another party against loss or damage from specific liabilities.

Injunction A court order instructing a party to either perform or stop performing some activity.

Integration In contract law, a written contract that is intended to be the complete and final agreement between the parties.

Integration Clause A contract clause which states that the written agreement is complete and that all oral and other agreements are integrated, or merged, into it.

Intentional Misrepresentation An incorrect or false statement that is made deliberately. Intentional misrepresentation is also referred to as *fraud.*

Intentional Tort A deliberate act that causes harm to another, for which the injured party may sue the wrongdoer. Fraud is the tort of intentional misrepresentation.

Interstate Commerce Any commercial transaction that crosses state boundaries or involves more than one state.

Joint and Several Liability When two or more defendants are joint and severally liable for a judgment, the plaintiff can collect the entire judgment from one defendant or may collect varying amounts from each of the defendants until the judgment is satisfied.

Joint Venture A partnership formed to achieve a specific objective.

Latent Ambiguity Errors or discrepancies in the documents that do not become apparent until construction has started.

Lawsuit A claim brought in court to obtain a judgment against another party for injuries that result from a wrongful act.

Liability   A situation in which one party is legally responsible for another party's loss. Liability is created when the law recognizes the existence of an enforceable legal duty and the failure to perform the duty in accordance with applicable legal standards.

Liquidated Damages   An amount of damages established in advance by parties to a contract that one party promises to pay to the other in the event that it breaches the contract.

Litigation   The process by which parties submit their disputes to a court for resolution.

Miller Act   A federal law that requires general contractors working on federally funded construction projects to obtain performance and payment bonds. The Miller Act applies to all U.S. government construction contracts valued at more than $100,000.

Misrepresentation   Under contract law, when a party to a contract misrepresents material facts that the other party relies on. Misrepresentation can be either intentional or negligent.

Mitigation of Damages   A duty that the law imposes on an injured party to make a reasonable effort to minimize its damages after an injury.

Modifications   A change to a contract that is made after the contract has been executed (signed) by both parties.

Mutual Assent   The agreement of two or more parties to be bound to the terms of a contract. A contract is not legally enforceable without mutual assent.

Mutual Mistake   Under contract law, a term applied when both parties misunderstood a material contract term at the time the contract was entered into, thus rendering the contract unenforceable.

National Conference of Commissioners on Uniform State Laws (NCCUSL)   An organization founded to promote uniformity of state law through the promulgation of uniform statutes. It has published a number of uniform codes; the one most applicable to the construction industry is the Uniform Commercial Code.

Negligence   The failure of a party to act in accordance with the standard of care required by law. The law requires all persons to exercise that degree of care which a reasonable person would exercise under the same or similar circumstances. Design professionals are required to exercise that degree of skill, care, and diligence that other design professionals would exercise under the same or similar circumstances.

Offer   A proposal by one party to perform a service or do something that invites another party's acceptance. The person who makes the offer is called an *offeror*, and the person who receives the offer is called an *offeree*. A bid is an example of an offer.

Ordinance   A law passed by a city or county.

Parol Evidence   Oral or written evidence of statements made by parties to a contract, prior to or at the same time as the signing of the contract that may vary or contradict the writing in the contract.

Parol Evidence Rule   A rule that requires courts to exclude parol evidence when interpreting a contract that has an integration clause. The rule also applies if there is no integration clause in the contract, but the court decides that the contract was intended to be a final expression of the parties' agreement.

Partial Performance   Under contract law, a term applied when a party has not fully performed all of its contractual obligations. A party that has only partially performed its contractual obligations generally has no right to enforce the contract against the other party. The party may, however, be able to recover under *quantum meruit.*

Partnership   An association of two or more people to conduct business for profit as co-owners.

Patent ambiguity   An obvious discrepancy. Bidders are typically required to request clarification of patent discrepancies in the bid materials before submitting their bids.

Payment Bond   A bond issued by a surety that provides funds to pay subcontractors and suppliers that have not been paid by the contractor.

Performance Bond   A bond which guarantees that if the contractor fails to complete the project in accordance with the terms of the construction agreement, the surety will either complete the contract itself or arrange for another contractor to complete the contract.

Personal Property   Generally, all property that is not real property. Personal property includes tangible goods, such as furniture, cars, books, and equipment, and intangible goods, such as money, notes, bonds, and stocks. Personal property can be owned by a business or a government agency as well as by an individual.

Plain Meaning   A rule of contract interpretation in which a word is given its ordinary meaning.

Plaintiff   The party that initiates a lawsuit against another party.

Principal   Under agency law, a principal is one who authorizes another (an agent) to act on its behalf and to legally bind the principal as though the principal had acted directly.

Privity of Contract   The relationship between the parties to a contract. Privity of contract creates contractual rights and obligations.

Professional Liability Insurance   Insurance carried by a design professional to cover liability arising out of its negligent acts, errors, or omissions.

Professional Standard of Care   The degree of care that the law requires all professionals to exhibit in their work.

Property Title   The right of ownership in real property.

Proximate Causation   Under tort law, a plaintiff must prove legal causation in a negligence case by showing that the harm that occurred was a reasonably foreseeable consequence of the wrongful act.

Proximate (Legal) Cause   A legally sufficient causal connection between the breach of duty owed under the applicable standard of care and the injury suffered by the party to whom the duty was owed.

Punitive Damages   Punitive damages (exemplary damages) are awarded not to compensate the plaintiff for losses incurred but to punish the defendant for its wrongful conduct and serve as an example to potential wrongdoers.

Quantum Meruit   A method of valuing the work done when there is no contract between the parties, or the contract has been breached.

Quasi-contract   An obligation imposed by law under which a party that received a benefit must compensate the party that provided the benefit, despite the absence of an actual contract between them.

Ratification   A principal's agreement to be bound by its agent acts, despite the fact that the agent acted outside the scope of its authority.

Real Property (Real Estate)   Land and anything permanently attached to or part of the land, such as buildings, walls, fences, driveways, garages, swimming pools, trees, and shrubs. Real property also includes fixtures (items that are permanently affixed to a building, such as light fixtures and cabinets).

Remedy   A court's action to redress an injury suffered by the plaintiff.

Restitution   A court-ordered money award that is intended to restore the parties to the financial position they were in before the contract was formed.

Schedule of Values   A breakdown of a fixed-price bid according to the various items of the work.

Simplified Acquisition Threshold   Federal contracts for an amount below the simplified acquisition threshold are not subject to the standard federal procurement requirements for full and open competition.

Spearin Doctrine   A common-law doctrine that makes the owner liable for any delays or cost increases due to defects in the plans or specifications.

Standard Rules of Interpretation   Rules that a court applies to interpret ambiguous contract language.

Statute   A law enacted by a federal or state legislature. Laws enacted by city and county governments are typically referred to as *ordinances*.

Statute of Frauds   A state law that requires certain contracts to be in writing.

Statute of Limitations   A state law that bars a claim unless the claim is brought either within a specified period of time after the event giving rise to the claim has occurred or within a specified period of time after the party bringing the claim knew or should have known of the event.

Statute of Repose   A state law that bars a claim unless the claim is brought within a specified period of time after the event giving rise to the claim has occurred, regardless of when the injured party became aware of the injury.

Substantial Performance   A party's performance of most of its contractual obligations. Substantial completion usually entitles the party to payment of most of the contract price.

Surety   An entity that agrees to be legally responsible for the debts or performance of a third party.

Surety Bond   A legal instrument under which one party agrees to be legally responsible for the debts or performance of a third party.

Termination for Default   A party's right, established under the terms of the contract, to terminate the contractor due to the other parties' material breach. Also referred to as *termination for cause*.

Third-Party Beneficiary   A person or entity who benefits from a contract but is not a party to the contract. A third-party beneficiary can be either an intentional or an incidental beneficiary.

Title Search   A search of the history of a title to real property to identify any defects or encumbrances.

Tort   A civil wrong, other than a breach of contract, for which the court provides a remedy in the form of damages. A tort is not a criminal offense but a civil offense that arises by operation of law rather than contract.

Trespass   To enter real property owned by another without having the legal right to do so.

Unconscionability   With respect to contracts, when one party takes advantage of the other party's inexperience or lack of bargaining power.

Uniform Commercial Code (UCC)   A model law developed to govern commercial transactions.

Uniform Partnership Act (UPA)   A model law developed to govern partnerships.

Vicarious Liability   When one individual or business entity is held liable for another person's actions or failure to act. Employers are vicariously liable for negligent acts or omissions committed by their employees in the course of employment.

Warranty   A general term for a promise concerning the future performance of goods, property, or services. If the performance falls short of the promise, there is a breach of warranty.

Zoning   A form of public control over land use.

INDEX